DRUG ABUSE

OPPOSING VIEWPOINTS®

Other Books of Related Interest in the Opposing
Viewpoints Series:

DRUG ABUSE

OPPOSING VIEWPOINTS®

David Bender & Bruno Leone, *Series Editors*

Karin L. Swisher, *Book Editor*
Katie de Koster, *Assistant Editor*

OPPOSING
VIEWPOINTS
SERIES®

Greenhaven Press, Inc.   PO Box 289009   San Diego, CA 92198-9009

Library of Congress Cataloging-in-Publication Data

Drug abuse: opposing viewpoints / Karin L. Swisher, book editor ;
    Katie de Koster, assistant editor.
        p.   cm. — (Opposing viewpoints series)
    Includes bibliographical references and index.
    Summary: Presents differing opinions on the causes of drug
abuse, the effectiveness of the war on drugs, drug testing, and
other related issues.
    ISBN 1-56510-060-3 (lib. bdg. : alk. paper) — ISBN 1-56510-
059-X (pbk. : alk. paper)
    1. Drug abuse. 2. Drug abuse—Prevention. [1. Drug abuse.] I.
Swisher, Karin, 1966–   . II. de Koster, Katie, 1948–   . III.
Series: Opposing viewpoints series (Unnumbered)
HV5809.5.D78 1994
362.29—dc20   93-12375
                                                                    CIP
                                                                    AC

"Congress shall make no law . . .
abridging the freedom of speech,
or of the press."

First Amendment to the U.S. Constitution

The basic foundation of our democracy is the first amendment
guarantee of freedom of expression. The Opposing Viewpoints
Series is dedicated to the concept of this basic freedom and the
idea that it is more important to practice it than to enshrine it.

Contents

Why Consider Opposing Viewpoints?

"The only way in which a human being can make some approach to knowing the whole of a subject is by hearing what can be said about it by persons of every variety of opinion and studying all modes in which it can be looked at by every character of mind. No wise man ever acquired his wisdom in any mode but this."

John Stuart Mill

In our media-intensive culture it is not difficult to find differing opinions. Thousands of newspapers and magazines and dozens of radio and television talk shows resound with differing points of view. The difficulty lies in deciding which opinion to agree with and which "experts" seem the most credible. The more inundated we become with differing opinions and claims, the more essential it is to hone critical reading and thinking skills to evaluate these ideas. Opposing Viewpoints books address this problem directly by presenting stimulating debates that can be used to enhance and teach these skills. The varied opinions contained in each book examine many different aspects of a single issue. While examining these conveniently edited opposing views, readers can develop critical thinking skills such as the ability to compare and contrast authors' credibility, facts, argumentation styles, use of persuasive techniques, and other stylistic tools. In short, the Opposing Viewpoints Series is an ideal way to attain the higher-level thinking and reading skills so essential in a culture of diverse and contradictory opinions.

In addition to providing a tool for critical thinking, Opposing Viewpoints books challenge readers to question their own strongly held opinions and assumptions. Most people form their opinions on the basis of upbringing, peer pressure, and personal, cultural, or professional bias. By reading carefully balanced opposing views, readers must directly confront new ideas as well as the opinions of those with whom they disagree. This is not to simplistically argue that everyone who reads opposing views will—or should—change his or her opinion. Instead, the series enhances readers' depth of understanding of their own views by encouraging confrontation with opposing ideas. Careful examination of others' views can lead to the readers' understanding of the logical inconsistencies in their own opinions, perspective on why they hold an opinion, and the consideration of the possibility that their opinion requires further evaluation.

Evaluating Other Opinions

To ensure that this type of examination occurs, Opposing Viewpoints books present all types of opinions. Prominent spokespeople on different sides of each issue as well as well-known professionals from many disciplines challenge the reader. An additional goal of the series is to provide a forum for other, less known, or even unpopular viewpoints. The opinion of an ordinary person who has had to make the decision to cut off life support from a terminally ill relative, for example, may be just as valuable and provide just as much insight as a medical ethicist's professional opinion. The editors have two additional purposes in including these less known views. One, the editors encourage readers to respect others' opinions—even when not enhanced by professional credibility. It is only by reading or listening to and objectively evaluating others' ideas that one can determine whether they are worthy of consideration. Two, the inclusion of such viewpoints encourages the important critical thinking skill of objectively evaluating an author's credentials and bias. This evaluation will illuminate an author's reasons for taking a particular stance on an issue and will aid in readers' evaluation of the author's ideas.

As series editors of the Opposing Viewpoints Series, it is our hope that these books will give readers a deeper understanding of the issues debated and an appreciation of the complexity of even seemingly simple issues when good and honest people disagree. This awareness is particularly important in a democratic society such as ours in which people enter into public debate to determine the common good. Those with whom one disagrees should not be regarded as enemies but rather as people whose views deserve careful examination and may shed light on one's own.

Thomas Jefferson once said that "difference of opinion leads to inquiry, and inquiry to truth." Jefferson, a broadly educated man, argued that "if a nation expects to be ignorant and free . . . it expects what never was and never will be." As individuals and as a nation, it is imperative that we consider the opinions of others and examine them with skill and discernment. The Opposing Viewpoints Series is intended to help readers achieve this goal.

David L. Bender & Bruno Leone,
Series Editors

Introduction

"It seems an impossible dream to recall that for most of human history . . . people and societies have regulated their drug use without requiring massive education, legal, and interdiction campaigns."

Stanton Peele, *Visions of Addiction*, 1988.

People have always used intoxicants. For centuries Andean peasants chewed coca leaves for a mild stimulus; Asians smoked opium made locally from poppies; and indigenous peoples throughout the Americas used drugs in religious ceremonies. In early America coca and opium were common ingredients in popular patent medicines. Today, however, abuse of long-popular drugs has caused concern in the United States. According to the Department of Justice, there were approximately 250,000 drug abusers in a population of 76 million people in 1900. By 1991, the number had jumped to about 16 million in a population of 250 million, a 20-fold percentage increase, more than any other industrialized nation. Experts have pondered what changed between previous centuries and this one to make drug abuse a major cause for concern. It appears that two things changed: the drugs and society.

In the twentieth century, scientific advances changed the properties and potencies of long-used drugs such as opium and coca, transforming them into heroin and crack cocaine, and also made possible a variety of new synthetic drugs. The new forms of these drugs are more potent and thus make addiction more likely.

Opium is one drug that science made more potent. It was introduced into the United States in the early 1700s in patent medicines used for a host of ailments. Since the opium had to go through the digestive process, it entered the bloodstream slowly from the stomach. In 1803 a German pharmacist isolated morphine, a more potent form of opium. A few decades later, the hypodermic syringe was invented, allowing drugs to be injected directly into the bloodstream, making their effects quicker and more powerful. According to James A. Inciardi in *Handbook of Drug Control in the United States:* "The use of morphine by injection in military medicine during the Civil War . . . granted the procedure legitimacy and familiarity both to physicians and the public."

In 1874 heroin was first isolated from morphine. Bayer and Company began marketing this powerful narcotic in 1898 as a sedative for coughs and as chest and lung medicine. The medical community, aware of morphine's addictiveness, at first believed that heroin was nonaddictive. According to one physician writing in the *New York Medical Journal* in 1900, "Habituation [with Heroin] has been noted in a small percentage of the cases. All observers are agreed, however, that . . . none of the symptoms . . . of chronic morphinism have ever been observed." By the time doctors recognized its addictive power, it had become the abusers' drug of choice.

In recent decades, such refinements on long-used drugs were joined by new illicit compounds, such as LSD and PCP, and discredited prescription drugs, such as Quaaludes and Ecstasy. Many of these now form the base of "designer drugs"—analogs that are slightly different in formula but often far more potent in effect. Since the development of the first designer drug in 1979, a massive proliferation of street drugs has led to what researcher Maureen Croteau and Wayne Worcester have called "one of the most dangerous and vexing trends in drug abuse: dangerous because no one knows the true effect of the drugs until they actually are used; vexing because kitchen chemists seem able to produce new drugs whenever the need arises." Thus today's drug abusers are exposed to a vast smorgasbord of readily available substances that are far more potent than those used by their predecessors.

The other change—a dramatic change in attitude—also began in recent decades. In the past, social and cultural barriers made drug abuse a rarity. As Inciardi notes, "Both the medical and religious communities defin[ed] it as a moral disease."

These barriers began to fall in the 1950s. Young people, the product of a new, prosperous middle class, were able to share in their parents' prosperity. As a result, as David Halberstam states in *The Fifties*, "The young formed their own community. For the first time in American life, they were becoming a separate, defined part of the culture: As they had money, they were a market, and as they were a market, they were listened to and catered to." The nation's youth gave their allegiance to each other, rather than to their parents' socioeconomic, religious, or ethnic groups.

The young always rebel, but the rebellion of the 1960s and 70s was different. This "baby boom" generation formed a population bulge. Their numbers and prosperity gave them power, and cultural artifacts such as television contributed to their cohesion, as well as to their understanding and frustration about the state of the world. Humanity had developed the power to destroy the entire earth, and in a cold war that occasionally grew heated, the

United States and Russia busily built and tested atomic weapons. Nuclear brinkmanship, accented by "duck and cover" drills at schools, fostered nihilism—rejection of traditional values—among the young; many believed the world would end before they were thirty. Some turned to a live-for-today hedonism. Some became antiwar protesters, insisting that America get out of Vietnam, or took up other rebellious social causes, such as civil rights and women's equality. Along with thousands of young American soldiers who became familiar with illicit drugs in the jungles of Vietnam, they met in the new drug culture, which variously promised escape, physical pleasure, enhanced spiritual insights, or just a sense of belonging. James A. Inciardi concurs:

> Concomitant with [the] emergence of a new chemical age, a new youth ethos had become manifest, one characterized by a widely celebrated generational disaffection, a prejudicial dependence on the self and the peer group for value orientation, a critical view of how the world was being run, and a mistrust of an "establishment" drug policy the "facts" and "warnings" of which ran counter to reported peer experience. Whatever the ultimate causes of the drug revolution of the sixties might have been, America's younger generations, or at least noticeable segments of them, had embraced drugs.

The new openness of a large segment of the population to the use of drugs, combined with the scientific advances that made them more powerful and easier to use—and thus to abuse—helped create that 20-fold increase in the percentage of the population that abused drugs. As Inciardi recaps, "The abuse of drugs as such can be traced to a number of factors—advances in chemistry and medicine, the discovery of new intoxicants, and a variety of social and political changes."

The impact of these changes in drug-taking behavior continues to be felt. The chapters in this newly revised edition of *Drug Abuse: Opposing Viewpoints* debate the problems of drug abuse and the controversies over how to solve them by examining the following questions: How Serious a Problem Is Drug Abuse? How Should the War on Drugs Be Waged? Should Drug Testing Be Used in the Workplace? How Should Prescription Drugs Be Regulated? How Can Drug Abuse Be Reduced? The issues of drug use and abuse remain volatile. As drug researcher Steven Wisotsky points out: "People take drugs, as they have throughout history and across cultures, because they need and like the experience. Unlike the politicians and drug enforcers, they do not see themselves as victims of the drug they take. Yet a balanced view of the matter must also respect the legitimate concerns arising from drug use. What about those who become addicted? Are they not victimized, and doesn't the law find its greatest justification in trying to prevent that disaster?" These are among the questions debated in the viewpoints that follow.

How Serious a Problem Is Drug Abuse?

DRUG ABUSE

Chapter Preface

Determining the seriousness and extent of drug abuse is difficult. Hard-core drug abusers—those who use the most illegal drugs—are hard to find and talk to unless they come in contact with the criminal justice or health care system. Because obtaining reliable information is difficult, drug abuse researchers must rely on a variety of methods to determine what drugs are used, how often, and in what quantities. One method is to give drug tests to arrestees and track what drugs they use. Other methods are to study the frequency of drug-related emergency room visits and to study the rates of admission to drug treatment programs to learn about health problems related to drugs. While this information is useful, it is not hard evidence. Clearly, determining the seriousness of the drug problem is difficult.

One current debate concerns the belief by some researchers that a 1970s-style heroin epidemic has begun. Heroin is an addictive and destructive drug. Experts fear that if the epidemic is real, it would strain America's already overburdened health care and criminal justice systems. Law enforcement agents report that the quantities and purity of heroin are increasing while the street price is declining, allowing addicts to purchase larger quantities of better-quality heroin. At the same time, heroin-related emergency room visits are increasing in regions where heroin is most common. For example, one New York state agency notes that in the first nine months of 1991 emergency treatment for the adverse effects of heroin was up by more than half the 1990 rate. Admissions to treatment programs for heroin addiction are up as well. Many experts believe these factors indicate that heroin use is increasing and will once again become a serious problem.

Other experts are skeptical about evidence of increased heroin use. They maintain that the rate of positive tests for heroin use among arrestees—a primary indicator of drug trends—has remained stable. According to Eric Wish, director of the Center for Substance Abuse Research in Maryland, "The trend in opiate positives for arrestees tested in Washington, D.C. . . . has remained flat, as has been the case for arrestees tested in other large cities." Wish suggests that increased heroin purity is causing more health problems among users, leading to more emergency room visits and treatment admissions. There is no increase in the number of users, he concludes—just an increase in the number of heroin-related health problems.

Because there are so many interrelated factors, determining the extent of drug abuse—whether the drug is heroin, PCP, or crack—is very difficult. Experts debate the seriousness of heroin and other drug use in the following viewpoints.

16

"Figures suggest that the drug epidemic is far from over."

Drug Abuse Is a Serious Problem

Mathea Falco

Mathea Falco is a visiting fellow at New York Hospital-Cornell Medical Center in New York City. She was the assistant secretary of state for international narcotics matters from 1977 to 1981. In the following viewpoint, Falco contends that widespread drug abuse continues to be a serious problem for many Americans. She maintains that law enforcement efforts at reducing the supply of drugs have largely failed, and that the social problems related to drug abuse, such as crime and poverty, continue to plague the United States.

As you read, consider the following questions:

1. What signs lead Falco to conclude that drug abuse continues to be a problem?
2. According to the author, how have international efforts to reduce the supply of drugs failed?
3. Despite the failure of law enforcement efforts, why is Falco hopeful that drug abuse can be stopped?

The United States has the highest rate of drug abuse of any industrialized country in the world. Twenty-six million Americans used illicit drugs in 1991, almost half of them at least once a month. The vast majority of drug abusers are also heavy consumers of alcohol and tobacco. The National Academy of Sciences estimates that 5.5 million Americans have serious drug problems that require treatment.

Drug abuse is at the heart of what many people think has gone wrong with America. It appears as either the cause or the effect of a wide range of problems which seem out of control: urban blight, the destruction of families, the failure of schools, the loss of economic productivity. Drug abuse is also harder to ignore than most social problems. A Gallup poll in 1989 reported that 40 percent of all Americans had had personal experience with drug abuse and drug dealing themselves or in their family or community.

A Major Threat

In recent years, Americans have come to consider drug abuse as a major threat to the nation's well-being, ranking with economic recession and environmental destruction. We worry about how to protect our children from addiction; we fear drug-related violence; we feel drugs are corroding our competitiveness in an increasingly difficult world.

Daily news reports feed our concerns. The horrors of drug abuse have become depressingly familiar: crack-addicted mothers abandoning their babies; young children dealing drugs instead of going to school; innocent citizens killed in gang shoot-outs; and sports stars dying from overdoses. Everyone wants to know what can be done.

The emergence of crack cocaine in the mid-1980s created a sense of national crisis. Cheap and rapidly addictive, crack—named for the cracking sound it makes when smoked—produces an extraordinarily intense euphoria that lasts ten to fifteen minutes. The sharp letdown that follows leaves users depressed and anxious. Driven to recapture the high, they become trapped in a cycle of compulsive use. Unlike heroin or marijuana, crack makes users aggressive, violent, and paranoid. The consequences are often tragic. As one young mother who had sold her baby for more crack explained, "This drug will make you do anything. There's nowhere it won't make you go."

Crack

Crack quickly spread across the country, overwhelming America's law enforcement, drug treatment, and social service programs. Especially popular among women who dislike the disfiguring "track marks" which come from injecting drugs, crack fu1ther weakened many fragile single-parent families. Children became crack's indirect victims. Foster-care placements jumped by nearly a third from 1987 to 1990, mostly in communities hard hit by the drug. More than one hundred thousand "crack babies" are born each year; many are mentally retarded and physically damaged. Some of these infants also carry the AIDS virus from their mothers, who often become infected selling sex for drugs.

Pat McCarthy. Distributed by Heritage Features Syndicate. Reprinted with permission.

Crack has also fueled an epidemic of drug-related crime. In the five years before crack appeared, from 1981 to 1985, violent crime in America—robbery, rape, murder, aggravated assault— fell steadily. But after the emergence of crack, violent crime exploded. From 1985 to 1989, aggravated assaults increased by nearly a third and robberies by 15 percent. At the same time, murders in Washington, D.C., more than doubled, while in New York City murders jumped by half. By 1990, 50 to 60 percent of all those arrested in the nation's largest cities tested positive for cocaine and crack, regardless of the charge at arrest.

Nor is crack the only problem. More recently, heroin use has been on the rise as well. Because of its calming effect, heroin is popular among drug addicts trying to come down from crack binges. Traditionally, heroin sold in the United States has been so diluted that it must be injected to maximize its effect, but the heroin available today is so inexpensive and pure that it can be smoked and still provide a powerful high. Since smoking eliminates the need for needles, this "new" heroin may also attract users who have previously been discouraged by the fear of contracting AIDS.

Still other drugs are on the horizon: "designer" drugs, which can be made in home laboratories from easily available chemicals; LSD and other hallucinogens, which are enjoying renewed popularity among young people nostalgic for the 1960s; and smokable amphetamines such as "ice," which produce even more intense highs and lows than crack. We can be sure of only one thing: in the future, new products will emerge to feed America's appetite for drugs. The problem will never go away. Something must be done. . . .

Drugs and Law Enforcement

Defining drug abuse as a law enforcement problem has long been an automatic response for politicians as they face voters alarmed by escalating rates of addiction and crime. Since 1981, Americans have spent over $100 billion in federal, state, and local taxes to support drug enforcement programs. Gauged by the traditional goals of these programs—higher drug prices and reduced availability—these efforts have been a dismal failure. Yet there has been no public inquiry into drug enforcement's effectiveness, even as the costs continue to rise. The General Accounting Office reported in 1991 that the flow of drugs into the United States had not declined despite massive expenditures for interdiction. . . .

The chief goal of interdiction is to increase the cost of drugs to American users, but we have learned that interdiction has very little effect on street prices. The largest profits from the drug traffic are made not in foreign poppy or coca fields or on the high seas but at the street level. Economists at the Rand Corporation estimate that only 10 percent of the final street price for cocaine goes to those who produce coca or smuggle it across the borders. Even if we were able to seize half the cocaine coming from South America—a wildly optimistic prospect—cocaine prices in American cities would increase by less than 5 percent. With a vial of crack selling in most places for less than the cost of a single admission to the movies, such increases would not likely affect consumption. . . .

Decline in Demand

The progress we have made against drugs during the past decade has resulted not from reduced supply but from reduced demand. Cocaine and marijuana use have substantially declined since 1988, largely because of greater awareness of health dangers and increasingly negative social attitudes about drugs. At the same time, cocaine and marijuana are readily available, suggesting that drug scarcity and high prices—the traditional measures of law enforcement success—are not responsible for the declines. . . .

Social Decay

In the inner cities, drug use is clearly out of control. In Washington, D.C., the infant mortality rate, already among the highest in the U.S., increased by nearly 50 percent in the first half of 1989 because of a surge of babies born to cocaine-addicted women. An estimated 169 babies died before their first birthdays during the first six months of 1989, an infant mortality rate of 32.3 deaths per 1,000 live births, according to preliminary city data. By contrast, the infant mortality rate for all of 1988 was 23.2 deaths per 1,000. "It is like a bomb has gone off," said one city official. "No one in this area knows what to do. I don't know what to do about social pathology and decay in half the city."

Drugs, sadly, are part of a larger social pathology in our inner cities and throughout the larger American society as well. More and more children find themselves in one-parent families and do not receive the care and nurturing which previous generations took for granted. Three reports issued by the U.S. Census Bureau in September, 1989 show that over the past generation, there has been a dramatic change in the American family, marked by a soaring rate of divorce and a sharp increase in single-parent families, as well as a mounting illegitimacy rate.

J.A. Parker, *The Lincoln Review*, Winter 1990.

This progress, however, is largely limited to better educated Americans who are more inclined to respond to health information. Cocaine use declined from 1985 to 1990 almost twice as much among those who had attended college as for those who did not. Teenagers who plan to continue their education after high school are also less likely to use drugs. Dr. Peter Reuter, director of the Rand Corporation's Drug Policy Research Center, points out that "the deaths of sports stars Len Bias and Don Rogers riveted national attention on the dangers of cocaine. Better educated Americans who used cocaine occasionally were the first to quit."

Despite these encouraging reductions among some segments of society, the latest surveys indicate that addiction is getting worse, not better. The Office of National Drug Control Policy estimates that there are at least 1.8 million "hard-core" cocaine addicts, triple the number of earlier estimates, as well as an additional 600,000 heroin addicts. In 1991 the number of Americans who reported using cocaine at least once a week jumped 25 percent from the previous year. Among young adults aged eighteen to twenty-five, drug use increased after several years of steady declines. Cocaine and heroin overdose cases, as reported in hospital emergency rooms across the country, have also gone up. These figures suggest that the drug epidemic is far from over. . . .

Drug Abuse Affects the Poor

Although drug abuse cuts across all social classes, it is far more visible among the poor, who are at much greater risk for unemployment, AIDS, homelessness, and crime. Their children are more likely to be sick, to drop out of school, or to be placed in foster care. Treatment is far less available to them than to those who have health insurance or can afford private programs.

As drug use declines among affluent Americans, the drug problem is increasingly identified with poor, inner-city minorities. Criminal justice statistics reinforce this perception. Blacks constitute only 12 percent of the total population, but they account for 41 percent of drug arrests and a third of criminal drug convictions nationwide. Because minorities are so closely linked with illegal drugs in America, our political leaders, with strong popular support, have increasingly turned to law enforcement as the major weapon in the war on drugs.

Drugs and Immorality

The view that drug abuse is above all a criminal problem is rooted in our nation's deep, unacknowledged feelings about the dangerous immorality of addicts. This is true even in the communities most affected by drug abuse. I discussed this with a black doctor who grew up in Detroit and continues to live there even though most of his friends have moved to the suburbs to escape the crime, drugs, and violence. He told me, "These guys brought this on themselves; they don't have to be junkies. Most days I think they deserve to be locked up."

These attitudes are understandable coming from citizens driven by fear, rage, and frustration, but they prevent us from taking a hard look at our efforts to combat substance abuse. They often blind us from seeing what works and what doesn't. Until we begin to build on what we know rather than on what we feel, we will be no closer to finding durable solutions. Half a million Americans are behind bars for drug-related crimes. But tens of millions on the outside are prisoners of their own attitudes about the nature of our drug problem and how to begin to solve it.

"The [drug] problem does not appear nearly as severe as newspaper headlines and TV 'sound bites' suggest."

The Seriousness of Drug Abuse May Be Exaggerated

Sam Staley

Drug abuse has been cited by many as one of America's worst social ills. In the following viewpoint, Sam Staley contests this analysis, and maintains that the seriousness of the drug problem has been inflated in two ways. First, according to Staley, many researchers do not distinguish between casual users, abusers, and addicts, making the number of abusers seem larger. Second, the addictive properties of drugs have been exaggerated, Staley argues, making it appear that anyone using a drug occasionally is destined to become an abuser. Staley, an expert in public policy and urban development, is the author of the book *Drug Policy and the Decline of American Cities*, from which this viewpoint was taken.

As you read, consider the following questions:

1. What conclusions does the author draw from studies done on drug abuse in young adults?
2. According to Staley, how do legal drugs like alcohol and tobacco compare with illegal drugs like cocaine and heroin?
3. How has the American public responded to trends in drug use, according to the author?

From Sam Staley, *Drug Policy and the Decline of American Cities*, © 1992 by Transaction Publishers. Reprinted by permission.

Drug use in the United States is extensive, although trends since 1975 suggest a slight decline. Lloyd D. Johnston, Patrick M. O'Malley, and Jerald G. Bachman, of the University of Michigan's Institute for Social Research, have published the most widely recognized analysis of trends in drug use. Their analysis of survey data from 1975 to 1986 reveals that older age groups have higher levels of "lifetime" experience. In other words, older people experiment with more types of drugs. The authors, however, did not find a corresponding increase in the daily or monthly use of drugs in this age group. Thus, despite the fact that young adults continue to experiment with drugs, few become heavy users.

Cocaine use appears as a unique exception. They observe,

> *Cocaine* presents a somewhat unique case in that lifetime, annual, and current use *all* rise substantially with age, at least through age 24. . . . In 1986, lifetime prevalence by age 27-28 was roughly 40%, vs. 17% among today's high school seniors (and 10% among the 27-28 year-old cohorts when they were seniors in the mid 1970's). Annual prevalence for 27-28 year-olds today is about 20% and 30-day prevalence around 8%—again, appreciably higher than for 1986 seniors. Clearly this is a drug which is used much more frequently among people in their twenties than among those in their late teens; and at the present time this fact distinguishes it from all of the other illicit drugs. (Emphasis in original.)

In contrast, experience with marijuana rises from under 50 percent to 76 percent by the time students are nine to ten years out of high school. Yet, daily use remained the same. In contrast, daily alcohol consumption increased with age (at least through age 28).

These data are confirmed by earlier studies tracking the age of first use among drug users. A study of over 27,000 participants in federally supported drug-treatment programs between 1973 and 1975 found that most were exposed to heroin and cocaine at later ages than marijuana. While over half of the participants had used marijuana before they were fifteen, only 14 percent had used heroin. Exposure to cocaine, however, tended to spread out more evenly, with peak exposure occurring between sixteen and twenty years old.

Legal Drugs

In fact, the percentage of high school seniors ever having used marijuana, cocaine, or heroin has declined. The most popular drugs are the ones most entrenched in American social custom: alcohol and cigarettes. The prevalence of alcohol among seniors increased from 90.4 percent in 1975 to 93.2 percent in 1980, although alcohol use seems to have declined somewhat during the

1980s. While tobacco is the second most used drug, its use has declined significantly since 1975.

These data should be qualified, since a general trend exists toward lower-tar cigarettes and less-potent alcoholic beverages such as beer. Even though alcohol and tobacco remain the most used drugs, their use has been accompanied by reduced health risks. Nevertheless, in absolute terms, smoking has declined among high school seniors from 73.6 percent in 1975 to 67.6 percent in 1988.

In contrast, the proportion of high school students reporting use of either marijuana, cocaine, or heroin is substantially lower. Nevertheless, marijuana remains the most popular of the three drugs. It is important to note that the proportion of high school seniors indicating that they had used marijuana at least once declined from 60.3 percent in 1980 to 47.2 percent in 1988. Perhaps more important, cocaine experienced an increase in popularity in the 1980s but has declined substantially toward the end of the decade.

These trends persist when frequency is considered. In 1986, over half of the high school seniors surveyed indicated that they had used marijuana. Only 23 percent, however, indicated that they used marijuana within the last thirty days. Only 6 percent of high school students indicated that they had used cocaine in the last thirty days. Although cocaine use increased significantly since the mid-1970s, cocaine users remain a small minority of the drug-user population. The heroin user formed a negligible part of the general drug-user population and has not increased significantly in recent years. On the other hand, almost two-thirds of the students polled said they had used alcohol.

Little Daily Use of Illegal Drugs

When seniors were asked about their daily consumption of these drugs, very few students indicated they used them on a daily basis. Based on data for the years through 1986, the most frequently abused illicit drug appears to be tobacco: almost one-fifth of high school seniors said they smoked on a daily basis. Daily cocaine use and heroin use constituted less than 1 percent of the drug use among American high school seniors. Even the popular drugs alcohol and marijuana were used daily by only 4 percent.

Thus, while almost 17 percent of the high school seniors surveyed in 1986 said they had tried cocaine, less than 1 percent used cocaine at least once every day. While over half of the students polled said they had tried marijuana, only 4 percent indicated they used marijuana daily. Given that the indicators of use have steadily declined during the late 1980s, daily prevalence has probably also continued to decline.

To the extent that these data reflect actual trends in drug use, the drug-abuse story appears extremely complex. Whether illicit drugs are a "social problem" depends at least in part on where you start. Clearly, currently illicit drugs are less prevalent than the more socially acceptable substances such as alcohol and tobacco.

If the yardstick used to gauge the extent of the "drug problem" is the proportion of children ever having used a psychoactive drug, then the numbers reported by Johnston, O'Malley, and Bachman are serious. If, on the other hand, the standard is daily prevalence, then the problem does not appear nearly as severe as newspaper headlines and TV "sound bites" suggest. Without a doubt, addiction will adversely affect the lives and families of the students and their friends. Yet, heavy regular drug use does not appear to be the norm among high school students.

Indeed, the "drug problem" is normally defined as the rate of addiction to any psychoactive substance. Illicit drugs are considered dangerous because of their addictive qualities and the inability of users to control their personal behavior when on these drugs. The data suggest that substantial control is exerted by drug users, even teenagers. Only a small minority—with the notable exception of users of tobacco—use psychoactive drugs on a daily basis.

Moreover, these controls are substantial given the availability of these drugs. Although data were not reported for alcohol and tobacco, their extremely high use rates reported by seniors suggest that supplies are plentiful. Of more interest for this discussion, however, is the prevalence of the more traditional illicit drugs, marijuana, cocaine, and heroin.

Eight out of every ten high school seniors surveyed in 1989 claimed that marijuana is either "fairly easy" or "very easy" to get. Over half the seniors (58.7 percent) felt that cocaine would be easy to obtain as well. Even heroin was obtainable, if they wanted it, by almost one-third of the seniors polled. Moreover, the availability of these drugs increased throughout the 1980s. Given the availability of these drugs and the experimental nature of younger people, the proportions of students ever using these drugs may be considered remarkably low. Other factors are clearly important in decisions by young people to experiment and use illicit drugs. . . .

The Persistence of Drug Use in America

Drug use is an indelible part of the American sociological landscape. But drug use moves far beyond the limits of illicit drugs. Alcohol also alters human behavior and is a psychoactive substance despite its social acceptability. What differentiates alcohol use from other drug use is its legal status. Similarly, cigarettes are highly addictive and arguably alter human behavior. Users build up a tolerance to alcohol and tobacco, as they do to other psychoactive drugs. Tobacco smoking can even develop into a physical dependency. Thus, in evaluating the psychological and physical effects of illicit drugs, comparisons to other socially acceptable drugs provide a useful context. . . .

Drug use has emerged as an important force in American life in the twentieth century. While use among adults has been endemic in American culture, the spread of drugs to children and adolescents dates only to the mid-twentieth century. The use of drugs by children and their growing spending power has [according to Joseph Westermeyer] "stimulated the search for cheap, readily available psychoactive substances in the home, school, workplace, grocery store, and hardware shop." Thus, cheaper forms of traditional drugs, such as crack cocaine, have become more commonplace. . . .

None of the rates in drug use appear to differ significantly among occupations. The percentage of respondents using alcohol within the last thirty days ranges from a low of 74 percent for farm laborers to 86 percent for managers and sales workers. Cigarette use appears to vary the most, ranging from only 30 percent among professionals to a high of 57 percent among general laborers.

Illicit substance use does not vary greatly either. The least popular drug was cocaine. Only 10 percent of farm laborers reported using cocaine in the last thirty days while only 17 percent of craftsmen and service workers indicated use. Marijuana, the most popular of the illegal drugs, ranged from a low of 30 percent for farm laborers to a high of 49 percent for service workers. . . .

Drugs and Public Health

A cost of drug use is a public health concern. Drug users place themselves at risk more than nondrug users. This, of course, is true for all drug users regardless of whether the drugs are legally tolerated or not. For example, the risks of tobacco place smoking at the top of the list among potential killers. Similarly, the risks to users associated with illicit drugs may also be extremely high. While this argument plays well at first, evidence on deaths per capita by type of drug use reveals that drugs other than cocaine, heroin, and marijuana pose far greater health hazards.

James Ostrowski determined the per capita death rate for several drugs: tobacco, alcohol, heroin, cocaine, and marijuana. In his calculations, Ostrowski attempted to isolate only those deaths that were "intrinsically" connected to the drug being used. In other words, he attempted to determined whether an alcohol death was related to the use of alcohol per se rather than to some other influence. Thus, deaths resulting from diseases directly related to alcohol use are included while others such as DUI traffic deaths are not.

The data show that tobacco remains the number one killer, claiming 650 deaths per 100,000 users. Heroin use results in half the death rate of alcohol per capita. Not one death has been attributable to marijuana use. In fact, based on data concerning the number of repeat users of these drugs, Ostrowski notes that the illicit substances are less likely to lead to repeat use than either alcohol or tobacco.

Estimated per Capita Death Rates for Selected Drugs

Drug	Users	Deaths Per Year	Deaths/100,000
Tobacco	60 million	390,000	650
Alcohol	100 million	15,000	150
Heroin	500,000	400	80
Cocaine	5 million	200	4

Source: James Ostrowski, "Thinking About Drug Legalization," Cato Policy Analysis No. 121 (Washington, D.C.: Cato Institute, 1989), 47, table 4.

Note: Deaths attributed to heroin and cocaine were adjusted downward to include only deaths attributed to drug use (e.g., not suicide). The unadjusted figure for heroin is 400 per 100,000 and for cocaine, 20 per 100,000.

Tallying the number of people killed through substance abuse is only one method of determining its risk. Another risk is dependence. Substantial numbers of people are psychologically dependent on drugs (although the degree of this dependence is contestable). Nevertheless, for the 10 to 20 percent of each drug user population that is dependent, the effects can be devastating.

Drug dependence, however, is manageable. Heroin addicts can lead productive lives even if they require four or five doses a day. The debilitating effects of heroin are related to the drug's availability and affordability, which in turn are due almost exclusively to its legal status.

Cocaine, in contrast to heroin, is more debilitating and interferes more with work performance. Yet, cocaine's effects typically become negligible within two or three hours. After twenty-four hours, cocaine cannot be chemically traced in human urine (two days with heavy doses). Scientific evidence indicates that regular cocaine use affects the heart and causes cardiac death, heart attack, irregular heartbeat, and damage to the muscle tissue surrounding the heart. Other physical problems associated with chronic cocaine use are deterioration of the liver, high blood pressure, convulsions, respiratory failure, and destruction of the nasal passage.

Nevertheless, as the table detailed, the risks of cocaine are not as significant as those other drugs that are legally and socially tolerated. The number of chronic or compulsive users is probably very small, despite the results of the study released by the Senate Judiciary Committee. Thus, Steven Wisotsky concludes,

> The data lead to one conclusion: even allowing for legitimate concerns about the health consequences of cocaine and fears about the spread of cocaine dependency, the legal prohibition of cocaine and its severe penalties cannot be justified solely on the grounds of public health. At the very least, the health and death toll of legal drugs—cigarettes and alcohol—runs far higher. . . . But for that 10-20 percent minority, . . . a destructive, accelerating pattern of compulsive use can develop over time. Approximately the same percentage fall "victim" to alcoholism or heroin addiction. . . .

In sum, the demand for illicit drugs in the United States will continue despite their legal status. Moreover, the physical and psychological effects of the major illicit drugs—heroin, cocaine, and marijuana—appear much smaller than previously thought. A realistic assessment of the drug problem suggests that dependence on illicit drugs should be treated as a health problem similar to smoking and alcohol use. In fact, at current usage rates, the public health risks associated with illicit drug use are far lower than those for alcohol and smoking.

Moreover, unlike currently illegal drugs, the risks associated with the legal drugs will probably persist through their popularity. As James Ostrowski has noted, "not only are alcohol and tobacco inherently more dangerous than heroin and cocaine, but because they are more popular, their danger is magnified." Despite widespread access, illicit drugs appear far less popular than alcohol or cigarettes. Even those who experiment with these drugs are much less likely to use them again.

Dependence Through Prolonged Use

The true costs of substance abuse lie in the dependence users develop through prolonged use of the drug. In some cases, such as cigarette and alcohol abuse, the physical effects become life-threatening.

Alcohol and cigarette use, however, appear to be declining over time. The proportion of current smokers in the U.S. population has declined from 42 percent in 1955 to under one-third in the late 1980s. Moreover, recent drinking trends show a general move to beverages with lower alcohol content, such as light beer and wine.

Drug use is part of a far reaching cultural tradition. The most traditional forms of drug use manifest themselves in alcohol and tobacco consumption. These forms have been socially tolerated for centuries and have been an omnipresent fact of American life. Illicit drugs have also been around for centuries, but have received more attention in the late twentieth century.

The reasons for the resurgence of public interest in the most common illicit drugs lie principally in the perceived social devastation that lies in its wake. Indeed, social control over these drugs began in the late nineteenth century as politicians responded to heightening public criticism of cocaine and special interests sought to expand their power. Similarly, the recent trend toward widespread intolerance of psychoactive drugs reflects the rising public outcry against "soaring" addiction rates, the diffusion of drug use into schools, and the violence associated with drug trafficking. Against the backdrop of economic devastation in many American urban areas, drugs became an easy target of public criticism.

Declaring War

Indeed, the recent declaration of "war" against drugs can be viewed as a reaction to the rising social devastation evident in urban areas. As this viewpoint has detailed, while heroin, cocaine, and marijuana have addictive qualities, none of them approaches the levels of use or addiction evident in socially tolerated drugs such as alcohol or tobacco. Indeed, the numbers of chronic users are substantially lower than perceptions gleaned from newspaper headlines and evening news reports. Moreover, the classification of users of illicit drugs as addicts or compulsive users is highly suspect. Many so-called addicts demonstrate substantial control over their drug intake and use.

The issue is not whether people will use drugs, but how much is demanded on the market at a given price. For the vast majority of consumers, drug use is not addictive. "Recreational" drug use, or use of drugs in the same sense that most drinkers use alcohol, is reasonably safe and enjoyable although the potentially negative long-term consequences of drug use may become important. Drug use becomes a problem only when a physical or psychological dependence emerges for the drug or individual behavior becomes individually or socially destructive.

"Drug-treatment experts report seeing an alarming rise in heroin use."

Increased Heroin Use Is a Serious Problem

Mark Miller

Heroin use, once stereotyped as dangerous, unappealing, and vi-
ciously addictive, has undergone an image change, according to
Mark Miller, a correspondent at *Newsweek*, a weekly news-
magazine. In the following viewpoint, Miller argues that more,
purer forms of heroin have become available, which allow users
to smoke or inhale the drug, rather than inject it, increasing its
appeal for many. The new methods of ingesting it, Miller concludes, have led many to believe, erroneously, that heroin is a
safe, nonaddictive drug.

As you read, consider the following questions:

1. Who are the new heroin users that the author describes?
2. What are some of the effects of prolonged heroin use,
   according to Miller?
3. What evidence does Miller cite that abuse of heroin is
   increasing?

Mark Miller, "Fatal Addiction." This article originally appeared in the November 1991 issue of *Mademoiselle* magazine and is reprinted with permission.

It is Friday night in the East Village of Manhattan, a neighborhood where self-proclaimed anarchists rub elbows with starving artists and other eccentrics. Susan (names have been changed), a 22-year-old former social worker, is standing with about 20 other people on a broken, rippling sidewalk beneath construction scaffolding. The line moves fairly quickly, five per minute, and when it's Susan's turn, she runs across the street to an old, decrepit apartment building where a group of longtime residents sit on the steps like living gargoyles.

Susan goes through the entranceway and waits in a small vestibule with the others. A peephole opens suddenly and a man peers out, then unlocks the door to allow the group to go inside the building. A fluorescent light flickers and hums in the hallway as Susan walks down to the bottom of the stairs to meet a man wearing an apron—drugs in one pocket, money in the other. She gives him $10, and he gives her a small plastic bag of off-white powder. Almost no words have been exchanged, and the whole process—from the sidewalk to entry to exit—takes no more than five minutes.

Susan has just scored heroin. The supply will last her one night. And if this is a typical weekend for her, she'll probably be back for more when Saturday night rolls around.

Smack Is Back

Heroin. Smack. Horse. By whatever name, this seemingly passé remnant of the '70s is back. And it's more plentiful, more potent and cheaper than ever before. In the '80s, the war on drugs for all intents and purposes meant a war on cocaine. Now the drug of choice is heroin—only this time it isn't just poor, wiped-out, needle-wielding junkies who are using the stuff. When Susan looks around at the people waiting in line with her to score heroin, almost half of them are "people who seem like your average person. People like me."

The difference is that Susan and her friends aren't shooting up; they snort their heroin or sometimes even smoke it. For Susan, the fact that she doesn't use a needle makes it easier to rationalize her dependency on heroin. In thinking that is typical of an addict, she tells herself that real addicts use needles; therefore, they're the only ones in danger of getting hooked on smack. The truth is that heroin, no matter what form it comes in, is extremely addictive. And the number of young women like Susan using the drug is growing daily. "I think heroin could be the drug of the nineties," says Felix Jimenez, chief of the heroin-operation section of the Drug Enforcement Administration [DEA] in Washington, D.C.

What happened? How can heroin, which never really entered the mainstream last time around, be making such a comeback and be seducing a whole new generation? Some experts actually predicted a resurgence in the popularity of the drug, based on the theory that drug epidemics are cyclical, and that an epidemic of stimulant abuse—like cocaine and crack—is naturally followed by a surge in the use of depressants like heroin. And often there is a certain crossover, with treatment centers today reporting large numbers of crack addicts who are also hooked on heroin.

New Addicts

But many of these new heroin users have never used crack, or even, like Susan, much cocaine. And they certainly don't fit the old, stereotypical profile of the strung-out junkie. They are young, educated, smart and maybe just a little too anxious to be on the cutting edge, at the forefront of every new trend.

Like Louise, 29, a graduate of a prestigious Southern university and a successful novelist. She summers at the Long Island shore and while she isn't rich, she's more than comfortable. She also snorts heroin.

Nikki is 23 and attended an exclusive liberal-arts college in the Northeast. She's trying to break into the movie industry by writing screenplays. Often, she's out prowling the same mean streets as Susan—but she's not looking for ideas to turn into scripts. She's out trying to score her drug of choice: heroin.

A Fashion Statement

For Susan, Louise and Nikki, snorting heroin holds the same attraction that snorting cocaine held for the privileged and well-off young women who were drawn to that drug in the '70s: It's decadent, nonconformist and dangerous. At one popular restaurant in Manhattan's East Village, the manager reports that in the past year he's had to chase several heroin-snorting patrons from the bathrooms. The tip-off is a line at the door, particularly for the men's room, which is tucked away in a corner and therefore less conspicuous. "They're mostly in their mid-twenties or early thirties," he says of the heroin-users he kicks out. "It's almost like it's become a fashion statement or some sort of *Sid and Nancy* thing."

In fact, it *was* that biographical film about Sex Pistol Sid Vicious and his girlfriend, Nancy Spungen, that first made Nikki curious about heroin—in spite of the fact that the movie did nothing to glamorize addiction (both Vicious and Spungen die as a result of their drug abuse). Nikki tried snorting heroin not long after that, with some friends at college. By the end of her senior year, they were doing it three times a week or more, stopping only temporarily when they had finals to take or major papers to write. When she graduated, Nikki moved to New York

City to try to get her film career started. Instead, she's using heroin even more frequently and working only sporadically.

"The problem with heroin is that you become disinterested in what you are doing, and isolate yourself with an I-don't-care, everyone-is-an-idiot attitude," Nikki says. "I've lost interest in most of my acquaintances. Heroin removes a lot of the joys of going out and meeting new people. But it also removes some of the struggle."

The Killer Drug

In the world's primary opium-growing regions—Southeast Asia, Southwest Asia and Mexico—the Drug Enforcement Administration has found an "explosion" of increased production. As a consequence, law enforcement authorities are reporting a tremendous increase in the purity of the cut heroin sold on the street—often five times the level normally found.

The higher its level of purity, the more easily a dose of street heroin can be smoked, experts tell us. Today's purer heroin is attracting users who previously avoided the drug because of the fear of needles and AIDS. Moreover, a deadly mixture of cocaine and heroin has resurfaced as well. There are reports that a new and even more deadly drug combination of heroin and crack—nicknamed "moon rock," "speedball" and "parachute"—has also hit the streets.

Charles B. Rangel, *The New York Times*, August 14, 1990.

Now she fears she may be becoming addicted. After two months in the Caribbean writing a screenplay, Nikki returned to New York City and promptly "binged for like two weeks" on smack. That was when she began to fear she might have a serious problem—"after the binge, I was completely dependent on it," she admits—and has stopped using it, at least for now. "I decided not to do it, but I haven't decided not to do it forever," she says. "I'm trying to set limits, like not doing it all of next month, because I don't want to put too much pressure on myself. Once you do smack you will always want to do it. Once you've gotten off on it, you always want it again. I will always feel that way."

Psychological Addiction

Unfortunately, Nikki is probably right. Heroin's addictive powers are distinctly different from cocaine, which alters the brain's chemistry to create a craving. When used as infrequently as once a week, heroin produces a psychological addiction. On a more frequent basis, the addiction becomes physical, and very difficult to break. And the high produced by snorting or smoking heroin is also quite different from cocaine's. "It's a very physical feeling," Louise says. "It's not really a head trip, it's more subtle. Sometimes you can get really overwhelmed and you can't keep your eyes open. You're not tired, it's like you drift. You're humming on the inside."

The morning after she has snorted heroin, though, Louise wakes up in what she calls a "low-grade depression," thinking about doing more heroin to get over it. In fact, Louise believes her heroin use may have triggered the serious and prolonged depression she went through. (Other side effects include nausea, painful headaches and constipation.) "It's insidious, because when you do it, you wake up the next day and if you have any left over, you just think how you want to do it. I can see how it could worm its way into your life."

Euphoria and Dependency

Aside from the euphoria and dependency it produces, a large part of heroin's appeal lies in the fact that it's still seen as the last unexplored chemical frontier in an age where cocaine has come and gone and marijuana smoke seems to overpower cigarettes at most parties. Indeed, Louise attributes her curiosity about heroin to its being the last remaining taboo substance in drugland. "I had dreams about it because I'd forbidden myself to try it," she says. She'd smoked pot and popped Ecstasy pills; cocaine didn't interest her much. What had stopped Louise from trying heroin was the prospect of using a needle. So when a younger friend told her heroin can be snorted—and showed her how—she quickly tried it.

The new heroin craze isn't just an East Coast phenomenon. Reports from Los Angeles are disturbingly similar. Julia, a 30-year-old photographer's assistant and frequent clubgoer, says heroin use in her circle is "extraordinarily commonplace," and seems to cut across a lot of social lines to include "children of wealthy people, people with careers, the actor-model set, people with money and regular people, too. It's just very common, and it's perceived as something you can do without the world knowing what's going on." Heroin isn't used as a social lubricant the way cocaine was during the days when it was openly snorted in clubs like Studio 54. In some ways, it makes perfect sense that the drug of choice for the stay-at-home '90s would be heroin, whose users typically snort the drug at home alone or with friends. Occasionally, Susan or Nikki will go to bars after they've gotten high, but they seldom drink alcohol, which in combination with the heroin can induce nausea.

It is probably safe to say that most of the young women using heroin today would not do so if getting high entailed shooting up, as it did in the '70s. The difference is that today's heroin is much more potent than it was just a decade ago, which means that casual users can snort it and get the same high—and the same quick addiction—as yesterday's junkies.

In the early '70s—the days of the infamous French Connection—most of the heroin in this country came from opium grown in the Southwest Asian countries of Pakistan and Afghanistan, and in Turkey. It was shipped across Europe to be refined into heroin in French labs; from there, it was smuggled into the United States.

The Golden Triangle

Now, however, more than half of the heroin entering the United States is produced in Southeast Asia—specifically, Myanmar (formerly Burma), Laos and Thailand, the so-called Golden Triangle. Large loads arrive in the United States aboard commercial ships, concealed amidst the legitimate cargo. As with cocaine, small amounts of heroin are worth large amounts of money, making it an ideal drug in which to traffic.

Once the Southeast Asian traffickers established their dominance, the quality of the heroin on the streets in this country increased dramatically. In the early '70s, when Jimenez worked the streets for the DEA, the heroin he saw was usually no more than 2- to 5-percent pure. (The remainder is composed of material used to dilute the drug and get the most out of a kilo.) Today, the heroin sold on the streets can be as much as 50-percent pure. Again, this is a direct result of the increase in production of opium—traffickers can afford to radically increase the potency of the drug because more of it is being produced than ever before. Another by-product of this increased production is a street price for heroin that's considerably less than it was in the '70s, when being an addict required access to large sums of cash.

Heroin Use Increasing

For now, neither the experts nor the users see this country's latest drug fad slowing down. Drug-treatment experts report seeing an alarming rise in heroin use. And, while hard statistics on the actual number of heroin users are virtually impossible to obtain, federal authorities estimate that the number of heroin users has increased from the '70s—and they expect that rise to continue in the '90s as the number of cocaine users continues to drop. "We are seeing a lot more heroin use than we ever did, and that has to do with the fact that in the past, heroin use was fairly confined to a relatively small subsection of people," says Anne Geller, M.D., chief of the Smithers Center in Manhattan. "Now we are seeing people who are employed, who are much more socially stable in many ways than the classical picture of the seventies heroin addict."

The same is true at Yale University's School of Medicine Substance Abuse Treatment Unit. In the late '80s, the cocaine-treatment center was full, with a long waiting list. Now, it's the heroin-treatment section that is filled and the waiting time to get in can last as long as six months, says Thomas Kosten, M.D., the program's director.

What experts like Dr. Geller have found is a whole new group of young people who are as ignorant today of the destructive power of heroin as we were about cocaine in the late '70s. "Cocaine has had such abysmal press that people have finally become terrified of it, and those who want to get high but who would have been deterred by the use of needles now find they can get a very pleasurable high with heroin by snorting or smoking it," says Dr. Geller. "They think heroin is probably the 'safe' drug of the nineties—just as cocaine was the 'safe' drug of the seventies." Dr. Geller hears dangerous myths and misconceptions every day, like Louise's idea that "it is pretty hard to get addicted if you are snorting it."

The strongest words of caution about casual heroin use come from former addicts themselves. Like Julia in Los Angeles, who has seen two friends lose or quit their jobs when they began getting high so often they simply dropped out of mainstream society. "It's extraordinarily difficult to shake. It's just got an incredible grip," Julia says. "The trendiness is the real peril, because anything new is tantalizing and this is considered new again."

A True Addict

As frightening as it is to think that women choose drugs like clothes or restaurants—based on what's hot and who's doing it—it's precisely this mind-set that turns women like Susan into addicts. She quit her job as a social worker when she became too burnt-out and unable to cope with the daily responsibilities it entailed. Unemployed and with lots of free time on her hands, she continues to use heroin on a regular basis. She acknowledges she might be dependent on the drug, but insists that she can control it. But when she describes just how she does that, you realize she's in deeper than she knows. Because when Susan has a headache or backache or chills, she doesn't reach for aspirin or cold medicine like the rest of us. Instead, she takes "a little Valium or a little bit of heroin or another sort of opiate, and then I'm fine." Spoken like a true addict.

"To date, there is remarkably little hard evidence that a new heroin epidemic has begun."

Evidence of Increased Heroin Use Is Inconclusive

Mark A.R. Kleiman and Jonathan P. Caulkins

Mark A.R. Kleiman is associate professor of public policy at the John F. Kennedy School of Government at Harvard University in Cambridge, Massachusetts. He is the author of *Against Excess: Drug Policy for Results.* Jonathan P. Caulkins is assistant professor of operations research and public policy at Carnegie Mellon University's School of Urban and Public Affairs in Pittsburgh, Pennsylvania. In the following viewpoint, Kleiman and Caulkins contend that there are few reliable ways of determining whether heroin use is increasing. Typical addict populations are difficult to find to interview, and heroin use by students, an easily accessible population, is low, the authors maintain. They accede that the street supply of heroin is increasing, but contend that heroin's frightening reputation and the fear of transmission of the AIDS virus through injection needles could prevent an increase in heroin use.

As you read, consider the following questions:

1. According to the authors, what factors have traditionally kept heroin use from increasing significantly?
2. According to the authors, how could arrest records and treatment center admissions help track the incidence of heroin use?
3. What are some of the methods Kleiman and Caulkins suggest to increase the amount of information available about heroin use?

From Mark A.R. Kleiman and Jonathan P. Caulkins, "Heroin Policy for the Next Decade," *Annals of the American Academy of Political and Social Science* 521 (May 1992): 163-74. Copyright 1992 by The American Academy of Political and Social Science. Reprinted with permission of Sage Publications, Inc.

By several measures, the supply of heroin to the U.S. market has been increasing over the past several years, after more than a decade of relative stability. The frequency of large-scale seizures has risen substantially, and the sizes of individual seizures continue to set records. Wholesale (kilogram-level) prices are substantially below those of the early 1980s. Retail-level purity has soared; levels higher than 40 percent are now routine in many large urban markets. The average retail price per pure milligram for 1990 in the largest market, New York City, was estimated to be barely over $1, a figure comparable, in inflation-adjusted terms, to the price that prevailed at the beginning of the last great heroin epidemic, in the mid-1960s. . . .

Higher Prices

The high price of heroin heretofore may have exerted a restraining effect on the tendency of some heavy cocaine users to combine the two drugs, either to obtain a polydrug effect or simply to ease the crash following a cocaine binge. It also made it less likely that heavy cocaine users, particularly crack smokers, would switch to heroin. As heroin prices fall, the migration path from cocaine use to heroin use will tend to become easier.

On the other hand, several mechanisms restrain the consumption of heroin, whatever happens to its price. The miserable condition of most of the highly visible heroin addicts has attached a substantial stigma to heroin use as perceived by virtually every social group and subculture. The association of heroin with acquired immune deficiency syndrome (AIDS) has driven the lesson home even more firmly. If there were a sudden upsurge in heroin initiation, the presence of many (temporarily) happy consumers for the drug would tend to change the drug's street reputation, but in the meanwhile the reputation itself helps to block the very phenomenon that would change it.

In the absence of supply changes, the trend in heroin use would likely be down. The existing user base is being steadily eaten away by cessation of use and by mortality, already high and now aggravated by aging and AIDS. The massive revulsion from illicit drug use resulting from the cocaine experience of the past decade is probably making itself felt even in the social milieus from which heroin users have traditionally been drawn. Growing supply may be relatively unimportant in the face of shrinking demand.

Moreover, price and purity represent only one aspect of the heroin supply situation. Retail availability, determined by the number, social and geographic distribution, and aggressiveness of retail dealers, shapes consumption patterns by determining the cost, in time and inconvenience, of searching for the drug. In the case of crack, the spread of the epidemic from city to city was limited less by wholesale supplies, which were always ample, than by the existence of retail distribution channels.

The number of retail heroin dealers today is surely a small fraction of the number of retail cocaine and crack dealers, and the falling price of heroin itself—the raw material of retail dealing—does little directly to change that lack of distribution capacity. . . .

Poor Data Collection Methods

To date, there is remarkably little hard evidence that a new heroin epidemic has begun. But this may say as much about the data collection systems in place as it does about the existence—or not—of significant trends.

The seizure data themselves provide strong evidence that the physical volume of heroin being consumed has increased. In the very short run, increased shipments need not reflect increased consumption; slack demand can create involuntary inventory buildup of illicit as well as licit goods. But just as unsold automobiles on car dealers' lots eventually lead to reduced production, unsold heroin in retail dealers' stashes will reduce demand at wholesale, and importers will quickly learn that even a technically successful smuggling venture fails to earn an economic reward. Thus the fact that seizures have risen, not for one or two quarters or even for a year, but for several years in succession, strongly suggests that more heroin is going into users' bodies now than was the case five years ago.

This rise, in turn, must reflect some combination of more users and more consumption per user. Increasing tolerance and possible shifts to less efficient modes of administration—away from intravenous injection to smoking or insufflation—imply that the number of hours or days each user spends under the influence of heroin will grow more slowly than the physical dosage per user. The physical consumption of heroin would double, for example, if the user population and doses per user per day both remained fixed while the heroin content of each dose doubled as a result of a purity increase from 10 to 20 percent.

More Users or Increased Consumption?

The question, then, is how much of the additional consumption supply of heroin is attributable to an increase in the number of users—by increasing rates of initiation and relapse from abstinence or by decreasing quit-attempt rates—and how much is attributable simply to an increase in consumption rates by existing users. The former set of effects is far more worrisome than the latter.

Survey evidence is of little value here. Heroin use is too rare and too socially marginal an activity to be reliably measured by

40

administering questionnaires to national probability samples. Street ethnography, particularly the systematic variety as practiced by the Street Studies Unit in New York City, has better prospects for noticing—though not for measuring—changes, but street ethnographers of necessity start from known populations of users and may easily miss pockets of new users developing at a social distance from existing users. In addition, the capability of New York's street studies is unique; there is no comparable capacity to detect the early stages of a microepidemic in Boston or Kansas City. The Community Epidemiology Work Groups are only a partial substitute.

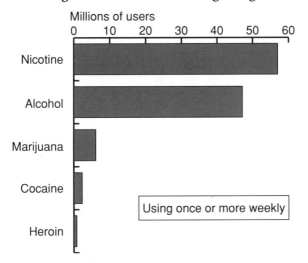

Regular Users of Addicting Drugs

Source: Data for 1990 from several U.S. Government sources.

The other systematic data collection efforts tend to count drug users in trouble and thus to miss drug users just starting out. The Drug Abuse Warning Network (DAWN) counts users injured or killed, the Drug Use Forecasting (DUF) system counts arrested users, and the drug treatment system counts users who have lost control of their habits. Any of these systems would notice a truly massive upsurge; if the number of heroin users had doubled, almost certainly the numbers of injuries, deaths, arrests, and—somewhat later—treatment entries would reflect that fact. But if the number of initiations had merely gone from a few tens of thousands—roughly replacement level for a chronic

41

user population in the hundreds of thousands—to twice that level, the addition of a few more tens of thousands of new, and consequently low-problem-incidence, users to the existing population might not show up for several years. Furthermore, despite their names, these data collection efforts are lagging, not leading, indicators of initiation rates, because most users do not experience such severe problems immediately upon initiation. . . .

Preventing Increases

If heroin becomes increasingly available, the value of prevention efforts aimed specifically at heroin will tend to increase. Unfortunately, the populations most likely to start using heroin are among those least likely to be receptive to officially generated messages. Nevertheless, in addition to reinforcing heroin's already bad reputation, there would be some value in warning potential new users that the risk of addiction is generic to the drug, not specific to intravenous injection. The danger here would be that prevention efforts could have the effect of spreading the message that heroin can be snorted or smoked as well as injected.

One low-cost preliminary step would be to launch a pilot study of a sample of young adults from high-HIV-seroprevalence census tracts in New York City to determine their attitudes and beliefs about heroin. The results of the study would be an aid to the design of appropriate messages for prevention efforts.

In addition to choosing messages, a prevention campaign needs to consider target audiences and communications vehicles. Even if the heroin-using population grows substantially, it is likely to remain heavily concentrated geographically and sociologically; if there is a new population of heroin users, it will probably look like the existing population but twenty years younger—and perhaps more evenly divided by gender. This concentration makes the use of mass media not only inefficient but substantively unwise; there is no point in stirring up curiosity about heroin in those who would otherwise never think of it without a shudder.

Again, if heroin follows its previous patterns, the value of school-based programs will be limited by the fact that heroin initiation tends to take place in young adulthood rather than adolescence and that those most likely to become its users are most likely to be frequent absentees and early dropouts. One common characteristic of many of the 1967-73 cohort of heroin users was their early involvement with the criminal justice system, an involvement that tended to predate their heroin use. This suggests that big-city arrestee populations, including juveniles, may be good targets for anti-heroin messages. Even given the obvious problems, jails and police lockups are probably underutilized as sites for drug education. In addition, there might be value in giving drug prevention training and materials to pa-role and probation officers and to criminal defense lawyers, in-cluding public defender staffs and other publicly paid counsel.

Neither supply control nor prevention efforts are likely to be sufficient to forestall all of the increase in heroin consumption that greater availability could cause. This raises the question of how to protect, insofar as possible, a new cohort of heroin users from the risks of heroin use and to protect their neighbors and families from the behavioral consequences of the use of an ex-pensive and dependency-inducing drug. Achieving this protec-tion means designing a new set of secondary and tertiary pre-vention efforts to match the characteristics of the new heroin-using population and adjusting the treatment system to meet a new set of demands.

The Fear of the Needle

The fear of the needle has been one layer of protection between the United States and a new heroin epidemic. A second is simply the word *heroin*. Not only do people fear the drug, they also do not want to think of themselves, or have others think of them, as heroin addicts. The next sign that a heroin wave may be upon us would be the introduction of a new term for the drug in a new form, as far from *heroin* as *ice* is from *crank* (the slang term for methamphetamine). A packing innovation like the crack vial could also make a difference.

To date, none of the national monitoring systems shows evidence of a new wave of heroin use. That is reassuring as far as it goes. But if the price keeps falling and the purity keeps rising, the threat of growing use will intensify. Heroin does not now have the enormous retail distribution system that has built up around cocaine and crack, but the diminution of demand for crack will leave a large number of unemployed or underemployed drug dealers ready to respond to new demand if it arises.

Mark A.R. Kleiman, *Against Excess: Drug Policy for Results*, 1992.

The most novel tertiary-prevention issue is how to persuade those who begin to use heroin intranasally or by smoking not to switch to injection as their growing drug habits begin to put pressure on their budgets. (In this connection, a great deal could be learned by conducting interviews with a sample of recent-onset intravenous heroin users entering treatment to determine how many of them started as intranasal users.) Even more than primary-prevention efforts, these messages would have to be narrowly targeted to appropriate audiences to avoid an unwanted advertising effect.

The other post-primary prevention, treatment, and treatment-outreach issues are all familiar ones. Just as a treatment system too centered on the problems of forty-year-old male heroin injectors had to be reshaped to meet the cocaine epidemic, the rising generation of heroin users, if there is one, will require services appropriate to its needs. At first, neither the existing heroin programs—still focused on the older cohort—nor the existing programs for younger users—still focused on cocaine—will be fully ready to do the job.

Methadone programs will face a peculiar set of pressures if the typical daily street habit rises. On one hand, the dose of methadone required to induce treatment entrance and prevent withdrawal discomfort and consequent dropout is likely to be higher for clients entering with larger habits. On the other hand, using larger doses with new clients will make it more difficult to keep existing clients content at current dosages. European clinical experience, gained in a setting of low prices and high doses, may become more relevant for the United States than it has been heretofore.

Monitoring Systems

The foregoing discussion suggests that there are substantial policy choices to which the question of how fast the number of heroin users is growing would be directly relevant. This raises the question of how to find out.

To some extent, existing data sources can be tapped for evidence. Stratification of DAWN heroin reports by age of patient, for example, would help to separate out incidents involving new, younger users from those that involve the existing heroin cohort and would thus create a more sensitive measure of initiation rates. Similarly, analysis of treatment-entry data, including time since first use for heroin users and secondary drugs for those whose primary drug is other than heroin, could be illuminating.

Some of the most powerful evidence is likely to come from targeted surveys and from street ethnography. The problem is to identify appropriate sample frames for surveys—here again, criminal justice populations leap to mind—and appropriate starting points for ethnographic investigation—new treatment entrants, if they can be located though the veil of confidentiality, might be a good place to start. The DUF system, which asks its interviewees about their year of first use, will tend to detect a rise in recent initiations before most other data collection efforts. The expansion of the sample size for the National Household Survey on Drug Abuse, and the deliberate oversampling of young adults in high-prevalence areas, will also be helpful in measuring changes in the prevalence of heroin use.

Unfortunately, the survey does not ask about duration of use and therefore provides no direct evidence on incidence.

Finally, the independent variable in the causal equation—the price and purity of heroin sold on the street—could be measured with far more precision. Simply creating a national data base analogous to the Drug Enforcement Administration's System to Retrieve Information from Drug Evidence that included data from all local, state, and federal enforcement agencies would be a great first step. But any attempt to use enforcement data to study the retail drug markets will be limited by the fact that undercover drug purchases are not designed or executed with research purposes and standards in mind. There may be a need for systematic retail drug-purchase activity designed explicitly as a research tool, with careful attention to issues such as sampling frames, test-retest validity, and the like. Statistically valid local price and purity data for the cities with the dozen largest heroin markets could be obtained for relatively little money. To these could be added a panel survey of users to attempt to measure search time and other nonprice components of availability.

While it is implausible that the United States is about to experience a heroin epidemic comparable in scope to the current cocaine epidemic, it is almost equally implausible that the continued availability of heroin at historically low prices and high purities will have no effect at all on the number of new heroin users. Since undue delay can be expensive, and most of the existing sources of data are likely to lag substantially behind the problem itself, it may be wise to take some relatively low-cost actions now, while simultaneously increasing monitoring efforts.

These low-cost actions might include criminal-justice-system-based education programs designed to deter intravenous drug use and to inform potential users that heroin can be dependency-forming even if it is not injected. There may also be a need to expand and redesign treatment programs to accommodate younger heroin users. If the enhanced monitoring programs discussed in the preceding section give signs that another heroin epidemic is under way, then more expensive options such as redirecting enforcement resources toward heroin may be appropriate.

Heroin's Danger

At this point it is difficult to predict what will happen. Supply conditions are not unlike those that preceded the last heroin epidemic, but other things have changed. Knowledge of heroin's danger is more widespread, and AIDS adds a new dimension to those dangers. It would be unwise to either do nothing or to act as if a new epidemic were certain.

"Cocaine use is on an upswing, and a big one at that."

Cocaine Abuse Is a Serious Problem

Charlie Knox

In the following viewpoint, Charlie Knox argues that government surveys indicate that many people are continuing to abuse cocaine. This abuse contributes to serious problems such as poverty, child abuse and neglect, and crime, Knox contends. He is a staff writer for the *Prison Mirror*, the biweekly newspaper for the Minnesota Correctional Facility-Stillwater.

As you read, consider the following questions:

1. Why have law enforcement efforts to reduce cocaine abuse been ineffective, according to the author?
2. What measures does Knox advocate to stop the abuse of cocaine?
3. How does cocaine affect those who use it, according to the author?

Charlie Knox, "Law of Gravity Check: What Goes Down May Come Back Up." Reprinted from *The Prison Mirror* (Minnesota State Prison at Stillwater), January 27, 1992.

One of the mainstays of the conservative verbal quiver of armaments in the "war on drugs" has been the notion that "cocaine use has fallen dramatically over the last half of the past decade." Often such pearls of wisdom (remember: never cast pearls before swine) are delivered by law enforcement personnel or lawmakers involved in instituting harsh (or harsher yet) legislation pertaining to powder or crack cocaine. While offering the usual impenetrable statistical fog of governmental-agency-produced numbers, those principals involved on one side—the right side—of the battle against drug use sometimes lose sight of the bigger picture. And the bigger picture, according to the latest survey by the National Institute on Drug Abuse, paints a picture far different from that presented by those fighting the good fight: Cocaine use is on an upswing, and a big one at that.

Cocaine Use Is Rising

The NIDA report stated that cocaine use (used at least once a month by those surveyed) between 1991 and 1992 rose by about eighteen percent. In real numbers that translates into about two million new users; two million more people who have been unaffected by the bureaucratically inept machinations attempting to pace the Mephisto waltz of cocaine use and abuse. And the upswing in new users is from a broad-based constituency: minorities, the unemployed, and persons over the age of 35.

Moreover, the NIDA has estimated that something on the order of 855,000 individuals are currently habitual users of cocaine; habitual use being defined as cocaine ingestion on a weekly basis. Those numbers are virtually the same numbers that existed in 1988. While that realization in itself is troubling, perhaps greater consequence should be made of this: According to the Drug Abuse Warning Network (yet another hawker in the Reagan/Bush "drug war" sideshow), cocaine- and heroin-related emergencies in the nation's hospitals rose by more than 30 percent. Such figures lead one to question just how effective recent "drug-war" policies have been.

Even so, there are plenty of experts who find a way to cast a positive light on the obvious negative connotations of the recent numbers. William Bennett, the former drug czar who now works for the conservative oracle, *National Review*, has pooh-poohed the NIDA and DAWN results. "We said a number of times we'd see declines followed by plateaus." And then he offered a classic Reaganesque rhetorical pontification: "One has to question what would have happened without the effort we made." No, Bill, one has to question what would have happened had more money been spent on the educational and treatment aspects of drug use/abuse instead of the interdiction and incarceration angle.

Fortunately there are a few experts who can see the forest for the trees. Charles Rangel, U.S. Representative of New York and chairman of the Select Committee on Narcotics Abuse and Control, happens to be one of them. "The administration is constantly talking about . . . reports. They're always looking for good news. But the truth of the matter is they don't want to acknowledge that . . . there is still an explosion of cocaine use."

BOILEAU

All of this couldn't come at a worse time economically. Towns, cities, states and the nation as a whole are operating in the throes of a recessed economy. Drug treatment—both illicit and licit—programs are being cut in a willy-nilly fashion. According to a recent article in the *Washington Post*, almost one-quarter of this nation's states have cut back on such programs, among them Florida, Colorado, Connecticut, Georgia, and Pennsylvania. Those cut-backs fit in nicely with general governmental trends, but they contravene what politicians have been fervently spouting about amplifying the "war on drugs."

Let's do a quick reality check: More people may be using drugs, so say various groups who chronicle that type of number game. This is happening while literally billions of (shrinking) local, state, and federal dollars are being spent to prevent such an occurrence. The Bureau of Justice Statistics has released figures that show just what use of chemicals brings: crime. We don't have to take a great logical leap to see that one leads to the other in a hand-by-hand fashion. But that is where the logic seems to come to a screeching stop.

Law Enforcement Will Not Work

Programs that rely on the at-large law enforcement community to help solve the nation's drug problem surpass the ludicrous and step right up to the asinine. Law enforcement has a vested interest in keeping the drug money flowing into their hands as opposed to treatment and/or education programs, despite their protestations to the contrary. Until that realization is properly addressed interdiction programs will continue to be the prevailing force in the "war on drugs." And they will continue to fail miserably.

Drug use rents the fabric of lives. It creates a nightmarish scenario of despair and hopelessness that transforms into life's guiding force. It provides a flight from reality that too often becomes a one-way trip to a place of irreality; a destination resort called Club Dead in the tropical environs of the hell of mindless abuse. Until lawmakers truly use their resources in a deliberative fashion to stop the declination of those who use, the country will have to become accustomed to the wasted souls that drug use creates. Americans will have to understand that what goes down must come up . . . and up . . . and up . . .

"*Cocaine is not a significant source of crime, violence, addiction, heart disease, brain damage, unhealthy babies, student apathy, low productivity, or terrorism.*"

Cocaine Abuse Is Not a Serious Problem

Bruce Alexander

Cocaine is thought by many to be an especially harmful or damaging drug. In the following viewpoint, Bruce Alexander challenges this idea and discounts most studies that have been used as evidence that cocaine is addictive and damaging. Instead, the author suggests that cocaine use should be considered risky but not dangerous. Alexander is a professor of psychology at Simon Fraser University in Burnaby, British Columbia. He is also the author of the book *Peaceful Measures: Canada's Way Out of the "War on Drugs."*

As you read, consider the following questions:

1. What is the "propaganda of the drug war," and why does Alexander call it that?
2. What studies does the author discount and how does he do it?
3. According to Alexander, how should cocaine be categorized and why?

In the propaganda of the drug war, cocaine is an unmitigated evil, perhaps symbolized most vividly by one of those none-too-subtle images from the Partnership for a Drug-Free America: a revolver with its barrel aimed up the user's nostril. At other times and in other places, however, the drug has been known as a benign stimulant and a marvelous tonic for a variety of major and minor ills. . . .

Cocaine Is Not Highly Addictive

In spite of widespread availability and declining prices, most people never use cocaine; of those who do, most use it only once or a few times; of those who become casual or regular users, most do not become dependent or addicted; of those who become dependent or addicted, most return to moderate use or voluntarily abstain without treatment; and of those whose addiction becomes serious enough to require treatment, most had lives that were marked by severe alienation or misfortune before they first used cocaine. None of this is intended to deny the horrors of severe addiction to cocaine, but rather to challenge the view that these horrors prove cocaine is a highly addictive drug.

Whatever the drug's power, the vast majority of Americans have managed to resist it. Cocaine use appears to have peaked by 1979, leveling off in the early 1980s. The National Household Survey on Drug Abuse indicates that at the peak, less than 10 percent of Americans had ever used cocaine and less than 2 percent had used it even once in the year in which they were surveyed.

The "addictive liability" of a drug is not a precisely defined term, but it should be reflected in the difficulty that people have in terminating use. When the National Institute on Drug Abuse questioned high-school seniors who were considered recent users of cocaine in 1983, 3.8 percent reported that they had tried to stop using cocaine and found they could not. By comparison, 18 percent of cigarette smokers reported that they were unable to give up tobacco. Other American surveys of more geographically limited populations have produced similar results.

Taken together, the survey data indicate that cocaine is used by a minority of Americans and that only a small fraction of this minority uses very much. Of course, general population data like these tell little about special populations, such as school dropouts, in which more people may use cocaine and a higher proportion may become addicted. . . .

Smokable Cocaine

It's widely reported in the news media and medical literature that smokable cocaine is much more addictive than snorted cocaine hydrochloride. Crack, in particular, is frequently said to

51

be "instantly addictive" or the "most addictive drug on earth." Some eminent scholars take these claims about smokable forms of cocaine seriously. But others note that these claims are suspiciously similar to the unsubstantiated stories that were told about marijuana, glue, heroin, and cocaine hydrochloride when they first became matters of public concern.

Smokable cocaine reaches the bloodstream much faster than does nasally administered cocaine hydrochloride. This in itself does not prove that smokable cocaine is more addictive than other drugs. The speed with which smokable cocaine reaches the bloodstream is no greater than that with which smoked marijuana or nicotine (or intravenously injected cocaine hydrochloride) normally enters the bloodstream.

Horror Stories

After an extensive search of the literature, I have concluded that the widespread conviction that moderate use of cocaine is dangerous is based on horror stories that are accepted uncritically and on medical research that is misinterpreted because of the presuppositions of the war on drugs.

The misinterpretation of medical research entails each of the following errors: (1) exaggerating the amount of sickness and death that is associated with cocaine; (2) gratuitously assuming that people harmed by using cocaine are moderate rather than heavy users: (3) neglecting indications that medical emergencies that befall heavy cocaine users could just as well have resulted from their other drugs, activities, or pathologies; (4) gratuitously assuming that cocaine purchased by users who experience medical emergencies was unadulterated; and (5) ignoring the fact that many legal drugs and activities are just as dangerous as cocaine.

Bruce Alexander, *Reason*, December 1990.

Pharmacologically, the effects of smoking crack should be similar to those of smoking coca leaves because the active ingredient, the cocaine alkaloid, is the same. Parke, Davis & Company introduced coca-leaf cigars and cigarettes in 1885, and other drug companies offered similar products, primarily as treatments for respiratory infections. Although cocaine in general was gaining a bad reputation in this period, no one claimed that these smokable forms were especially addictive. In fact, some users publicly endorsed them as mild and effective remedies.

In spite of many media testimonials about the addictiveness of smokable cocaine, the only experimental evidence that I have found to support them comes from a single study on smoking coca paste in Lima, Peru. The subjects were all described as nondependent, "occasional" users. All subjects (the total number does not appear in the report) became anxious before smoking, all expressed an "extreme desire" for alcohol during the experimental sessions, and two reported "an inability to resist smoking" during the sessions. Nonetheless, all subjects must have resisted smoking enough to stop voluntarily, since no injuries or deaths were reported, even though the subjects were allowed as much coca paste as they wanted during two of the three experimental sessions in which each participated.

No Evidence of Widespread Use

There is no statistical evidence of widespread use of crack or any other form of smokable cocaine in North America. In the United States, 5.6 percent of high-school seniors surveyed in 1987 had ever used crack (as compared to 15.2 percent for all forms of cocaine). Only 1.5 percent reported use in the 30 days preceding the interview (as compared to 4.3 percent for cocaine in general). Thus, crack did not cause "instant addiction" in the great majority of people who tried it.

A study in Miami found that juvenile delinquents generally preferred cocaine hydrochloride to crack, because its effects last longer. Many of them used crack in addition to cocaine hydrochloride, however, because it was sold in smaller, cheaper doses. The study also found that addiction to crack was rare among the subjects. Taken together, these data suggest that there is no difference in addictive liability between crack and cocaine hydrochloride. . . .

False Impressions

It's widely accepted in North America that crack and other forms of smokable cocaine are especially dangerous. Some of the reports on which this impression is based are simply false. For example, *USA Today* attributed 563 deaths to cocaine and crack in the first six months of 1986. After a careful study of the official government reports and available medical literature, Arnold Trebach, president of the Drug Policy Foundation, found that none of these deaths could be confirmed.

Some articles in medical journals claim that crack, free-base, coca paste, and other forms of smokable cocaine are significantly more harmful than cocaine hydrochloride. However, apart from the well-established fact that smokable cocaine reaches the bloodstream faster than orally or nasally administered cocaine, these articles offer little data to support this assertion. The authors seem to have relied on uncritical assumptions about evidence.

I do not mean to claim that harm never results from moderate use of cocaine. All drugs, including cocaine, can hurt people. However, the existing research does not justify the claim that using cocaine in moderation is an unusually dangerous practice.

When a person dies as a result of jogging, playing squash, driving a car, or engaging in sexual intercourse, the event may lead people who engage in these activities to reassess the costs and benefits. It does not provide the occasion for a War on Jogging, a War on Squash, a War on Cars, or a War on Sex. The kind of research that has been taken as serious proof that cocaine regularly causes heart attacks and other dire consequences in moderate users only proves the existence of an extraordinary, warlike mentality. This kind of thinking forfeits a normally critical perspective to embrace spurious justifications for the war on drugs. . . .

Deeply Rooted Problems

In this century we have overreacted to the dangers of cocaine with a futile attempt to ban it from the world. This campaign stains the earth with blood and corrupts the fragile institutions of democracy. Worst of all, it diverts our attention from the real causes of the misery and conflict that surround us. Cocaine is not a significant source of crime, violence, addiction, heart disease, brain damage, unhealthy babies, student apathy, low productivity, or terrorism in the Third World. The real danger is the destructive illusion that we can relieve these deeply rooted problems by attacking cocaine.

Periodical Bibliography

The following articles have been selected to supplement the diverse views presented in this chapter.

American Medical Association	"Drug Abuse in the United States," *Journal of the American Medical Association*, April 24, 1991.
Stephen Chapman	"Could We Become a Nation of Zombies?" *Conservative Chronicle*, March 28, 1990. Available from PO Box 11297, Des Moines, IA 50441.
Steve Hochman	"Heroin: Back on the Charts," *Rolling Stone*, September 27, 1992.
Philip Jenkins	"Fighting Drugs, Taking Liberties," *Chronicles*, May 1992. Available from The Rockford Institute, 934 North Main St., Rockford, IL 61103-7061.
Lincoln Review	"The Scourge of Drug Addiction: A Challenge for the Black Community," Winter 1990. Available from The Lincoln Institute for Research and Education, 1001 Connecticut Ave. NW, Washington, DC 20036.
Clarence Lusane	"Illegal Drugs, the African American Community and the New Economic Order," *Crossroads*, December 1992/January 1993.
Michael Massing	"Crack! Girls like You on Drugs like This," *Mademoiselle*, May 1990.
Salim Muwakkil	"Drugs and the Black Community," *Utne Reader*, May/June 1991.
Charles B. Rangel	"The Killer Drug We Ignore," *The New York Times*, August 14, 1990.
Joseph B. Treaster	"Drug Use Is Growing, Study Says," *The New York Times*, July 9, 1992.
Cecil Williams	"Crack Is Genocide, 1990s Style," *The New York Times*, February 15, 1990.
Gordon Witkin	"A New Assault on Cocaine," *U.S. News & World Report*, January 11, 1993.
Robert C. Yeager	"Kids Who Can't Say No," *Reader's Digest*, February 1991.

How Should the War on Drugs Be Waged?

DRUG ABUSE

Chapter Preface

For more than a decade, the federal government fought the war on drugs by enforcing strict laws against the import, sale, and use of drugs. This effort has been supported by those who believe criminalizing drug use is the best way to reduce abuse.

Other Americans, dissatisfied with the results of the federal government's war on drugs but unwilling to decriminalize drug abuse, are offering new ways to reduce drug abuse and wage the drug war. One dramatic new idea, proposed by authors Daniel K. Benjamin and Roger Leroy Miller, is to remove the federal government as the leader of the drug war and empower state and local governments to take over. Benjamin and Miller argue, "This move will eliminate the federal monopoly on drug policy, at the same time that it will force state and local governments to undertake new initiatives that match the preferences and circumstances of their citizens." Giving the states control over drug policy, they argue, would satisfy many more people than the federal policy has.

Another new idea is to link drug treatment more closely with the criminal justice system. Roger Connors, coauthor of *The Winnable War: A Community Guide to Eradicating Street Drug Markets*, maintains that this proposal might include "self-funded treatment as a condition of parole, court-mandated AA or NA, driver's license forfeiture, or a car seizure." More severe measures might include court-mandated drug testing, home detention, or property seizures. The most severe would be mandatory drug treatment while in prison. This emphasis on treatment, Connors argues, would get and keep people off drugs, reducing the U.S. demand for them.

These proposals are just two examples of the creative new ways experts are seeking to wage the war on drugs. The viewpoints in the following chapter debate the effectiveness of these and other ways of waging the drug war.

"It is essential, for once, that we become truly serious in our efforts to combat the flow and use of illegal drugs. "

The War on Drugs Should Be Prosecuted More Vigorously

Joseph D. Douglass Jr.

The war on drugs is more than ten years old. According to the author of the following viewpoint, the federal government's efforts to win the war have been negligible. Author Joseph D. Douglass Jr. compares the war on drugs to the Vietnam War both in human and monetary costs and in the lack of will to win the war. As a solution, Douglass, a national security affairs consultant, argues that the war on drugs can be won if the government commits its political, financial, and military might to the cause.

As you read, consider the following questions:

1. According to Douglass, why have efforts to win the war on drugs been unsuccessful?
2. Into what three areas is the annual drug budget divided? What problems does the author find with each of these three areas?
3. Why does the author compare the drug war to the Vietnam War?

From Joseph D. Douglass Jr., "How Goes the 'War on Drugs?'" *Conservative Review*, January 1992. Reprinted with permission.

It has been ten years since President Reagan began a serious attack on the illegal drug business. The annual budget for the war on drugs in 1981 was $1.46 billion. In 1992 it [was] close to $12 billion, a 700 percent increase.

It is difficult to say whether the problem has worsened, lessened, or just changed over the past decade. The amount of money budgeted to combat the illegal drug problems has greatly increased, jails are filled to overflowing, and drug seizures each year set record highs. While the number of casual users has significantly decreased since its peak in 1986, the number of addicts seems to have increased or remained relatively constant. Violent crime and homicides continue to increase. Domestic marijuana production is down but overseas drug production—coca, poppies, and marijuana—is up and growing areas are more widely distributed. Drug-related physical and mental health problems continue to increase. Cocaine use, which had been decreasing, is again on the rise, up 18 percent in 1991 over 1990.

Drugs' Costs to Society

One way to gain an impression of how serious the drug problem has become is by adding up all the various costs that can be attributed to illegal drugs. These costs are difficult to assess because the statistics are not readily available and those that are seem to be changed every few years. . . .

What is immediately alarming about these figures is that *the annual cost of illegal drugs, both monetary and human casualty costs, is comparable to the total ten year cost of the Vietnam War*, and with many of the most serious costs of illegal drugs—such as political corruption, white collar crime, moral disintegration, and breakdown in family units—not even included in the totals! Consider the national outcry if we fought and lost an entire Vietnam War every year. Yet, that is precisely what is happening in the battle against illegal drugs.

A second disturbing aspect of these statistics is their cumulative nature. Many of the costs would continue even if the flow and use of drugs were instantly reduced to zero. Addiction recovery costs would continue to mount as would special education needs of drug-impaired children. AIDS cases caused by drug use will continue to increase, probably for at least ten years. The accumulated profits—globally over $200 billion new profits each year—that are used to finance other criminal activities and to transfer assets such as businesses, banks, and industries into the hands of criminal enterprises grow larger each year and clearly would not suddenly disappear if trafficking stopped.

A third insight that can be gleaned from these figures is that most of the problems are associated with the *use* of the drugs; that is, they are not, as many people would like to believe, simply due to the fact that the drugs are "illegal." The argument, "Just make drugs legal and the problem will disappear," is deceptively enticing—until you take a close look at all the problems and recognize that most of them arise out of the use of the drugs, which is *why* they are illegal. Should drugs be legalized, drug use likely will increase and the problems associated with the use will increase, probably in direct proportion. About the only costs expected to decrease are those due to crime, homicides, administration of justice, and that portion of the drug war that is not associated with education and treatment. Everything else increases; for example, mortality, morbidity, health, special education, and lost productivity. Nor does it make any sense to talk about legalizing only one drug, such as marijuana, because most of the problems are associated with more potent drugs and legalizing marijuana would only serve to increase the demand for more potent drugs and, hence, exacerbate all the most serious problems.

Out-Gunned and Out-Maneuvered

The statistics on the magnitude of drug sales provide an additional interest into what might be the essence of the drug war problem. The U.S. Treasury in 1988 estimated the size of the U.S. sales volume at $110 billion, of which they estimated 80 percent was pure profit. The *proceeds* of the global drug trafficking business was estimated by the State Department in 1991 to be over $300 billion, of which slightly more than a third came from the United States. Thus, it seems that the size of the enemy—the illegal international drug business—as best as can be determined today is in the range of $200 to $300 billion.

Contrast this with the size of the war on drugs, around $12 billion, of which only about $8 billion is used to fight the drug traffickers, both domestic and foreign. That is, the enemy is well over a factor of twenty times larger than the drug-war forces.

Even more important than the monetary comparison is a comparison of the nature of the forces and methods that are involved in the war. The anti-drug forces are law abiding and answerable to Congress and to both civil and criminal courts. In contrast, the enemy is dedicated, aggressive, innovative, well-financed, politically connected, ruthless, seldom answerable to the courts—indeed, the enemy controls many of the courts—and totally unprincipled. It is safe to say we are out-manned, out-gunned, and out-maneuvered. Is it any wonder that progress in the war seems to be so slow?

Judging from the nature of the illegal drug business—specifically, its enormity and what it is doing to our children and to our society—*perhaps it is time for all of us to become more informed and more critical of our own attitudes and programs to com-*

bat the drug plague. It now seems unlikely for the drug problem simply to cure itself. It is also unlikely to fade away if we just gradually increase our efforts each year as we have been doing—there is simply too much momentum, too much money to be made, too much support structure, and too many markets readily available for exploitation. Nor can we afford to allow the illegal drug costs to continue to accumulate at their present rate; unless, of course, we simply do not care what happens to our children and our way of life.

Cost Comparison Between the Vietnam War and the War on Drugs

Vietnam War—Total Ten-Year Costs	
Deaths	58,000
Wounded/casualties	300,000
Monetary costs	$150-230 billion
Drug War—Approximate Annual Costs	
Deaths	
Drug-related homicides	over 8,000
Drug-dependent deaths	15,000
Total annual deaths	over 23,000
Wounded/casualties	
Medical emergencies	371,208
Gun shot wounds	30,000
Drug-impaired babies	300,000
Students (grade 6-12)	
use cocaine weekly or daily	223,000
tried cocaine last year	690,000
new users of heroin	80,000
Hard-core users	
cocaine	2,200,000
heroin	940,000
marijuana	over 5,000,000
Monetary Costs	
Drug sales (just U.S.)	$50 to 110 billion
Justice, health, and lost productivity	over $60 billion
War on drugs program	over $12 billion

The manner in which the drug war is being approached is presented in the annual *National Drug Control Strategy*, which is prepared by the Office of National Drug Control Policy (ONDCP) and submitted to Congress each year. The budget is allocated within three major areas: demand reduction, domestic law enforcement, and international initiatives. . . .

Part of the problem is inherent in the approach, as set forth in the above budget figures. Border interdiction ($2 billion plus per year) is exceedingly difficult, as we should have learned during the Vietnam War when, notwithstanding major efforts, we were unable to stem the flow of weapons and material into South Vietnam. Interdiction imposes a cost on traffickers, but it does not stop the flow.

The principal accomplishment of criminal justice ($5 billion per year) is to fill the courts and jails to overflowing. The problem with the criminal justice approach is that the law enforcement agencies are organized to arrest, prosecute, and jail people. But, the objective of the war on drugs should be to stop drug trafficking and drug use, and arresting and jailing people is only useful to the extent it contributes to the cessation of trafficking and use, which certainly does not appear to be the case. *If anything should be clear, it is that the business of illegal drugs has gone way beyond the ability of the law-and-order mechanisms to control the activity.* That is, illegal drug trafficking is fundamentally not a law-and-order problem any longer.

International cooperation ($.9 billion per year) is a farce, and is well known to be a farce! This is easy to understand when you start to recognize the astronomical magnitude of the profits that are involved and the associated extent of drug money corruption in foreign countries, both non-industrialized and industrialized countries. Corruption figures of 75 percent and higher at the top levels in politics, business, finance, police, military, and justice are not uncommon. Except in a few very exceptional examples, there is no international cooperation, nor is there any reason to expect any to develop.

Education is certainly one means to be employed to reduce demand. Unfortunately, however, the U.S. educational system is not even succeeding in teaching reading, writing, and arithmetic fundamentals. Moreover, the U.S. educational system itself contributed to the problem when it stopped teaching right and wrong and instead began promoting relativistic morals and "do your own thing" decision-making in the 1960s. As for education through advertisements, the states are more interested in promoting get-rich lotteries than staying away from drugs. . . .

A Successful Approach

If you sweep away the rhetoric and look at what is really happening, there seems to be only one area where the approach has been truly successful. That is the anti-drug program that was implemented within the U.S. military services in the mid-1980s.

The U.S. military had been a primary target of international drug traffickers since the early 1950s. The effects were most noticeable during the Vietnam War, not only in Vietnam but at U.S. military bases in the United States and Europe as well. In the early 1980s, a good ten years after the massive U.S. military drug use problems were recognized and efforts to counteract this use were undertaken, use rates well over 30 percent in deployed military units were still being reported.

In the mid-1980s, after some disastrous accidents and adverse publicity, the military finally decided to get serious and clamp down. Their approach was the essence of simplicity: randomly test everyone each year for drug use and discharge identified users who do not immediately stop. Drug use in the military went from a range of 35 to 50 percent to less than 3 percent almost overnight. What caused the decrease was not education, or treatment, or law and order. It was simple fear—fear of being caught and thrown out.

How Serious Is the War on Drugs?

There are also a number of problems that do not show up in the *National Drug Control Strategy*. For example, to better coordinate operations, Congress created the ONDCP. Presumably, ONDCP is in charge of strategy and plans. Nothing could be more misleading. As insiders recognize, there is still no one in charge. The head of ONDCP, the so-called *drug czar*, is mainly a figurehead, a spokesperson, a single point of contact for Congress. The drug czar is a "commander" with no troops, no real budget, and no authority. The *National Drug Control Strategy* that ONDCP issues each year is only an organized description of all the anti-drug agency programs. There is no real strategy or plan, which is why in the fall of 1991 the Maryland Governor's Drug and Alcohol Abuse Commission in its published recommendations urged ONDCP to come up with a plan and a strategy.

Another good example is the interagency fight over a national drug intelligence center (NDIC) that emerged in 1989-91. NDIC was to be a strategic intelligence center. Deputy drug czar Stanley Morris described the rationale for the center most succinctly in June 1990: "We have very little effective strategic information on which to design a drug war."

After NDIC was approved by the President, it was sabotaged in Congress by several of the drug war agencies, most notably DEA [Drug Enforcement Administration], which already had a strategic intelligence division that was more abused than used by the DEA leadership. Next, it was captured by Justice, which is adept in crime, the courts, and politics, but not strategic intelligence. Why it would report to Justice, rather than ONDCP, is especially curious insofar as its main purpose was "to serve the strategic needs of policy making," which presumably was ONDCP's responsibility.

Justice's victory, however, was short-lived because the department was unable to convince the Appropriations Committee that there was a need for such a center and the committee decided not to fund the new initiative. Then to almost everyone's surprise the NDIC suddenly appeared as approved pork-barrel legislation in the Department of Defense (DoD) budget with its base of operations specified to be Pennsylvania, of all places!

Strategic Intelligence

The real tragedy of this example is that good strategic intelligence on all facets of the illegal drug and organized crime business should have been the first and highest priority action undertaken by the drug czar, *if not by the President himself.* Congressional approval was no more necessary to do what was needed than it was back in 1982 and 1986 when the CIA increased its narcotics intelligence efforts in response to two national security directives or in 1989 when the CIA formed a Counter Narcotics Center. Rather than question the whole NDIC funding fiasco, one should more properly ask, "Why now?" What has our national intelligence community been doing since President Nixon first identified drugs as a major threat to our nation and began a war on drugs in 1969? How can you devise an effective, efficient, and intelligent strategy to fight the war unless you begin with good strategic intelligence on where the enemy is and how he operates? Obviously, you can not—which speaks volumes about the depth of interest in the drug war in Washington, D.C.

When all is said and done, there is simply no war on drugs or even any serious interest in a war on drugs that is identifiable anywhere in the U.S. Government, including Congress, with two exceptions, the military services and the ranks of the men and women of the various anti-drug agencies who are on the front lines, out in the field, fighting the battle. But, aside from these people, the "war on drugs" has been and still is mainly a political mirage. Occasionally, an individual who is truly serious and does try to stem the flow of drugs as a high priority action surfaces; but, such an individual is a rare exception and lonely in Washington, D.C. For the most part, the war on drugs is used to build budgets, expand political power, and provide unlimited material for publicity and propaganda. . . .

The Need to Get Serious

It is because of the enormous costs and their insidious impact on our children, our society, and our way of life, that it is essential, for once, that we become truly serious in our efforts to combat the flow and use of illegal drugs. Those who would rather not become involved or are satisfied with the various Presidential pronouncements that we have "turned the corner" or are "on the road to victory" are encouraged to examine with care the costs. Dare any of us sit on the sidelines?

It would be nice if one could say, as many people seem to be saying, "If they want to fry their brains out, let them." Or, "Do not worry, AIDS will enable the drug problem to solve itself within ten to fifteen years." Or, "Do not worry about the rising number of homicides. It's only the drug dealers killing each other." Unfortunately, it is not that simple. The drug users and drug dealers are taking all of us—and our children—down with them.

Unless and until we get serious and decide to really fight back, the costs set forth in the table will continue to mount until stability and security in the United States is not much different from the deplorable conditions in Colombia or Mexico. This is the risk we face in not addressing the war on drugs with the same seriousness and attention that was marshalled in Desert Shield and Desert Storm. Don't American victims of illegal drug trafficking deserve at least the same degree of concern and response that was so freely given to the citizens of Kuwait?

"Today's punishment-oriented policies will not generate long-term success with addicts, even if they manage to discourage some casual users."

The War on Drugs Should Be Abandoned

Daniel K. Benjamin and Roger Leroy Miller

In the following viewpoint, Daniel K. Benjamin and Roger Leroy Miller argue that the war on drugs can never be won and should be abandoned. While the war's law enforcement measures effectively dissuade casual drug users, the authors conclude that most hard-core addicts are impervious to such measures. Because hard-core abusers and addicts are responsible for the vast majority of the demand for drugs, the authors argue that rather than continuing the war on drugs, efforts must be made to reduce drug addiction. Benjamin and Miller are the authors of *Undoing Drugs: Beyond Legalization*, from which this viewpoint was taken.

As you read, consider the following questions:

1. The authors state that drug addiction should be treated as a disease, not a crime. Why?
2. What do the authors mean when they say, "We can dissuade 70 percent of the users; we cannot eliminate 70 percent of the use"?
3. According to Benjamin and Miller, what should be the goal of any effort to fight drug abuse?

The current federal approach to fighting the war on drugs, which is essentially identical to that used during Prohibition seventy years ago, is based on two fundamental errors concerning drug use, abuse, and addiction. First, the drug warriors believe that drug consumers can be permanently and effectively dissuaded from ingesting their drugs of choice if the costs of doing so are high enough. For casual users of psychoactives, this stance is no doubt basically correct; most casual users will respond to an increase in the cost of an activity by doing less of that activity. Thus, Prohibition reduced alcohol consumption in America, and the fear of being arrested today induces many casual users to "just say no."

In principle, this theory also applies to addicts whether the costs are self-inflicted or externally imposed. After all, a dead addict is no longer a practicing addict. And there is evidence to suggest that death is not the only deterrent to drug use by addicts. For example, during Prohibition, the number of actively practicing alcoholics probably fell by as much as 20 to 30 percent, a (very) rough estimate based on the observed decline in cirrhosis deaths and other alcohol-related deaths during Prohibition. World War II proved even more disruptive to practicing heroin addicts in America, whose numbers may have fallen by as much as 50 percent during the war due to the worldwide disruption of heroin supplies.

Addiction Is a Disease

Nevertheless, the approach of the drug warriors ignores a fact that is recognized by every specialist in the field of drug and alcohol treatment: Addiction and alcoholism are diseases. Addicts and alcoholics who are forced to abstain from their drug of choice due, say, to imprisonment or threat thereof are, in the nomenclature of the field, "dry" rather than "sober." They are still addicts and alcoholics, whose practice of their addiction has merely been interrupted. Short of being executed or physically isolated from their psychoactive of choice, the overwhelming majority will sooner or later (and more likely sooner than later) return to drugs or alcohol, thereby starting the cycle anew. Involuntary incarceration, or the threat thereof, at best produces abstinence; it does not produce recovery from the underlying disease.

Addicts and alcoholics are not hopeless cases, however, fit only for abandonment or permanent incarceration. Treatment programs have been developed (and are steadily being improved) that empower these individuals to refrain completely from consuming their psychoactive of choice, and to do so in a manner that enables them to live "as though" they are not addicts or alcoholics. These programs, which generally require a lifelong commitment to self-monitored follow-up programs (such as Alcoholics Anonymous or Narcotics Anonymous), help addicts and alcoholics become recovering addicts or alcoholics—sober (or "clean") rather than merely dry. Those treated remain at risk of returning to the depths of practicing addiction if they resume drug or alcohol use, but they learn how to establish an effective set of barriers against such resumption of use, barriers that the dry addict or alcoholic does not have.

The current approach to the drug wars is imperiled by its refusal to acknowledge addiction as a disease rather than a crime. When it comes to their psychoactive of choice, addicts (and alcoholics) simply don't respond to incentives the way rational people do, because they are not—in this dimension—rational. By the very definition of the term, an addict has "given himself up" to his drug. Truly draconian measures, including punishment, will induce some addicts to temporarily forgo their drug of choice, but most will refuse or simply switch to legal substitutes (such as alcohol) while awaiting the opportunity to return to their drug of choice. Unless they obtain treatment (and not just punishment), they are at best "just one hit away from their next high."

Drug War Fallacies

Another fallacy underlying the current approach to the drug wars is the belief that if casual users can be prevented from consuming drugs, the market for psychoactives will collapse. Let's consider the facts. The consumption of psychoactives generally follows the lognormal distribution, which means that the vast majority of the population either does not use the psychoactive or uses it only casually, and a small minority of the population accounts for the vast bulk of the total consumption of the psychoactive. Consider alcohol. About 80 percent of all adult Americans either don't drink, or drink in such moderation that, as a whole, this part of the adult population drinks only 20 percent of the alcohol consumed in the United States. The other 20 percent of the adult population—the "heavy drinkers"— consume the remaining 80 percent of the alcohol. In fact, the 10 percent of adult Americans who drink the most consume more than 50 percent of the total amount of alcohol drunk in the United States.

This pattern has been true in the United States for as long as such statistics have been kept, and holds (plus or minus a few percentage points) in all countries for which statistics are available. And although the percentages that fall into each category differ across different psychoactives, the character of the lognormal distribution generally holds true: Most people consume drugs either not at all or casually, but most of the consumption is accounted for by a small percentage of people, who systematically either abuse or are addicted to the psychoactive in question. This pattern is true not just when most people are nonusers, as with heroin. *Even when casual use is widespread, as it is with marijuana and cocaine, most of the drug in question is being consumed by the abusers and addicts.* This point cannot be overemphasized. Casual users ingest less than half of the illegal drugs in question, while the bulk of all illegal drug consumption (between 60 percent and 80 percent) is engaged in by abusers and addicts. And it is these individuals who are the least responsive to the measures advocated by today's drug warriors.

The upshot is sad but simple. If we spend enough money and deprive enough people of their liberties, we can, in principle, dissuade people from casual use, and even induce some addicts to give up. But a core of abusers and addicts will remain who, though small in number, will keep overall consumption high. This core demand is sufficient to keep the basic infrastructure of the drug market profitable and in place. *We can dissuade 70 percent of the users; we cannot eliminate 70 percent of the use.* And achieving even this would require efforts on a scale far beyond what we are trying now; after all, not even the most ardent proponents of today's policies claim that we have eliminated casual drug use. Perhaps more importantly, and distressingly, even a 30 percent reduction in total consumption by means of today's policies would require significant additional resources permanently devoted to this task. The moment we lessen our efforts or relax our constraints, casual users will return to the market, and drug dealers will immediately leap into the breach, ready, willing, and able to supply all comers.

Prohibition History

History is clear on this point. Despite fourteen years of all-out war against alcohol during Prohibition, the suppliers survived, and when Repeal brought a resumption of legal production, the cocktail hour returned to millions of homes across the country. Despite seventy-five years of all-out war on heroin in this country, the suppliers and addicts remain. One out of 400 Americans is addicted to heroin today, just as roughly one out of 400 was addicted eighty years ago. The faces and names have changed, but the addiction has not.

The resilience of users, addicts, and suppliers is not unique to the United States, nor does it exist simply because we haven't been "tough enough." Malaysia and Singapore, for example, both impose the death penalty for drug trafficking. For run-of-the-mill drug users, the penalties range from whipping to two years in boot-camp-style "rehabilitation" facilities, where push-ups and hard labor are the order of the day.

"Punishment must be strict, or otherwise the penalty has no meaning," says Roh Geok Ek, the director of Singapore's central narcotics bureau. The assistant director of the Malaysian anti-narcotics force, Tey Boon Hwa, claims that "we hang anyone convicted who exhausts their appeals." Apparently, officials in both countries mean what they say. Since Malaysia introduced the death penalty for trafficking in 1983, some 235 people have been sentenced to death; as of early 1990, 81 had been hanged. Singapore, whose population is about the same as that of Dallas or Boston, has imposed the death penalty for drugs since 1975. Thirty-seven people have received the death sentence for trafficking; at last count, twenty-five of them had been executed. According to the prime minister of Singapore, Lee Kuan Yew, "death is the best deterrent we have." It's difficult to argue with the prime minister's logic, but drugs have not disappeared from the streets of his nation. Despite the prospect of whipping and forced labor, the arrest rate for drug possession in Singapore is still only about 30 percent below that in the United States. Meanwhile, the rehabilitation camps in both Malaysia and Singapore continue to grow in size, and hangings continue unabated.

Ineffective Government Policies

Years of ineffective government policies have done little to reduce drug sales or consumption. All they have done is establish an inner-city drug culture that grows like a tumor on our neighborhoods. . . .

No society has ever been able to eradicate drug or alcohol use. The real challenge is to reduce the horrible *impact* the illegal trade has on a neighborhood. I'm not sure what it will take, but it is high time to consider more creative, possibly radical, alternatives. Perhaps we should set up zones in nonresidential areas for the dealers to do their business. Hell, for all the money our government has been spending on its impotent little "war," we could probably just buy the whole drug crop every year!

Victoria McKernan, *Time*, September 21, 1992.

On the home front, it appears that even the weight of the presidency is not enough to swing the scales. Early in 1989, President Bush vowed to make Washington, D.C., a "test case" in the war on drugs. Assisted by U.S. marshals and led by Drug Enforcement Administration agents, the Washington, D.C., police began the most intensive drug-eradication effort in our nation's history. Within six months it was clear that the effort had been an abysmal failure, as the use of drugs in Washington was as high or higher than ever. Publicly, William Bennett, Bush's first drug czar, said, "From April to October, the length of a baseball season, may be enough to establish a winner in the World Series. It is not enough to win the war on drugs in this city or in any other city." One of Bennett's aides privately admitted to journalists that "twenty-five years was probably not enough either."

1984 in the Making

An illegal drug transaction involves a voluntary exchange between buyer and seller. The sale, purchase, and consumption of illegal drugs therefore constitute what are commonly labeled "victimless" crimes, in the sense that there is generally no aggrieved party who is likely to serve as a criminal witness. As a result, the legal authorities must do without the most important ingredient in a successful prosecution—the victim. Without victims to report drug deals and drug use, and to serve as material witnesses at trial, the drug warriors typically must rely on covert operations, including the use of informants and undercover activities, in their endeavors. Most Americans rightly regard such operations as being inherently antithetical to the heritage of our nation—suitable perhaps against foreign spies, but surely not appropriate for everyday police work. Unfortunately, covert operations have quickly transformed the federal government's war against drugs into a war against its citizens.

Americans are an intensely private people, as is evident in our lifestyles. Single-family dwellings are far more prevalent in the United States than anywhere else in the world, in part because houses offer more privacy than do apartments. Once ensconced in single-family dwellings, we continue our quest for yet more privacy by purchasing houses with larger lots, building fences, planting dense shrubbery around our homes, and so forth. Our craving for privacy even shows up in our modes of transportation, for Americans are notoriously averse to using public transportation, preferring the privacy of cars. Our entire lives are structured in ways that maximize our privacy—which is to say, in ways that make it difficult and costly for the government (or our neighbors) to spy on us.

Freedom from Government Intrusion

Even more fundamentally, the American people are intensely individualistic. Many people who originally immigrated to the United States did so in part because it offered freedom from the intrusions of others—government officials and nosy neighbors included. Some immigrants had been repelled by the repressive governments of their homelands, and the secret police and informants that accompany such governments. Others were attracted by a country in which individual freedom was prized above all else. The U.S. Constitution reflects this spirit of individual freedom, for it protects our fundamental rights to say, believe, and worship what we choose. And although the Constitution does not specifically guarantee our right to privacy, opinion polls reveal that most Americans either think it does, or feel it should. The bottom line is that the government's use of covert operations against its own citizens is antithetical to the foundations on which America was established, and thus is likely to be met with both resentment and opposition by those citizens.

Nonetheless, the drug warriors have persisted in urging Americans to inform on each other. Television commercials have appeared urging viewers to "rat on a rat," the rodents being alleged drug dealers, or even drug users. In some cases, police departments have advertised openly for private citizens to serve as buyers in sting operations, offering the citizens a share of any assets confiscated from dealers as a result.

To date, appeals such as these have met with relatively little success, perhaps because the thought of informing or being informed upon is so repugnant to most people. As a result, the government has relied heavily on the use of undercover agents in its efforts to ferret out participants in drug deals. But even this approach is unlikely to produce much success in the long run, in part because there are tens of millions of Americans who consume illegal psychoactives each year. Undercover operations also take months (and sometimes years) to develop properly, as undercover agents must work slowly and carefully if they are to uncover the evidence without breaking the law or being uncovered themselves. Short of reimposing the military draft and putting the draftees under cover, we are not likely to uncover more than a trivial percentage of the drug trade through covert operations.

War Is Hell

Drug use in the United States is not confined to some narrowly defined, easily excised subculture. Tens of millions of Americans use illegal psychoactives each year, and they come from all walks of life. If we are to undo drugs in America, our policies must reflect the fact that *we* are the users, the abusers, and the addicts.

Although the bulk of all users of psychoactives are casual users, the bulk of all use is by abusers and addicts. And most of the damage done to and by users occurs as a result of addiction and abuse. This is true whether we focus on the adverse health consequences for the users (such as lung cancer for nicotine addicts), adverse health consequences for third parties (such as people killed by drunk drivers), or other adverse effects (such as crimes committed by heroin addicts). Thus, only if we materially alter the behavior of addicts and abusers will our policies yield substantial benefits.

Unfortunately, the users whose behavior is the most difficult to modify successfully are the addicts. Not only is it difficult to get them to abstain or refrain for any given time period, but modifying their short-term behavior (e.g., via incarceration) is unlikely to have beneficial long-term effects on their drug use. Today's punishment-oriented policies will not generate long-term success with addicts, even if they manage to discourage some casual users. Eventually, addicts will simply return to their addictive behavior. Unless and until public policy is shaped to yield a permanent and substantial reduction in *use* rather than *users*, few beneficial consequences are likely to result from drug policy.

Although the battlefields are different, our tour of the home front reminds us of the Civil War general William Tecumseh Sherman's proclamation that "War is hell." When the opponents are psychoactives, it would appear that Sherman understated the nature of the problem—but, of course, Sherman had considerably more success than today's drug warriors are having.

"We have by no means won the 'war,' but we have made substantial progress. "

International Measures Can Help Win the War on Drugs

Melvyn Levitsky

Melvyn Levitsky is the former U.S. assistant secretary for international narcotics matters. In the following viewpoint, Levitsky maintains that the U.S. government's international policies for reducing the supply of drugs to the United States have been successful. According to the author, policies such as reducing the production of drugs in other countries, stopping drug trafficking into the United States, and uncovering international money laundering schemes have all meant progress in the war on drugs.

As you read, consider the following questions:

1. How have the U.S. international efforts helped reduce the production of illegal drugs, according to Levitsky?
2. What are the five myths the author discusses and how does he refute them?
3. What are some of the international efforts that have been most successful in stopping drug trafficking, according to the author? Why have they been successful?

From Melvyn Levitsky, "Progress in the International War Against Illicit Drugs," *U.S. Department of State Dispatch*, March 2, 1992.

Cocaine seizures in this hemisphere and worldwide have increased significantly, as have other operations and pressure against drug traffickers; law enforcement actions and coca eradication have contributed to a stabilization of cultivation; and international efforts against illegal money-laundering and diversion of essential chemicals are beginning to pay dividends.

President Bush and his counterparts from Colombia, Bolivia, and Peru met on February 15, 1990, at Cartagena, Colombia, to address the shared problem of drug use and trafficking in this hemisphere. That summit laid down a strong concept for concerted action against the drug barons and their cartels. . . .

Domestic Spending

The Administration increased domestic spending on drug law enforcement and treatment over 65% and committed itself to the long-term problems of changing attitudes that made drug abuse a "victimless" crime. Although everyone recognized that such an undertaking would take time, we are already seeing results. US demand for cocaine has been decreasing, especially among our youth:

• Past-month cocaine use in 1991 was 35% below the 1988 level, with 1.3 million fewer users. Despite an unsettling increase in 1991 over 1990, the overall trend is down.

• Occasional use of cocaine since 1988 dropped 22%, and adolescent use dropped 63%.

• Current cocaine use among high school seniors is down from 1.9% in 1990 to 1.4% in 1991.

• Student approval ratings of occasional cocaine use dropped by 47% since 1988.

To put this into some perspective, it has taken a generation to achieve sustained reductions among smokers, despite intensive information campaigns and scientific evidence of the inherent dangers. In this light, the drops in just the last few years in drug abuse, then, are even more encouraging and underscore not only the commitment of the Administration to reduce long-term abuse but to the changing attitudes that must go along with increased enforcement and treatment efforts.

As impressive as these have been, my focus is on the international effort to address drug abuse and trafficking, particularly of cocaine, in this hemisphere. Here, too, the results have been impressive, from the unprecedented degree of international cooperation and coordination that we have seen to the increased effectiveness of US efforts.

The strategy for tackling the cocaine threat . . . contains four major objectives:

• Strengthening the political commitment and institutional capability of the Andean governments to enable them to take

the necessary steps to disrupt narcotics trafficking activities;
- Increasing the effectiveness of military and law enforcement activities against the cocaine industry in the Andes;
- Inflicting significant damage on the trafficking organizations that operate within the three source countries by apprehending the trafficker leadership and disrupting or dismantling their operations; and
- Strengthening and diversifying the legitimate economies of the Andean nations to enable them to overcome the destabilizing effects of eliminating cocaine, a major source of income.

Our cocaine strategy translates these goals into action by

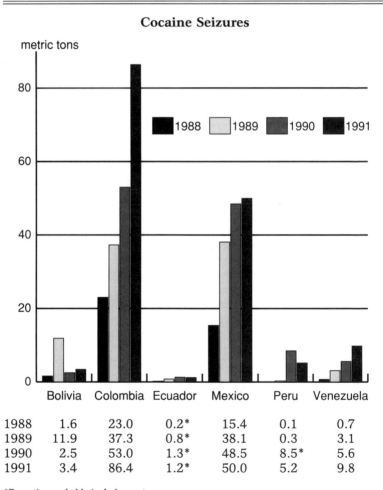

Cocaine Seizures

	Bolivia	Colombia	Ecuador	Mexico	Peru	Venezuela
1988	1.6	23.0	0.2*	15.4	0.1	0.7
1989	11.9	37.3	0.8*	38.1	0.3	3.1
1990	2.5	53.0	1.3*	48.5	8.5*	5.6
1991	3.4	86.4	1.2*	50.0	5.2	9.8

*Reporting probably includes paste.

focusing on working with the producer and transit countries to attack drug trafficking from its point of origin—beginning with coca and coca seedbed eradication and alternative development programs for farmers—and throughout its production and trafficking life cycles. The strategy uses security and economic assistance as well as trade incentives and the employment of sophisticated intelligence technology to deal with the problem in a comprehensive manner. We believe in attacking every link of the drug chain, from leaf to street.

These efforts are beginning to pay dividends. . . .

Unprecedented Cooperation

There have been unprecedented levels of cooperation among the governments of the region. Continuous consultations and communication take place from the highest political levels to the lowest technical levels. There have been, for example, numerous regional meetings on demand reduction issues. The governments of the region have participated in a series of joint anti-narcotics operations, known as "Support Justice," involving US and local government detection and monitoring assets and Andean government air interdiction assets which have had considerable success in disrupting the flow of cocaine products moving north from the Andean region. There are regular meetings of established inter-American forums on drugs, such as IDEC [International Drug Enforcement Conference], CICAD [Inter-American Drug Abuse Control Commission], and HONLEA [Heads of National Drug Law Enforcement Agencies].

This cooperation extends to efforts to control the flow of chemicals and money-laundering, in the Andean region and more broadly. Chemicals are necessary for the production of cocaine, heroin, and synthetic drugs. Using as a foundation the 1988 UN Convention Against Illicit Traffic in Narcotic Drugs and Psychotropic Substances and the Chemical Diversion Trafficking Act which the Congress passed in 1988, the Administration's efforts to internationalize this effort are yielding results.

The United States chairs the G-7 [Group of Seven] Chemical Action Task Force, which includes 26 other major chemical manufacturing countries. A series of extensive discussions between 1990 and 1991 resulted in a series of recommendations that include five basic chemical control procedures to be adopted at the national level to prevent illegal chemical diversion, and the expansion of the 1988 UN convention to include 10 additional chemicals. The Administration has also signed major chemical control agreements with Bolivia, Colombia, and Peru to facilitate the exchange of information that will allow law enforcement officials to check the legitimacy of chemical shipments.

Profits from the sale of illegal drugs generate hundreds of billions of dollars each year. Somewhere, somehow, this money must be "laundered" or "cleaned" in the world financial system so that it can be made to look as though it were legitimate proceeds from legal transactions. The Administration has cast a wide net in enlisting countries throughout the world to attack this critical link in the drug chain.

The tip of this spear is the Financial Action Task Force (FATF), an ad-hoc group of 26 countries that constitute the major financial centers of the world. This group has endorsed 40 measures to combat money-laundering which it has recommended other countries adopt. These recommendations call for the criminalization of money-laundering, cooperating in financial investigations, reporting suspicious transactions, and regulating non-bank as well as banking institutions.

The FATF's plan is to adopt these measures and, through an outreach program that already involves governments in Latin America, the Caribbean, Africa, the Middle East, and Asia, to persuade governments whose financial centers are vulnerable to laundering activity to adopt the FATF's recommendations.

The governments of the Andes, particularly Colombia, have assisted in the effort to control money-laundering. Colombia has provided assistance to international efforts against a number of money-laundering operations, [and] has raided key trafficker financial centers, arrested many financial managers, and seized numerous documents. Colombia also signed an asset sharing agreement with the United States.

Multilateral Efforts Successful

These numerous and varied efforts represent more than just mere activity. They are part not only of a growing cooperative effort but contribute to an overall strategic approach that focuses the efforts of many governments toward a common purpose. One of the most encouraging aspects of recent actions is the multilateralization of these efforts as more countries recognize the threat to their security from unrestrained illegal drug trafficking. The cumulative effect of this growing environment of cooperation and common action helped to increase the variety, number, and effectiveness of operations throughout the region.

As a result, we have seen significant results from the Andean strategy:

• Andean coca cultivation has leveled off, and there has been a net reduction of over 4% instead of the 10% or more annual increases of the early 1980s. In 1991, reductions took place in all three Andean coca producing countries.

• At Cartagena, we signed six bilateral agreements. Recently, we have signed agreements with Colombia on essential chemicals and asset sharing and a declaration of intent on evidence sharing; with Peru on drug control and alternative development and on money-laundering; and with Venezuela on a reciprocal shipboarding agreement.

• Drug kingpins of the Medellin cartel are either in jail (Pablo Escobar, the three Ochoas) or dead (Rodriguez Gacha). Twenty-six major Colombian traffickers were extradited between 1989 and 1991, when extradition was made unconstitutional in Colombia. Twenty-one traffickers have turned themselves in under a presidential plea-bargaining decree. Thousands of other drug-related arrests have been made each year in Colombia.

• In 1991, Colombia and Mexico together seized about 140 tons of coca products—40 tons more than in 1990 and 65 tons more than in 1989.

• In other significant transit countries, large amounts of cocaine were also seized in 1991: almost 9 metric tons in Venezuela, 17.5 in Guatemala, and 5.3 in the Bahamas.

Drug Seizures

These facts directly reflect the increased operational capability of local security forces, aided to a considerable degree by the flow of pledged US assistance. We have seen increased coordination and effectiveness from our own effort as well. The cumulative effect of this is an overall increase in operational effectiveness, as clearly indicated by seizure numbers. Although we cannot give a precise figure to the amount of cocaine produced, it is reasonable to assume around 700 metric tons after inefficiencies are factored in. Worldwide seizures in 1991 were about 300 metric tons. This means, conservatively, that we and our allies seized over 30% of total production. While the remainder can still meet US demand, that demand is dwindling, and we are making significant inroads into the market.

Nevertheless, we do not believe that the proper measure of our success should be the above "body count" type data on arrests, labs destroyed, and cocaine seized. These are indicative only of the qualitative improvements that must ultimately result for our programs, such as the degree to which we are encouraging host country political will to arrest, try, and imprison drug kingpins, to eradicate illicit coca crops, to disrupt the trafficking organizations, and to work cooperatively with us and their neighbors.

Our efforts must go, however, to the development of host country judicial institutions capable of operating securely to resist the threats, bribes, and other instruments of the enormously powerful and wealthy traffickers. We are increasingly seeing evidence that the Andean governments are moving positively in these directions with our assistance. . . .

I believe that criticisms of the Andean strategy are based on misconceptions or myths about what we are really trying to accomplish there. Many of these grow out of a desire to see quick results on an issue affecting the health and welfare of this country. I believe we all want to see results, but, in order to be effective, we must be prepared to sustain our engagement with the problem in all its complexity and not be diverted by simplistic panaceas or criticisms from solving a difficult long-term problem. As one observer put it, for every problem there is a solution that is simple, straightforward, and wrong. Let me outline, then, what I believe are some of the notions about the nature of the problem that we face that mislead many people.

Myths About the "Drug War"

Myth No. 1: The "drug war" is a war like other wars. The "war on drugs" is a metaphor, and, while there are battles and casualties, the nature of the conflict is not a straightforward, stand-up fight like Desert Storm. There are no frontiers and no fronts in this war. The "enemy" is not in uniform, and he does not fight in formations. The nature of the threat is indirect and underground. The trafficker fights his battles with subversion, terror, bribery, intimidation, and subterfuge. This type of attack, nevertheless, poses an immediate threat to the sovereignty and stability of the nations it puts at risk, for it undermines the very institutions upon which a free and open society is based, and it attacks the health and welfare of the people themselves. The nature of the response must take these facts into consideration.

Myth No. 2: We are not up against a traditional threat. I believe that much of the confusion that we see about the nature of our effort stems from a lack of understanding of the type of threat we are dealing with. In our counter-narcotics efforts, we are not seeking to invent a surrogate for the Cold War. We are not looking backward at guerrilla wars in Central America. We are seeking to look forward. There is nothing ideological, or even partisan, in this effort. Drugs are a new, emerging, transnational concern, similar to nuclear proliferation, environmental devastation, AIDS, and disaster relief. These are all issues which, if not addressed adequately, have long-term consequences that affect our future. We must make the decade of the 1990s one in which we obliterate narcotics as a threat to our societies and our democratic values.

Myth No. 3: "Militarization" of the drug war. Use of the metaphor of war has raised the question of an alleged desire by the US government to "militarize" the counter-drug effort. This is also a myth. Most of our "military assistance" for counter-narcotics is, in fact, going to Andean police organizations. Dealing with drug trafficking organizations is primarily and essentially a civilian law enforcement problem requiring that police be on the front lines. Our goal is not "search and destroy." We wish to indict, arrest, try, convict, and incarcerate criminals either in the United States or in their own countries—respecting their rights and those of ordinary citizens. This requires better equipped, more professional police and more streamlined judicial organs.

We have involved the US military in supporting roles to provide sophisticated assets for detection and monitoring, transport, training, and delivery of military assistance hardware and in providing communications, logistical, and intelligence expertise to US missions abroad. Host government militaries provide air intercept, transport, and airlift capabilities to their own police; security for law enforcement personnel; [and] riverine capabilities; and [these] are sometimes used directly for operations against large, outlying drug production complexes.

Illegitimate Wars

Recall, also, that, in Colombia and Peru, violent insurgent organizations that are waging illegitimate war on democratically elected governments are engaged in narco-trafficking themselves, and it is their considerable firepower in difficult, semijungle terrain that overmatches the police. Part of the myth of militarization ignores this fact and the responsibility for sustaining domestic violence and the drug trade.

Myth No. 4: Counter-narcotics assistance serves to violate human rights. We have little choice but to engage ourselves in combating the vicious organized criminal gangs which seek to penetrate our country. Some people seem to believe, however, that any assistance to Andean governments for anti-narcotics will result in or associate the United States with violations of human rights.

Our counter-narcotics programs include human rights training for both police and military, include efforts to professionalize and institutionalize police and the organs of justice which are the safeguard for human rights observance, and include conditions for human rights observance. Furthermore, we monitor our assistance to assure it is not used for other than counternarcotics purposes. We believe that the more closely we work with host government institutions, the less likely they are to engage in violations of human rights.

We must recognize that we have a responsibility to prevent the abuse of human rights from drugs and those that push them; we must recognize the key role that drug traffickers and their allies play in promoting the atmosphere of violence that produces the majority of abuses; [and] we must see that our goal of supporting democracy does not become a victim of ignorance of the threat posed by traffickers and their insurgent allies.

Myth No. 5: We have failed in our objective of stopping the flow of cocaine to the United States. We are dealing in an ambiguous environment in which it is difficult to know anything with absolute certainty. Drug trafficking occurs in the shadows, and traffickers take infinite pains to obscure the workings of their business. Progress, moreover, takes time, especially against a well-entrenched, ruthless foe who possesses incredible wealth. Nevertheless, we are making impressive gains in efforts to deal with the illicit flow of cocaine to the United States.

While it is difficult to know exactly how much is being produced, we know that, in a brief 2-year period, the Andean countries have staunched the rising levels of coca cultivation, [have] cut back on new cultivation through seedbed eradication, and have had increasing success in arresting major traffickers, breaking up narcotics networks, and seizing cocaine shipments. These reflect the increased commitment of the producing and transiting countries with the support of the United States.

The Threat of Drugs

The pressure is up, but we view this effort as a long-term one, and there will be no instant success against a deeply rooted problem. Increased assistance to the Andean governments was only approved in 1990. . . . If we do not have the patience and the stamina to persevere, we will not only lose the ground that we have gained, we will fail in the goal of reducing the threat to this country and to our friends and allies from drugs.

We have by no means won the "war," but we have made substantial progress. It remains for us to sustain those gains.

"[The] international drug war has proven a resounding failure and a mounting threat to U.S. and regional security interests. "

The International War on Drugs Is a Failure

Peter Andreas and Eva Bertram

In the following viewpoint, authors Peter Andreas and Eva Bertram refute claims that the international war on drugs has succeeded. They contend that U.S. government efforts to stop the supply of drugs from entering the United States have failed. Instead of ensuring U.S. national security by stopping drug trafficking, the international drug war has intruded on diplomatic relations with many drug-producing countries and has fueled anti-American sentiment. Andreas is a research associate and Bertram is an associate fellow of the Institute for Policy Studies, an organization in Washington, D.C., that analyzes U.S. domestic and international policies.

As you read, consider the following questions:

1. What evidence do the authors use to determine that the international war on drugs is a failure?
2. According to Andreas and Bertram, in what ways has the war on drugs hurt relations with other countries?
3. What policies do the authors suggest to replace the international war on drugs?

From Peter Andreas and Eva Bertram, "National Security and the War on Drugs in the Americas," a 1992 Institute for Policy Studies briefing paper. Reprinted with permission.

The conviction of Panamanian Gen. Manuel Noriega has been hailed as a major victory in the war against drugs, yet it is a transparent disguise for what has proven to be a policy of disaster.

The Bush administration made an unprecedented investment in this nation's continuing battle against drugs. Federal anti-drug funding has increased by 750 percent since 1981, to a requested $12.7 billion for fiscal 1993—with increasing levels going to the military to fight the foreign drug supply. Yet on its own terms, the international drug war has proven a resounding failure and a mounting threat to U.S. and regional security interests.

Funding the Drug War

Drug war funding is one of the few line items in the Pentagon budget that continues to grow in the post-Cold War era. The Pentagon's share of federal drug-war dollars has jumped from $440 million in 1989 to $1.2 billion in 1992. The number of military flying hours devoted to drug interdiction has increased sevenfold since 1990 while drug-related Navy ship days at sea have more than doubled. The drug war looms large on the U.S. military agenda: "Counternarcotics" leads the list of likely future conflicts presented to Congress by the Joint Chiefs of Staff in 1991's "Military Net Assessment."

The primary foreign theater in the drug war is Latin America, the source of virtually all of the world's cocaine. The U.S. Southern Command in Panama fields more than 500 soldiers in training and intelligence missions throughout the region. Military aid to Andean security forces has jumped from less than $5 million in 1988 to more than $140 million in 1990—placing the Andean region ahead of Central America as the leading recipient of U.S. military aid in the hemisphere. The drug war is rapidly intensifying, from Mexico to Argentina: Ten Latin nations now host U.S. "Tactical Analysis Teams" charged with gathering intelligence on trafficking organizations and activities.

Increased Supply

Despite periodic news stories of sensational drug busts and cocaine seizures by the ton, the failure of the policy to reduce overall levels of supply to the U.S. is well documented. More drugs are produced, processed and transported in more places than ever before. The General Accounting Office (GAO) reported in September 1991 that military "detection and monitoring efforts have not had a significant impact on the national goal of reducing drug supplies. The estimated cocaine flow into the United States did not decrease in 1989 and 1990."

The Drug Enforcement Administration [DEA] estimates that cocaine production in South America doubled from 1988 to 1990, increasing by a projected 40 percent in 1991. Production of coca, the raw material of cocaine, has surpassed 200,000 tons of coca leaf a year, enough to satisfy four times the estimated U.S. cocaine market. Heroin production has also risen ominously. Even the drug war's most celebrated victory—Operation "Just Cause" in Panama—appears hollow. Drug shipments through Panama "may have doubled" since the invasion, according to a July 1991 GAO report.

The rationale behind the drug war is deceptively appealing. Curbing the supply of drugs from abroad, officials calculate, will limit availability and raise the price of drugs on our streets—thereby reducing domestic drug consumption. The strategy combines enforcement at home and interdiction on our borders with the use of military, law enforcement and economic aid to curtail production in Latin America.

"The logic is simple," George Bush said in 1988. "The cheapest and safest way to eradicate narcotics is to destroy them at their source. . . . We need to wipe out crops wherever they are grown and take out labs wherever they exist."

Yet the mounting reports of failure suggest that the task . . . is not as simple as its logic. In fact, the evidence suggests that the strategy may be fueling the expansion of the drug trade. In part as a response to drug-control operations, the highly adaptable and mobile cocaine industry has now spread to countries such as Suriname, Venezuela, Brazil and Chile.

Escalation

The [Bush] administration responded to repeated reports of failure by escalating the drug war rather than re-evaluating it. But the record indicates serious flaws in the policy and suggests that the administration mobilized the wrong institutions in a misguided "war" abroad, badly miscalculating that more funds and firepower can reverse the trend.

The search for foreign solutions to our domestic drug problem is not new. The drug crisis was elevated to a "national security threat" by former President Ronald Reagan in an April 1986 national security decision directive stating that drugs destabilize governments, degrade U.S. society and harm the economy. At the peak of public concern over the spread of crack cocaine, President Bush took further steps to mobilize the nation's security apparatus. "When requested," he declared in September 1989, "we will for the first time make available the appropriate resources of America's armed forces" to assist Latin governments in the drug war.

While the drug war lacks the ideological content of the Cold War, a dangerous replication of Cold War strategies has been adopted in Latin America. The Pentagon identifies its counternarcotics mission as the newest form of "low-intensity conflict," the protracted U.S. war strategy used against popular insurgencies in the developing world. Honduran units assigned to patrol the Salvadoran border for guerrillas, for example, are to be converted into drug interdiction teams through U.S. Special Forces training, according to State Department plans.

Casting the drug crisis as a national security threat may have initially deflected attention away from the domestic roots of the drug crisis: Washington, it seemed, was "doing something." Yet something else is required now. A sober assessment of the strategic flaws in the U.S. drug war abroad and its damaging effects on U.S. and regional security interests needs to be made. And the steps necessary to forge a new debate and effective response to our nation's drug crisis should begin.

A Failed and Flawed Strategy

Drug strategists read reports of failure simply as an indication of inadequate funding and poor implementation of sound strategy, but in fact, the approach is wrong.

The U.S. strategy relies fundamentally on the cooperation of regional leaders. Yet the priorities of the Latin nations are distinct and sometimes contradictory to those of U.S. drug strategists. The reasons are obvious. Andean leaders in particular are consumed with issues of economic and political survival, and cocaine plays a central role. The crisis-stricken economies of Peru and Bolivia are kept afloat by the jobs and revenues generated by the cocaine trade, the most significant economic force in the region. The drug economy in Bolivia employs roughly 20 percent of the workforce and generates foreign exchange revenues equivalent to the total value of all legal exports combined. In Peru, coca provides employment for 15 percent of the workforce and is the country's largest source of foreign exchange revenues. A successful crackdown on the trade would threaten the immediate economic viability of either nation—and the political survival of its leaders.

The Latin security forces charged with carrying out of the U.S. drug strategy on the ground similarly have little real interest in joining the counternarcotics campaign. The major concern of the Peruvian and Colombian militaries, for example, is battling leftist insurgencies, not drugs—and they have made clear their intention to use U.S. counternarcotics aid to pursue their own objectives. Colombian military officials acknowledged in early 1990 that they would use $38.5 million of $40.3 million in 1990 U.S. drug-war assistance for counterinsurgency efforts in a region not known for drug trafficking.

A more insidious problem is the drug-related corruption that runs through the region's military and law enforcement agencies. Government salaries (a senior officer in Peru earns approximately $250 a month) cannot compete with traffickers' bribes. Peru is a "quagmire of deceit and corruption," according to a recent Pentagon internal memo which said, even before the recent coup, that "attainment of U.S. objectives is impossible." Reports abound of military personnel firing on anti-drug police, reselling cocaine seized in drug raids and allowing traffickers to use military-controlled landing strips. In his public resignation statement in January 1992, drug policy adviser to Peruvian President Alberto Fujimori, Hernando DeSoto, blamed state corruption for stalling the drug-control effort.

A Long Record of Failure

The premises and methods guiding the Andean drug control strategy are neither new nor untested and, unfortunately, have a long record of failure. After more than a decade of U.S. efforts to reduce the cocaine supply, more cocaine is produced in more places than ever before. Curiously, the U.S. response to failure has been to escalate rather than reevaluate.

Peter R. Andreas, et al., *Foreign Policy*, Winter 1991-1992.

DeSoto was the architect of the U.S.-Peruvian anti-drug accord; his resignation was both an embarrassment to the Fujimori government and a serious blow to Peru's drug-control program.

The problem is not limited to the Andes: Pervasive corruption has undermined drug-control efforts throughout Latin America for decades. According to a 1991 State Department drug-control report, "Corruption is perhaps the most difficult problem [the government of Mexico] faces." Mexico produces roughly half of the heroin and 70 percent of the marijuana imported into the U.S.

Market Logic

The most intransigent obstacle to success in the U.S. drug war, however, is the simple market logic of supply and demand. From peasant producers to traffickers, those involved in the drug trade are driven by one or both of two motives: profit and the lack of social and economic alternatives. As long as demand and profits run high in the U.S. and Europe, production and distribution in poor Latin nations will continue.

The logic of peasant coca growers should not be lost on Washington's "free marketeers." Lacking viable legal economic options, peasant growers and processors have little incentive to abandon drug production. Coca is easy to grow on poor soil and inexpensive to process. The market is virtually guaranteed: Traffickers fly into remote areas and pay peasants up front in dollars. Disruption of production in one area—through eradication or crop-substitution programs—has simply led peasants to replant elsewhere, often in new and more remote areas previously untouched by the crop. A similar dynamic applies to marijuana and poppy production in Mexico and Colombia.

Efforts to dismantle the operations of trafficking organizations are equally ineffective. The Colombian offensive against the Medellin cartel, for example, has only created opportunities and incentives for new traffickers to enter the trade. In the 10 months following the 1989 crackdown on Medellin, the competing Cali cartel boosted its share of the cocaine market to 75 percent, according to the DEA. Cali has emerged as the largest trafficking group in the world, and is now reportedly spearheading Colombia's diversification into the global heroin trade.

The analysis of economists such as Rand Corporation's Peter Reuter confirms the futility of supply-reduction strategies in the producer countries. Reuter demonstrates that the gap between the price peasant coca producers receive and the street price for the finished product is so large that traffickers and refiners can easily pay peasants more and persuade enough of them to stay in business to meet continued global demand. Even an inconceivable 50 percent reduction in the Latin drug supply destined for the U.S., Reuter has shown, would raise the street price by a mere 3 percent.

Casualties of War

U.S. drug-control efforts in Latin America are not only failing to make a serious dent in the drug supply but are also exacting a high price in regional stability. U.S. economic aid and diplomatic favor toward the Andean countries have been tied to compliance in the war on drugs—and, in particular, the acceptance of military assistance—while concerns over human rights have been subordinated to counternarcotics objectives. As one senior Bolivian official complained, "Our relations with the U.S. are completely 'narcoticized.'"

While the U.S. military is forbidden by law from engaging in domestic law enforcement, Washington has insisted that Latin militaries assume internal drug-enforcement missions—increasing the potential for corruption and human-rights abuses. Peru's military, long considered one of the most abusive security forces in the world, was condemned by the U.S. State Department for "widespread and egregious human-rights violations." The use of torture, rape and extrajudicial execution by Colombian and Peruvian security forces is rivaled only by Guatemala and El Salvador in this hemisphere.

The drug war threatens to further destabilize the region by helping to fuel the Shining Path insurgency now gaining ground in Peru. The guerrillas have effectively exploited the U.S.-sponsored counternarcotics campaign: They have established themselves as intermediaries in the coca zones, demanding higher coca prices from traffickers and offering protection for peasant producers. Peruvian officials argue that a sustained and effective crackdown on coca will drive desperate coca farmers into the hands of the insurgents. The growing U.S. presence has only bolstered the guerrillas' claims that they are the defenders of peasant interests against "Yankee imperialism."

The U.S. has taken the first steps toward direct involvement in the intractable 12-year civil conflict that has claimed more than 23,000 lives in Peru. The U.S. anti-narcotics mission in Peru deliberately blurs the distinction between counterinsurgency and counternarcotics and explicitly includes anti-insurgency support. The U.S. Army's counterterrorist unit, Delta Force, has reportedly provided training to the Peruvian army. In January 1992, a U.S. helicopter carrying anti-drug personnel crashed in Peru's Upper Huallaga coca-growing region, killing three U.S. contract workers. The Shining Path guerrillas claimed responsibility. If the U.S. role continues to grow, greater American casualties are inevitable.

A Fundamental Shift

Our current drug policy is exacerbating problems abroad and doing little to solve the drug crisis at home. What is needed is a fundamental shift in the means and methods of national drug policy. Miscasting drugs as a national security threat has diverted attention and funding from serious social and health problems to a high-tech military campaign on our borders and abroad. Few have questioned the mobilization of our national security institutions in a war effort abroad to battle a domestic problem: To do so is to risk the charge of being "soft" on drugs.

The "war" metaphor in U.S. drug policy is as misleading as it is stifling. War commonly has a clearly identifiable (usually foreign) enemy. It is limited in duration, high in intensity and ends in unconditional victory or defeat. A meaningful campaign to address the drug problem shares none of the characteristics. A real solution requires an indefinite multidimensional response and demands that we turn our attention to enduring issues of employment, housing, education and health care at home; economic development and multilateral cooperation abroad.

New Policy Needed

The record of the past decade is clear: Attempts to suppress the drug supply will not succeed as long as enough Americans want to buy drugs and profits run high. Efforts to wipe out drugs at the source only drive producers elsewhere; interdiction only leads to more sophisticated smuggling techniques and new supply routes; and arrests of traffickers only result in their replacement by others. Continued drug production and distribution overseas are largely the symptom and the consequence— not the source—of our domestic problems of drug use, abuse and addiction. Declaring war against the drug supply simplifies and obscures the real issues: Why do millions of Americans abuse and deal drugs, and what can we as a nation do about it? We must put our own house in order and abandon the hopeless and distracting search for a solution to the nation's drug problem in the distant coca fields of Latin America.

"The nation's fight against drugs will not be won overnight. . . . It's a fight that our military services can help our country to win."

Military Efforts to Stop Drug Trafficking Are Effective

Dale E. Brown

The U.S. military has been enlisted to help stop the flow of drugs into the United States from Latin America. In the following viewpoint, Dale E. Brown contends that this military intervention has been effective. He argues that the military is better equipped and better trained to handle the surveillance and intelligence aspects of drug interdiction than are civilian law enforcement agencies. Brown concludes that the military should continue to aid civilian agencies in the fight against drugs. Brown is deputy chief of operations for Joint Task Force Six, the military's drug enforcement program along the Southwest border of the United States. He is also the coeditor of a number of books, including *The Parameters of War*, *The Parameters of Military Ethics*, and *Military Leadership*.

As you read, consider the following questions:

1. Why does Brown argue that the military is better equipped for some anti-drug tasks than civilian organizations?
2. According to Brown, what role does the National Guard play in the drug war?
3. What are some of the operations the military has conducted to counter the influx of drugs into the United States, according to the author?

From Dale E. Brown, "Drugs on the Border: The Role of the Military," *Parameters*, Winter 1991-92. Reprinted with permission.

It was a twin-engined Beech, Captain Winters saw, the most common aircraft used by the druggies. . . . He pulled his F-15 level behind it, about half a mile back. This was the eighth time he'd intercepted a drug runner, but it was the first time he'd been allowed to do something about it. . . . When he got within four hundred yards, his finger depressed the button for a fraction of a second. A line of green tracers lanced through the sky. Several rounds appeared to miss the Beech ahead, but the rest hit right in the cockpit area. He heard no sound from the kill. . . . Winters reflected briefly that he had just killed one man, maybe two. That was all right. They wouldn't be missed.

—From *Clear and Present Danger* by Tom Clancy.

Mention military involvement in counter-drugs, and the scenario above may provide the sort of images that come to the average American's mind. Bloody, violent acts committed against culpable drug smugglers are the stuff of best-selling fiction, but they are just that—fiction. The reality of military support is not so dramatic, but it constitutes a solid contribution to law enforcement and valuable, real-world training for the participating units. This is true wherever the military is involved and especially on the Southwest land border.

A Threat to National Security

Although the military has provided counter-drug support for a number of years, the issue came to the fore in the fall of 1989 when President George Bush declared drug abuse to be the gravest domestic problem facing our nation and a threat to the national security. These sentiments were seconded by Secretary of Defense Dick Cheney, who declared, "The detection and countering of the production, trafficking, and use of illegal drugs is a high priority national security mission of the Department of Defense." Cheney further charged the military's major commanders with hemispheric responsibilities to draft plans on how they could contribute to the counter-drug effort. That these statements were reaffirmed one year later in the midst of Desert Shield is testament to their enduring importance and a tocsin call for military support.

The danger that drugs pose to our nation needs little elaboration. A report by a congressional subcommittee headed by Congressman Nicholas Mavroules concluded, "The chief threat to our national security in the 1990s may well come from hoards of red tomato cans [filled with cocaine, an actual smuggling technique] rather than hordes of Red communists." Stories about drug-related violence and human tragedy have filled our newspapers and local newscasts in recent years. The cocaine-related deaths of sports superstars Len Bias and Don Rogers and the theater of Washington Mayor Marion Barry's drug trial have captured the nation's attention. Accounts of hundreds of violent drug-related murders have compounded the horror. What should be done about the drug problem, however, is a matter of continuing debate. The drug control strategy has two facets: diminish the demand for drugs and eliminate their supply. With regard to diminishing demand within the military community itself, much has been accomplished through the DOD's demand-reduction education program and its progress with random urinalysis; yet military support of the strategy is almost entirely focused on the second facet—eliminating supply. No military authority believes elimination of supply is the definitive answer, but interdiction of the drug flow is the measure to which military assets are most applicable. . . .

Types of Military Support

Military support comes from all components of the Department of Defense. It is categorized into three areas: Title 10 forces (active duty and Reserve forces), Title 32 (National Guard), and logistical support through four regional offices.

DOD counter-drug involvement encompasses a number of major commands. Atlantic Command and Pacific Command have their own joint task forces—JTF-Four (Key West, Florida) and JTF-Five (Alameda, California)—which conduct aerial and maritime surveillance along the nation's coasts. Southern Command directs efforts to eliminate drugs at their Latin American sources through foreign military support and intelligence analysis. For example, SOUTHCOM [Southern Command] provided 49 mobile training teams and managed the delivery of $65 million worth of military equipment to Colombia in FY [fiscal year] 90. An additional $53 million has since been directed to Colombia and six other Latin American nations. (Questions have been raised in the press, however, about whether this aid is being used for counterinsurgency instead of counter-drug efforts.) North American Air Defense Command has contributed greatly to air interdiction through the use of its mobile ground radar units and AWACS [airborne warning and control system] surveillance assets; at one point in FY 90, 48 percent of all AWACS flying hours worldwide were devoted to counter-drugs. These assets are used to supplement a series of radar-carrying aerostats (tethered blimps) integrated into Customs control facilities. Actual intercept, however, is the province of the air branch of Customs.

The National Guard plays an important role in its capacity as a state militia. This status gives it certain powers not available to the active military, notably border inspection authority. Inspection of cargo at the nation's ports of entry is a time-consuming, manpower-intensive enterprise. With the Guard's help,

Customs is now able to examine 14 percent of containers originating from cocaine source or transit countries, a near threefold increase from FY 89.

Marijuana eradication is another significant Guard contribution. The Guard's FY 89 work in this regard netted over four million plants with a street value of at least $8 billion. Since eradication is not legally limited to the Guard, future missions will probably involve active duty forces. Yet such operations are not without controversy. A 1990 California eradication mission, Operation Greensweep, provoked an outcry from the local citizenry and a pending $100 million lawsuit. But eradication missions carry the strong political message to Latin American countries that the United States is willing to use military force to eliminate domestic drug production, the same thing we are asking them to do.

A Crucial Role

The Department of Defense has a crucial role in defending the United States from the scourge of illegal drugs. The Department will employ the resources at its command to accomplish that mission effectively. . . . The men and women of America's armed forces will fight the production, trafficking and use of illegal drugs, as an important part of the national effort to secure for all Americans a drug-free America.

Richard B. Cheney, speech given before the U.S. Senate, September 18, 1989.

All told, the National Guard contributed 532,899 man-days to the counter-drug effort while conducting 5155 missions in FY 90. There are limits, however, to the Guard's utility. Each state ordinarily can bring to bear only those types of assets that happen to comprise its force structure; New Mexico, for example, has no infantry or engineer units. This is one reason why active duty and Reserve forces are invaluable complements to the counter-drug campaign along the Southwest border.

Law enforcement agencies have a great need for military equipment with counter-drug applications. Items in greatest demand include secure radio gear and night-vision devices, but less glamorous equipment such as fuel pods are equally important. Loan of such items is coordinated by four Regional Logistics Support Offices nationwide. These offices also coordinate use of DOD facilities.

Joint Task Force Six was formed in November 1989 at Fort Bliss, Texas, to plan and coordinate active duty and Reserve military support to civilian law enforcement agencies along the

Southwest land border. The 129-member military and civilian staff encompasses all four uniformed services and includes liaison personnel from the Border Patrol, Customs, and the Drug Enforcement Administration. Its area of responsibility mirrors Operation Alliance, that being Texas, New Mexico, Arizona, and California as far north as Fresno.

JTF-Six support involves numerous activities and a wide spectrum of DOD units and capabilities. Support must meet legal scrutiny and, unless the requesting law enforcement agency will pay for the support or obtain special DOD funding, it must constitute bona fide military training. Only support requested by law enforcement agencies is provided; nothing is done unilaterally.

Smugglers' Routes

Reconnaissance operations are the most frequently requested form of support, and border areas are observed in a variety of ways. Manned observation posts are commonly provided. In all cases where a confrontation with potential smugglers is likely, soldiers or Marines are accompanied by members of the law enforcement agency requesting the support. DOD participants have no part in the subsequent seizure or arrest. While drug smuggling is possible anywhere along the 2000-mile border, there are specific routes located mostly in remote mountainous areas that have been smugglers' conduits to the north for centuries. These areas are ideal for use of trained recon elements such as Army Special Forces and Marine Recon teams with night-vision devices and long-range optics. Observation posts are both inexpensive and effective; they have successfully detected smuggling along the length of the border.

Remotely monitored sensors such as Army REMBASS and Marine SCAMP are used to supplement existing law enforcement agencies' sensors; the relatively small number of military sensor units are in great demand because they have proven to be an effective way to monitor large portions of the border area. A recently concluded sensor operation along the Texas border, for example, netted 15 drug seizures.

Relatively flat areas of the border provide excellent terrain for ground surveillance radar operations. A small number of radar teams can cover large border stretches, relying for example on the PPS-5 and 15 ground surveillance radars. Suspicious activity can be observed at relatively long range, giving law enforcement authorities ample reaction time.

Aerial reconnaissance is another useful form of support. Observation is accomplished by both fixed-wing and rotary assets and, on one mission, by a Marine Remotely Piloted Vehicle unit. The RPV was credited with aiding in the seizure of a truck loaded with more than a ton of marijuana. Aircraft with infrared detection systems are especially useful in the search for heat-producing methamphetamine labs, commonly found in the sparsely populated public lands in the border area. Six hundred lab sites were found in 1990 in California alone; the production chemicals also pose a significant toxic waste threat. Slow-flying helicopters are a useful tool for finding marijuana plots in the national forests; the choppers are an integral part of eradication campaigns such as the previously mentioned Greensweep and a highly successful sister operation in western Oregon, Operation Ghost Dancer.

Intelligence

Intelligence analysis is another valuable aspect of military assistance. Fusion of numerous intelligence sources is common in the military, but it is often beyond the resources and experience of law enforcement agencies. Military training teams instruct the law officers in analysis techniques as well as performing the procedures in specific instances. The proximity of the El Paso Intelligence Center, a repository of worldwide drug smuggling data headed by the Drug Enforcement Administration, is fortuitous in this regard. Military analysts working with law enforcement officials have been successful at using multiple sources of perishable intelligence to alert local agencies to expected border drug crossings. Care is taken not to maintain intelligence on US citizens, action that is forbidden by intelligence oversight laws. Similarly, military translators listen only to tapes of wiretaps, not to the actual conversations. Spanish translation is another highly prized form of military support for law enforcement. Lack of detailed border topographical products, a necessity for operational planning, has hampered law enforcement agencies in the past; the military has now filled part of this void with aerial photography and by updating outdated maps during ground reconnaissance missions.

Engineer support is not as glamorous as contributing directly to the arrest of drug smugglers, but it has proven to be an equally valuable form of aid. For example, the Laredo Border Patrol uses remotely monitored cameras to watch the Rio Grande. Over the years, scrub brush had grown so high as to obscure the view. An Army engineer company from Fort Carson was called on to clear away the brush; it additionally created 120 miles of road that could be monitored for illegal crossing activity. Another useful engineer project is repair of the San Diego border fence. While the simple act of welding panels made of pierced steel planking (the PSP used for temporary aircraft runways) was termed "fortification of the border" by civil rights groups, it stopped potential smugglers as well as illegal border-crossers in an area where roving packs of bandits routinely robbed and raped campesinos. The intent of the project was to channel immigrants to legal ports of entry.

Military transportation assets are also frequently requested by law enforcement agencies. Helicopters are especially useful for transporting agents to hard-to-reach areas of the Southwest border. Fixed-wing aircraft are used to transport large quantities of contraband.

Perhaps the most celebrated example of military support was the assistance rendered in the discovery of the Douglas, Arizona, drug tunnel. Customs officials had long suspected the existence of a tunnel under the border, but lacked sufficient evidence to justify search warrants. They requested assistance through Operation Alliance. It turned out that the Army had a long-standing interest in tunnel detection because of its experiences along the Korean border. Once the military team arrived on the scene in March 1990, it was only a matter of hours before the tunnel location was pinpointed. Subsequent search of a warehouse in Douglas by Customs authorities revealed a tunnel leading to the owner's residence in Mexico. The terminus was under a pool table raised from the floor by a hydraulic lift, a sophisticated device indicative of the smuggler's extensive resources. A search by Mexican authorities yielded two tons of cocaine and 14 tons of marijuana. The tunnel was thought to have been in use for two years and might still be a principal drug conduit if not for military involvement.

When military intervention in counter-drugs was first discussed, then-FORSCOM commander General Colin Powell envisioned deterrence of drug smuggling by units conducting normal training along the border. This idea has evolved into a concept known as terrain denial, whereby battalion-sized elements conduct primary mission training in proximity to the border. The concept entails no direct counter-drug effort, but the unit's presence alone disrupts the smuggler's patterns. . . .

Prospects for the Future

In the short time that the active-duty military has been involved in counter-drug operations along the Southwest border, considerable progress has been made toward understanding law enforcement agencies' efforts and procedures. Support that expands these counter-drug efforts as well as providing realistic training has been rendered in a wide variety of areas. The support has been well-received by law enforcement officials and has fulfilled both of its intents. Yet much remains to be done.

Mexico is the linchpin for ultimate counter-drug success. Without Mexican support the situation closely parallels a low-intensity conflict in which the guerrilla has perfect sanctuary. The two years of the Salinas Administration have seen dramatic improvement in Mexican drug efforts. In 1990, for example, Mexican agents seized $190 billion worth of drugs at a cost of 24 of their lives. The recent creation of Northern Border Response Teams ferried in US-provided helicopters is welcome. But smuggling is a time-honored profession along the border. The opinion among poor Mexicans that they are only providing what the *gringos* want is prevalent and will be hard to combat.

Law enforcement clearly needs more resources. More remote sensor assets are sorely needed and the aerostat system must be completed. Customs is not constrained from inspecting more cargo by a lack of personnel, but by cramped facilities; this problem would be exponentially compounded by the proposed free trade agreement between the United States and Mexico. A happy medium between examination of incoming cargo, possibly by new sensing technology, and the free flow of commerce must be found. Helicopter-borne interdiction teams are needed to overcome the border's great length and to respond to sensor activations. Similarly, Customs needs more aircraft to respond to aerial intrusions detected by the aerostats and other sensors. Until law enforcement agencies have all the resources they need, there will be a place for the military along the border.

The current legal constraints on military support are in place for a very good reason: Americans have a distrust of military involvement in civil matters that dates to their ancestors and Oliver Cromwell. Yet Congress may decide that military counter-drug involvement merits legislative relief. If Congress can authorize military protection of guano deposits—an actual authorized Posse Comitatus exception—then permission to accompany law enforcement agents onto private land or to give active-duty forces authority to examine inbound cargo is distinctly possible. Decisions in such matters are in civilian hands; meanwhile, the military is committed to providing the best possible support under the existing conditions.

How is JTF-Six doing? The command has steadfastly refused to use a Vietnam-style "body count" of drug seizures as a measure of effectiveness. This policy was lauded by the Mavroules subcommittee. The value of military support is measured by its worth as perceived by law enforcement agencies and its training value for the participating military units. The deterrent value of military involvement in terms of disruption of the smuggler's patterns or forcing him to take riskier, less-profitable routes cannot be quantified.

The nation's fight against drugs will not be won overnight. It will take progress in reducing demand as well as in supply interdiction. But it's a fight that is vital to our nation's future well-being, and it's a fight that our military services can help our country to win.

"U.S. military involvement in antidrug efforts is an inappropriate mission."

Military Efforts to Stop Drug Trafficking Are Ineffective

Center for Defense Information

The Center for Defense Information in Washington, D.C., analyzes U.S. defense policy. Its members support a strong but not excessive military, a reduction of waste in military spending, and avoidance of nuclear war. In the following viewpoint, the authors argue that military involvement in anti-drug efforts has not been proven effective and has become the Pentagon's justification for increased funding. The authors believe eradicating drugs in the United States is a problem for police and health officials, not for the military.

As you read, consider the following questions:

1. According to the authors, what message does using the U.S. military to fight drugs send to other countries?
2. Why will the military fail to reduce the supply of drugs into the United States, according to the authors?
3. What are some of the military anti-drug programs that the authors oppose and why do they oppose them?

From Center for Defense Information, "The Pentagon's War on Drugs: The Ultimate Bad Trip," *Defense Monitor*, vol. 21, no. 1, 1992. Reprinted with permission.

The Pentagon's greatest fear is to be without an enemy. That was the situation it faced during the late 1980s as the "evil empire" began to crumble. In order to justify its existence and budget requests a new villain had to be found quickly.

The Pentagon and Drug Trafficking

At the urging of the Reagan and Bush Administrations, along with most members of Congress, drug trafficking has been designated the newest national security threat. The Soviet commissars have been replaced by Colombian drug lords. According to the Bush Administration, the 1989 U.S. invasion of Panama was justified, in large part, because Manuel Noriega had been indicted for drug trafficking. To eliminate such traffic the Pentagon became the ultimate antidrug "Robocop."

In fact, antidrug activity has become the routinely invoked justification for almost all military programs and budget proposals. The U.S. Navy even lauds its Trident nuclear missile submarine for its value as a drug trafficking deterrent.

Yet such action flies in the face of both tradition and common sense. Using the Department of Defense [DoD] as law enforcement's "800 lb. gorilla" threatens the longheld policy of keeping the military out of domestic affairs. As then-Secretary of Defense Caspar Weinberger wrote in 1985, "Reliance on military forces to accomplish civilian tasks is detrimental to both military readiness and the democratic process."

Using the military to fight societal ills is to embark on a mission impossible. The problem of drug use in the United States is not new. For centuries people have regularly experimented with legal drugs such as alcohol and tobacco as well as illegal drugs. As long as there is a demand for drugs there will be a supply. Using military forces, whose primary mission is to kill people and destroy things, will not change this.

What it will do, however, is divert resources from the truly critical need: reducing domestic demand. It also threatens to strengthen antidemocratic military forces in such countries as Bolivia, Peru, and Colombia.

Furthermore, drug trafficking is a global problem. Building up a massive U.S. antidrug force flies in the face of President Bush's call for a "new world order" which should seek to solve international problems through a revitalized United Nations and strengthened multinational agencies.

Actually, growing reliance on the military is a tacit admission of failure in antidrug efforts to date. As Lt. Gen. Stephen Olmstead, a former Deputy Assistant Secretary of Defense for drug policy and enforcement says, "In describing our current antidrug abuse efforts I often hear the word 'war.' I have a few years of experience in war, and I don't think we're in a war.

War, defined by Clausewitz at least, is a total commitment of a nation. I currently do not find that. What I find is: 'Let's make the Army the scapegoat. We don't know what the answer is to the drug problem, so let's assign it to the Army and let them try and solve it."

Federal Antidrug Spending (millions of dollars)

	Total	DoD	%
1989	6,301.6	438.8	6.9
1990	9,377.7	745.8	7.9
1991	10,841.4	1,042.5	9.6
1992*	11,953.1	1,274.6	10.6
1993**	12,728.7	1,223.4	9.6

* estimated, ** requested

Sources: ONDCP, CDI.

A report by the congressional Office of Technology Assessment finds that "There is no clear correlation between the level of expenditures or effort devoted to interdiction and the long-term availability of illegally imported drugs in the domestic market. However, given the profitability of drug smuggling, a worldwide glut of drugs, and the view that the United States is the favored market for drugs, interdiction alone will probably never result in more than a short-term or relatively small reduction in drug availability."

In large part, committing the military to drug interdiction activities is based on a false premise. It is that the solution to the American drug-abuse problem lies in the hands of foreign nations that produce the most important illegal drugs. While the executive and legislative branches may argue over how much money to devote to "production control," unfortunately public officials raise critical questions about the wisdom or effectiveness of it as a basic strategy.

As Donald Mabry, a scholar at Mississippi State University, testified before Congress, "For almost a century American anti-drug policy has blamed foreigners for the American drug disease, thus preserving the myth that Americans are naturally good but corrupted by evil foreigners." Actually, the United States is the largest market for South American cocaine, sells the chemicals necessary to produce it and the firearms with which the major cartels arm themselves.

The failure of a strategy which focuses on limiting supply is inherent in the structure of the problem. Producer countries jointly lack either the motivation or the means to reduce total production. For the Andean countries in South America, cocaine is merely the latest manifestation of their dependence on producing export commodities for foreign consumption. Furthermore, even a vastly more effective interdiction program will make little difference with respect to such drugs as cocaine and, to a lesser extent, heroin. This is because the price of cocaine does not really rise until it is inside the United States.

The peasants who grow coca-leaf do not make any great profit. Growers sell a metric ton of leaf to middlemen for about $600. One ton produces about seven kilograms of finished cocaine. The price, when it leaves Colombia is probably something between $5,000 and $7,000 a kilo. Cocaine sells in Miami for about $15,000 a kilo. The effective retail price is on the order of $200,000 to $250,000 when it is broken down in one gram units. One can seize an enormous amount of cocaine that costs between $5,000 and $15,000 per kilo without making any major difference to the $250,000 street price. Thus, the grower gets only .0003% of the eventual street value of his crop.

As Peter Reuter, a senior economist with the Rand Corp., testified before Congress, "The only thing that interdiction can do is raise the price. It can't, at this stage, given the maturity of the cocaine business, affect the amount that enters this country. There's too much leaf capacity; there's too much production capacity. There are too many experienced adaptive smugglers. . . Interdiction simply works on a part of the system, at least with respect to cocaine, that is incapable of accounting for a large share of the cost of cocaine, given the risks that are faced by dealers within the United States.". . .

Past Antidrug Efforts

The Pentagon has been involved in drug interdiction efforts since at least 1971. Its assistance prior to 1981, however, was sporadic, uncoordinated, and very limited. In 1981, Congress modified the Posse Commitatus Act of 1878, explicitly allowing the military to support antidrug efforts. Prior to that, anyone who attempted to use the military for law enforcement, unless specifically authorized by Congress or the Constitution, was liable to a fine or imprisonment. The new legislation permitted the Pentagon to assist by providing information, equipment, facilities, training, and advisory services.

On April 8, 1986, President Reagan signed National Security Decision Directive 221 on narcotics and national security which, among other things, called for an expanded role for U.S. military forces in supporting counternarcotics efforts.

Between mid-July and early December 1986 U.S. military personnel went to Bolivia to support Operation Blast Furnace.

Working with Bolivian police, U.S. Army helicopters and military personnel sought to destroy coca-paste processing laboratories. It was the first U.S. military antidrug operation in the Andes. Long-term effects of the operation, however, were negligible since drug activities returned to previous levels soon after the operation ended.

The Anti-Drug Abuse Act of 1988 called for a substantial increase in military aid to those countries involved in U.S. antinarcotics programs, waiving a 1974 ban on aid to foreign police.

A New Mission

In September 1988 Congress passed legislation, as part of the FY 1989 National Defense Authorization Act, which marked the Pentagon's formal emergence as an antidrug warrior. DoD was required to undertake three statutory missions. These were: serving as the single lead agency of the federal government for the detection and monitoring of aerial and maritime transit of illegal drugs into the United States; integrating U.S. command, control, communications and intelligence (C3I) systems dedicated to the interdiction of illegal drugs into an effective communications network, and providing an improved interdiction and enforcement role for the National Guard.

Shortly thereafter the U.S. Justice Department's Office of Legal Counsel issued an opinion stating that U.S. military personnel can apprehend accused drug traffickers abroad—a power they do not have in the United States. Even more ominous is the fact that the U.S. military can act without host country consent.

When the U.S. invaded Panama on December 20, 1989, President Bush released a memo stating, "In the course of carrying out the military operation in Panama which I have directed, I hereby direct and authorize the units and members of the Armed Forces of the United States to apprehend General Manuel Noriega and any other persons in Panama currently under indictment in the United States for drug-related offenses.

"I further direct that any persons apprehended pursuant to this directive are to be turned over to civil law enforcement officials of the United States as soon as practicable. I also authorize and direct members of the Armed Forces of the United States to detain and arrest any persons apprehended pursuant to this directive if, in their judgment, such action is necessary."

Even before Congress passed supporting legislation, Secretary of Defense Dick Cheney sent a message to the various unified commanders in chief that reducing the flow of drugs to the U.S. was a high priority national security mission. The U.S. is the only country that assigns its military the mission of worldwide intervention. To that end it has established unified commands. These are geographically-defined commands that are made up

103

of two or more military services.

The Joint Chiefs of Staff were assigned responsibility for developing the necessary plans. Specifically, the Atlantic, Pacific, Southern Commands, and the Forces Command a year later, as well as the U.S. element of the North American Aerospace Defense (NORAD) Command, were assigned the counterdrug mission. The commands implemented the guidelines differently. The Atlantic, Pacific, and Forces Commands established Joint Task Forces (JTFs) to conduct their operations. At SOUTHCOM and NORAD the new mission was integrated into existing structures.

The Pentagon's War on Drugs

- The effectiveness of military antidrug efforts has not been confirmed.

- Congress continues to increase funding every year for state National Guard antidrug activities; up about 400% since FY 1989.

- Congress forced a reluctant Pentagon to take on an antidrug mission it did not want in 1988. Now the Pentagon finds it an expedient justification for budget proposals.

- The 1989 invasion of Panama by U.S. forces resulted in only a temporary reduction in drug traffic and money laundering there.

- There is no evidence to date that U.S. military activities in South American countries have diminished the introduction of drugs to the United States.

- Military assistance to South American countries for antidrug programs strengthens the overall influence of the military in those countries.

Besides the major unified commands and their subordinate task forces there are a host of other military agencies involved in antidrug efforts. The Defense Communications Agency is the single Pentagon agency responsible for implementing the Drug Enforcement Telecommunications Plan. It identifies specific secure telephone, radio, and satellite communications equipment needed to interconnect voice, data, and record communications among DoD and law enforcement agencies (LEAs). As part of its mission to provide secure antidrug communications systems the Pentagon has created a computerized Anti-Drug Network (ADNET). This allows LEAs to share information and access various databases.

The Defense Advanced Research Projects Agency is working on numerous projects in cooperation with LEAs. These include developing audio recording devices to aid in surveillance, re-searching chemical detection devices to help locate drug processing laboratories and detect drugs in transit, and using artificial intelligence systems to detect money laundering and aid in the analysis of surveillance and tracking data. Some systems are already in prototype stage and have been provided for field test and evaluation.

Researchers at the Los Alamos National Laboratory, whose primary mission has always been to design nuclear weapons, have made many proposals for developing high-tech weapons to combat drug trafficking. Many of the military's own research centers are trying to develop sensors, night vision, and surveillance equipment. Private contractors, sensing new opportunities, are also submitting proposals to develop and manufacture equipment.

Numerous other Pentagon agencies are heavily involved in antidrug efforts. The Defense Intelligence Agency has established a Counternarcotics Intelligence Support Office. The Defense Security Assistance Agency coordinates the distribution of military weapons, equipment, and training to foreign militaries. The Defense Mapping Agency has been busy developing maps of drug producing areas. DoD has assigned intelligence analysts to the Drug Enforcement Administration's intelligence center to organize and computerize its intelligence files.

There is a fine line between legitimate intelligence gathering and violation of basic civil liberties. Military actions to intercept communications and examine financial records because they are allegedly drug related are an increasing threat to the privacy of American citizens.

Home Front Warriors

One growth area for Pentagon narco-warriors has been the involvement of the National Guard. Their involvement began back in the 1970s when the Army National Guard was called out to support police in eradicating marijuana grown in Hawaii. The Guard, unlike the active forces, has no restrictions under the Posse Commitatus Act when acting in a nonfederal status. They are not, however, immune from liability arising from violation of constitutional rights.

The Guard forces have generally responded enthusiastically to this mission. In fact the Pentagon's National Guard Bureau had to restrain the Oregon National Guard from sending military police out in civilian clothes to help Portland police with drug busts and surveillance. Gov. James Blanchard (D-MI) called for using Guard troops to bulldoze crack houses in Detroit.

In accordance with the 1988 Congressional legislation the National Guard Bureau established a national-level structure in its Office of Military Support to coordinate drug-enforcement operations. As part of the process of obtaining funding for their antidrug missions all U.S. states and territories had to submit a plan describing their proposed activities for approval in the Pentagon. Using the Freedom of Information Act the Center for Defense Information obtained copies of all the plans for FY89.

A review of these plans show a huge expansion of the Guard's antidrug efforts. Some activities described in the plans include detection and monitoring of drug smuggling through aerial surveillance, radar surveillance, aerial photography and other imagery, long-range reconnaissance, and assistance in searching containers. Others are expanded training of law enforcement personnel, transportation of LEA personnel, equipment and seized substances, and increased loans of military equipment.

Guard authorities are not above exaggerating the problem in order to obtain support for their plans. For example, the Kansas National Guard plan stated, "More Americans are killed by drugs every 24 months than were killed in battle in Viet Nam. This figure is estimated as 60,000 fatalities." In truth, according to the National Institute on Drug Abuse the total number of drug abuse deaths in 1988 and 1989 was 14,016.

Guard units work in various areas. In 1990 Guard units in 21 states were working with the U.S. Customs Service to inspect commercial cargo entering the United States via sea, air, and land. Eleven states were working with the Border Patrol and the Customs Air Service to identify and track illegal ground and air drug traffic. In 1990 the National Guard established the National Interagency Counternarcotics Institute in San Luis Obispo, California, in order to enhance cooperation between the Guard and federal, state, and local agencies.

Although not used as extensively as the Guard, Reserve Forces have also increased their antidrug activities. Marine Corps Reserves have assisted both the Border Patrol and Customs Services. The Naval Air Reserve flies surveillance missions while Naval Reserve ships also participate.

Questionable Effectiveness

While the Guard has certainly benefited from the drug war, seeing its antidrug funding rising from $40 million in FY89 to $154 million in FY92, it is unclear how effective they have been. A DoD Inspector General's report released in July 1991 found that Guard components "had not fully identified their counternarcotics workload; sought feedback from the law en-forcement agencies (LEAs) on the Guard counternarcotics oper-ations; measured the effectiveness of the support provided; or conducted long-term planning, programming and budgeting for counternarcotics operations." It also found that the California National Guard did not justify the requirement for the National

Interagency Counternarcotics Institute. The FY93 request, however, increases the National Guard share of the DoD antidrug budget to $171 million.

Other Pentagon antidrug units have also come in for criticism. Another Inspector General report found that "JTF-5 duplicates counternarcotics capabilities" at other Pacific Command activities and creates unnecessary operational overhead. Furthermore, its location in California does not allow it to provide optimum support to the law enforcement community.

In late 1991 the Pentagon Inspector General issued a comprehensive report on Pentagon support to U.S. drug interdiction efforts. It found that DoD's counterdrug program has not been adequately coordinated with the law enforcement agencies at all levels to achieve maximum effectiveness. The DoD intelligence structure is not ideally designed to provide maximum support to the LEAs and measures have not been instituted that adequately measure the effectiveness of DoD's counterdrug support contributions.

Even the first major military antidrug action, the invasion of Panama, had no lasting effect. The State Department's 1991 International Narcotics Control Strategy Report found that "large seizures during 1990 indicated that traffickers continue to use Panamanian sea, land, and airspace to transship illegal narcotics—especially cocaine—destined for the U.S. and elsewhere." A 1991 GAO [Government Accounting Office] report found that "drug trafficking may be increasing and that Panama continues to be a haven for money laundering."

The Pentagon itself is reportedly having some second thoughts about its role. According to one recent report it rejected a proposal by the White House Office of Drug Control Policy that would have created a unified military authority to coordinate most U.S. counternarcotics operations in Latin America. This rejection reportedly reflected a Pentagon wariness about becoming too closely tied to a no-win cause. . . .

The Wrong Strategy

U.S. military involvement in antidrug efforts is an inappropriate mission. It is the demand by U.S. citizens which fuels drug trafficking. When the demand drops drug traffic will dry up. As it now stands the military is engaged in an endless and futile effort. It is gearing up to intervene in Third World countries when the real solution is to provide expanded education, prevention, and treatment programs. Drug use in America is ultimately a health and police issue, not a military one. Involving the military diverts scarce money from the necessary demand-side programs. It also threatens to undermine the wise policy of keeping the U.S. military out of the law enforcement business.

Periodical Bibliography

The following articles have been selected to supplement the diverse views presented in this chapter.

Dan Baum
"The War on Drugs, Twelve Years Later," *ABA Journal*, March 1993. Available from 750 N. Lake Shore Dr., Chicago, IL 60611

David Beers
"Just Say Whoa!" *Mother Jones*, July/August 1991.

William F. Buckley Jr.
"The War on Drugs Has Had Little Success," *Conservative Chronicle*, March 24, 1993. Available from PO Box 11297, Des Moines, IA 50340-1297.

Stephen Flynn
"Worldwide Drug Scourge: The Response," *The Brookings Review*, Spring 1993.

Marsha Freeman
"Yes, We Can Win the War on Drugs," *21st Century*, January/February 1990. Available from 60 Sycolin Rd., Suite 203, Leesburg, VA 22075.

Haven Bradford Gow
"Drug Experiment in Switzerland: A Glaring Failure," *Conservative Review*, January 1992. Available from 6861 Elm St., Suite 4H, Maclean, VA 22101.

Philip Jenkins
"Fighting Drugs, Taking Liberties," *Chronicles*, May 1992. Available from 934 N. Main St., Rockford, IL 61103.

Rensselaer W. Lee III and Scott B. MacDonald
"Drugs in the East," *Foreign Policy*, Spring 1993.

Clarence Lusane
"Racism in the Drug War," *The Drug Policy Letter*, Winter 1992. Available from 4801 Massachusetts Ave. NW, Suite 400, Washington, DC 20016-2087.

William S. Sessions
"Law Enforcement and the Community," *Vital Speeches of the Day*, May 15, 1991.

Sam Staley
"The War on Drugs Escalates Urban Violence," *The Wall Street Journal*, August 13, 1992.

Joseph B. Treaster
"Some Think the 'War on Drugs' Is Being Waged on the Wrong Front," *The New York Times*, July 28, 1992.

Should Drug Testing Be Used in the Workplace?

DRUG ABUSE

Chapter Preface

On January 4, 1987, 16 passengers died and 170 were injured when an Amtrak passenger train and a Conrail train collided in Maryland. After testing the trainmen, the National Transportation Safety Board concluded that the Conrail engineer and brakeman were both impaired from marijuana use. Such incidents have led many to believe that those who work in safety-sensitive occupations should be tested for drug use before they are hired and while they are on the job. "Testing is a vital tool with safety-sensitive employees who could kill or maim others," contends John W. Johnstone Jr., head of Olin Corporation.

Even those who do not work in dangerous jobs should be tested for drug use, some believe. This would have a double benefit: It would discourage drug use, since users would risk being caught by the tests; and it would enable companies to identify and help treat those who do use drugs, perhaps catching them before they become addicted. As Richard Willard writes in *How to Ensure a Drug-Free Congressional Office*, "The best way to cure drug addiction is to prevent it from ever occurring."

On the other hand, opponents see drug tests as unreliable and as an unwarranted invasion of employees' personal lives. There are several issues involved. For example, urinalysis—the most common kind of drug test—can reveal other information, such as pregnancy or certain diseases, that a person might wish to keep private. In addition, urinalysis reveals only by-products of drug use rather than current levels of drugs in the body. Thus, while a drug test might indicate that an employee used drugs on his or her own time, that employee may not currently be impaired. By the same token, a person under the influence of a drug might test negative if the by-products have not yet entered the urine. Charges Joseph Amma of the Mail Handlers union, "Drug tests are more unreasonable and more of an invasion of privacy and probably no more an accurate predictor of on-the-job behavior than the so-called lie detector tests."

Finally, drug tests can be inaccurate. The tests themselves are not infallible, and human error increases the number of mistakes. Eating certain foods, such as poppy seeds, or taking legal medicines, such as ibuprofen, may result in a false-positive test result. Since this may cost an employee his or her job, opponents believe that drug testing should not be allowed in the workplace.

"The war on drugs cannot be won in the United States until it is arrested in the workplace," asserts Edward E. Potter of the National Foundation for the Study of Employment Policy. Whether drug testing is a legitimate method to achieve that end is debated by the authors of the following viewpoints.

110

"Americans are supportive of drug-free workplace programs, and are willing to accept fair and effective drug testing as a part of those programs."

Employees Should Be Tested for Drug Use

G. John Tysse and Garen E. Dodge

Drug abuse in the workplace not only causes deaths and injuries, according to G. John Tysse and Garen E. Dodge, but also is an enormous drain on the nation's productivity. In the following viewpoint, the authors argue that drug testing programs can deter drug use both on and off the job. They believe pre-employment drug tests should be used to prevent the hiring of drug users. Tysse is a partner in the Washington, D.C., law firm McGuiness & Williams, and president of the firm's employment advisory services division. Dodge is an associate in the Washington, D.C., law firm Keller & Heckman, specializing in employment and labor law. They are the authors of the book *Winning the War on Drugs: The Role of Workplace Testing*, from which this viewpoint is excerpted.

As you read, consider the following questions:

1. According to the National Institute on Drug Abuse data, how do drug abusing workers compare to nonusers?
2. What findings of the Postal Service's study support the authors' assertion that screening applicants for drug use can increase workplace productivity?
3. What types of economic costs of drug abuse do Tysse and Dodge describe, besides injuries and deaths?

From G. John Tysse and Garen E. Dodge, *Winning the War on Drugs: The Role of Workplace Testing*. Washington, DC: National Foundation for the Study of Employment Policy, 1989. Reprinted with permission of the National Foundation for the Study of Employment Policy, © 1989.

Drug abuse exists in the workplace as well as in the home and on the street. According to the National Institute on Drug Abuse (NIDA), rates of drug abuse are consistently higher among persons in the 18 to 40 year old age group, in other words the core of today's (and tomorrow's) workforce. NIDA reports that among currently full-time employed 20 to 40 year olds, 22 percent used an illegal drug within the past year, and 12 percent within the last month. . . .

NIDA data also profiles the drug-abusing worker. He or she is late for work three times more often than a non-user; asks for time off or early departure more than twice as often; has more frequent and longer absences from work; uses three times the average level of sick benefits; is five times more likely to file a worker's compensation claim; and is three and one-half times more likely to be involved in an accident while on the job. The U.S. Postal Service, which conducted a major study on drug-abusing job applicants, found that they had a 43 percent greater chance of being absent from work than their non-using counterparts.

While the work-related consequences of drug abuse have been well-documented (for example, the tragic Amtrak crash in early 1987 in which 16 people were killed and 174 injured because of marijuana-caused negligence), drug abuse can also have less visible consequences in the workplace, including medical care expenses, tardiness and absenteeism, lost productivity, and damage to employee morale. In sum, the evidence makes clear that drug abuse in the workplace remains a serious problem. . . .

A consensus has developed in the nation that the workplace is an appropriate place to intervene in the process of individual substance abuse. Surveys indicate that the overwhelming majority of Americans are supportive of drug-free workplace programs, and are willing to accept fair and effective drug testing as a part of those programs. According to a public opinion poll conducted by the *New York Times*, 61 percent of the adult respondents said they would favor a policy that would require workers in general to be tested to determine whether they have used illegal drugs recently. . . .

The Drug-Abusing Job Applicant

Until recently, there had been little empirical data regarding drug use among employment applicants, although the evidence strongly suggests that drug abuse is just as, if not more, prevalent among those looking for work as it is among current employees. The release of preliminary data from a study by the U.S. Postal Service, the first large-scale test of its kind regarding employment applicants and drug use, establishes clearly that drug use among employment applicants is a clear indicator of future problems on the job.

During 1987 and 1988, the U.S. Postal Service administered drug tests to 5,465 applicants as part of a longitudinal study of pre-employment drug testing. Out of that population, 4,375 individuals were hired subject to a 90-day probationary period. This group composed the study sample. Among those hired as part of the group were applicants who had tested confirmed positive for illegal drug use. To avoid personnel actions based on the test results, only the research team at USPS was notified as to the results. Since their hire, the Postal Service has kept track of both those who tested negative and those who tested positive and the kinds of drugs for which they had tested positive. The data provides a unique perspective because in normal practice employers rarely will hire individuals who test confirmed positive for illegal drug use.

Drug Testing Is Critical for Safety

We should give drug testing a real chance to protect the public from those impaired by drugs. Drug testing is one cornerstone of Olin's substance-abuse prevention program. The other pillars of that program are rehabilitation and tough enforcement. For those of you unfamiliar with us, Olin's primary businesses are in chemicals, metals and defense/aerospace products. Like any responsible company, we take the care and handling of our chemical products and raw materials very seriously.

We not only train and retrain our employees in the safe handling of chemicals, we have also built sophisticated safety systems into our plants. Yet *all* of that training and *all* of that protective equipment could be for naught if a key operator is high on drugs.

That's why we see testing as an absolutely critical component of our program.

John W. Johnstone Jr., *Vital Speeches of the Day*, March 15, 1989.

Significantly, the USPS data shows that drug use was found to be linked to increased absenteeism—indeed those testing positive had a 43 percent greater chance of being absent during the probationary period than those testing negative. Broken down by *types* of drugs, high rates of absenteeism were found by 43 percent of employees that had used cocaine (compared with only 21 percent by those testing negative), and moderate rates of absenteeism were reported by 52 percent of marijuana-smoking employees (compared with 39 percent by those testing negative).

The USPS anticipates that "the strength of the observed relationship (between applicant drug use and job problems) will increase in magnitude as the study progresses." As a result of its preliminary analysis, USPS predicts that it could save as much as $4 million per year (not counting other costs such as a supervisor's having to rearrange schedules for absentees) by refusing to hire those who test positive for drugs. Simply on the basis of sound workplace productivity, the study strongly indicates that the significant unnecessary costs imposed by a new hire who has tested confirmed positive for drugs clearly supports the use of pre-employment drug screening.

In another study conducted by the Navy in 1985 involving recruits, a control group of approximately 500 male recruits who tested positive for marijuana at the time of induction (at the time the Navy accepted recruits who tested positive for marijuana, but not other drugs) was compared against a similar control group which tested negative. Retention data showed that 19 percent of the negative group and 43 percent of the positive group had been discharged from the Navy after 2½ years. Reasons for discharge for the positive group were much greater for drug and alcohol abuse or other behavioral or performance reasons. . . .

Hidden Costs of Drug Use

The most graphic results of the consequences of workplace drug abuse come in the form of death and injuries. But there are other effects, particularly economic and other less obvious costs. Indeed, it has been suggested that a company is likely to see the costs of substance abuse in at least one of four ways: 1) manifest direct costs; 2) latent direct costs; 3) manifest indirect costs; and 4) latent indirect costs.

1. Manifest direct costs are payments for treatment of substance abuse, including emotional care and detoxification programs. Health care insurers that cover such costs report that they are rising sharply. For example, a report issued by Blue Cross of Greater Philadelphia describing the medical insurance program covering the Philadelphia Council AFL-CIO [American Federation of Labor/Congress of Industrial Organizations] revealed that hospital admissions for treatment of drug or alcohol problems among subscribers rose dramatically in the period from 1980 to 1984. Different patterns become apparent when drug and alcohol hospitalizations are considered separately. According to the report, "the percentage of all days used for alcohol treatment has remained fairly stable since 1982; however, the percentage of days used for treatment of drugs rose steadily." The report also makes clear that the use of health care services by abusers, even for medical disorders unrelated to substance abuse, is higher than for the non-drug using population. In the Philadelphia AFL-CIO program, said the report, "the average length of hospital stays for alcohol and drug patients was about three times that of subscribers who were not admitted for drug and alcohol treatment in 1984." In addition, family members of drug and alcohol abusers, who themselves did not have a drug problem, were more likely to utilize mental health and hospitalization benefits.

Some employers are finding that they are paying much more for treatment of substance abuse and emotional problems than first thought. One Massachusetts company estimated initially that such expenses comprised approximately 8 percent of total health costs. However, when the company's data was examined carefully, it was discovered that 28 percent of all claims paid were for substance abuse and emotional problems. Similarly, another company study revealed that drug users were five times as likely to file a worker's compensation claim, and received five times the average level of sick benefits.

Drugs and Health Care Costs

Clearly, employer health care costs have increased at an alarming rate over the last several years, to the point where getting control over these costs is a major priority not only of the business community, but of the nation as a whole. A healthier workforce is a more productive workforce, and it is obvious that the drug-abusing worker is much more likely to need and use health care services. To the extent a drug testing program deters employee drug use, it will also help in reducing related health care costs.

2. Latent direct costs, the second category of loss in the workplace due to drugs, are the medical care expenses for illnesses that are not obviously associated with substance abuse, but which have an important emotional or behavioral element. Substance abusers appear to be high-cost consumers of health care, typically with repeated rather than one-time hospital confinements.

3. Manifest indirect costs, the third category of employer costs, include as major components factors such as absenteeism, employee turnover, waste, accidents and decreased productivity. The drug-abusing employee is more likely to be late, to request early dismissal or time off, to use more sick leave benefits and to file a worker's compensation claim than the non-abusing employee. In fact, studies have shown that employees with drugs in their systems are one-third less productive than non-abusing workers. . . .

4. Latent indirect costs, the fourth category, are those associated with damage to corporate image and employee morale. The costs of bad decisions, diverted and unproductive supervisory and managerial time, damage to equipment and products, and disciplinary and grievance actions are difficult to quantify, but obviously can be significant. . . .

This systematic categorization of costs to employers may provide a useful means of analysis. Substance abuse affects productivity (and thus profits), which affects a company's shareholders.

Sending a Signal to Incoming Workers

Looking at the issue more broadly, however, employers have an interest in the continued health and productivity of their employees. Stated simply, substance abuse harms an employer's human resources. In terms of corporate responsibility, it seems evident that an employer's contribution to the curtailment of substance abuse will have a beneficial impact upon society, which, in turn, will benefit the company. In sum, while it is not easy to quantify every cost, it seems clear that substance abuse is having a substantially negative effect on employees and their employers.

The data presented here indicate the tremendous human and economic stake that America has in ridding the workplace of drugs. [As stated in the final report of *The White House Conference for a Drug-Free America,*] "The business community has enormous power to deter illicit drug use in the workplace and community. . . . Sending a strong antidrug signal from the workplace to young people is one of the ways to ensure that incoming workers would understand that they were entering a drug-free environment." We believe that a drug-free workplace program which contains a drug testing component administered in a fair and careful manner can be an effective means of sending that signal, and in helping to solve the drug abuse problem in the workplace and the nation as a whole.

"We are all intensely interested in overcoming this country's current nightmare of drug abuse. But drug testing is not the answer."

Employees Should Not Be Tested for Drug Use

Glenn Berrien

In a U.S. Postal Service (USPS) study, job applicants were tested for drug use and their subsequent job performance was monitored. The USPS concluded that it could save money by rejecting applicants who tested positive for drugs. In the following viewpoint, Glenn Berrien, president of the National Postal Mail Handlers Union, argues that drug use should not keep workers out of the workplace, where they can get help for their drug problems while supporting themselves. He also challenges the USPS claim that money could be saved by rejecting applicants who use drugs.

As you read, consider the following questions:

1. Why does Berrien believe that rejecting job applicants who tested positive for drug use would be unlawful for the Postal Service?
2. What legal definition of drug users should protect them, under the Rehabilitation Act, from being discriminated against in the USPS hiring process, according to the author?
3. How will hiring drug users who are capable of working save taxpayers' money, in Berrien's view?

From Glenn Berrien's testimony before the House Subcommittee on Postal Personnel and Modernization during the April 12, 1989, hearing on the U.S. Postal Service's Pre-Employment Drug Testing Program.

The National Postal Mail Handlers Union is indeed appalled and totally opposed to drug abuse in the workplace in any form. The nationwide plague of drug abuse has reached epidemic proportions. Here in the nation's capital we are experiencing a drug related murder rate that grows daily, with many deaths occurring within a mile or two of even this House office building.

As the father of four young daughters and fearful for their future, I realize that an answer to this problem must be found. That answer is not to line up employees of the Postal Service in lavatories and test them for drugs.

The Postal Service proposes drug testing all job applicants for marijuana, cocaine, and a broad spectrum of other drugs, and denying employment to all applicants who test positive. Its proposal is based upon its study showing a statistically significant correlation between positive drug tests and absenteeism and involuntary termination during the first few months of employment.

The aim of this proposal is to save money; the dollars lost on absenteeism and training and breaking in replacement workers.

Unlawful Consequences

The Mail Handlers Union believes that this proposal will have unlawful consequences. It is contrary to the intent of Congress, as expressed in the Rehabilitation Act of 1973 and the 1978 amendments to that Act. It is designed to evade the Postal Service's statutory and contractual obligations to provide therapy and opportunities for rehabilitation to employees afflicted with alcoholism or drug addiction. And, it is unwise as a matter of social policy.

The study showed that 8.5 percent of the new hires between September of 1987 and May of 1988 tested positive; 65 percent of the positive results reported marijuana. Most of the new hires who tested positive were black males between the ages of 25 and 35.

The researchers found that new employees who tested positive had somewhat higher rates of absenteeism. They also found a higher rate of involuntary termination among those who tested positive. But this result was neutralized by another finding of an equally high rate of voluntary termination among new hires who tested negative.

The study showed no significant relationship between the overall turnover rate and the drug test results.

The Postal Service concluded that it could save approximately $4 million annually by refraining from hiring all applicants testing positive using the EMIT-100 test, and even more money by eliminating the presumably greater number who would test positive using the EMIT-20 test instead of the EMIT-100 test recommended by NIDA [National Institute on Drug Abuse].

The Rehabilitation Act of 1973 prohibits the Postal Service from discriminating against employees *and applicants for employment* on the basis of physical or mental handicap. The 1978 amendments to the Rehabilitation Act were intended to make the federal government a "model employer" of the handicapped.

© Gary Huck. Reprinted with permission.

The governing regulations prohibit the Postal Service from using employment tests or other selection criteria that screen out or tend to screen out qualified handicapped applicants, unless such tests can be shown to be job-related to the specific position. The same regulations require the Postal Service to make all reasonable accommodations to employees' handicaps that can be made without undue hardship. The statute and regulations establish clearly and unequivocally that the Postal Service cannot discriminate against job applicants on the basis of physical or mental handicap, and that the Postal Service has, as well, an affirmative obligation to offer employment to qualified handicapped applicants.

The definitions section of the Act expressly define as "handicapped individuals" alcoholics and drug abusers whose current use of alcohol or drugs does not prevent them from performing their job duties or threaten the property or safety of others.

In other words, the nondiscrimination and affirmative action employment obligations of the Postal Service apply to job applicants who are alcoholics or drug abusers able to perform the work without posing a threat to the health or safety of the rest of the work force.

The Postal Service's obligation to employ the handicapped, including alcoholics and drug abusers able to perform their jobs, is even greater once the applicant becomes an employee. As postal employees, alcoholics and substance abusers are entitled to participate in the Postal Service's Employee Assistance Program [EAP] and to be granted leaves of absence to undergo rehabilitation.

The Intention of Congress

The federal courts tell us that it was Congress' firm intention in enacting and amending the Rehabilitation Act to require federal employees to exert substantial affirmative efforts to assist alcoholic employees toward overcoming their handicap before firing them for performance deficiencies related to drinking.

The same regulations impose the same duty toward drug abusers.

In the absence of state handicapped statutes with provisions comparable to those of the Rehabilitation Act, private employers are, as a general rule, under no obligation to employ alcoholics and drug abusers. The same is not true of the Postal Service, however.

It is clear from the way Congress drafted its definitions that it intended the Postal Service and other federal employers to serve as a part of the solution to drug abuse problems in our society by providing employment to drug abusers who are reasonably employable.

Congress defined employable drug abusers rather narrowly, as either former addicts or present abusers who are able to perform their jobs and pose no danger to the work force. Applicants meeting these qualifications and who are otherwise qualified to perform the job are to be offered both employment and all of the accommodations available to them as postal employees, including EAP counseling and the opportunity to undergo rehabilitation.

There can be no doubt that the Postal Service's proposal will cause it to run afoul of its duty to refrain from discrimination against, and its affirmative duty to employ, the handicapped.

The Agency justifies its proposal to refuse employment to qualified drug abusers as a substantial money-saving measure. This justification is patently indefensible in light of Congress' decision to require the Postal Service, as a federal employer, to assume the higher cost of employing such job applicants.

If the Postal Service is permitted to deny employment to qualified applicants who are drug abusers, it is likely that the taxpayers will ultimately pay for their support in some other way. Congress has decided, and we think it has decided wisely, that we will all ultimately benefit by paying higher postal rates for any higher costs associated with offering employment to such applicants than by denying them an opportunity to live useful and productive lives as wage earners.

Rehabilitation Is the Proper Focus

We believe that the proper focus is on the quality of rehabilitation and counseling assistance offered to postal employees afflicted with drug abuse problems. A properly run Employee Assistance Program, including rehabilitation services, will cost more in the short run than purging all known drug abusers from the work force. In the long run, however, effective rehabilitation and counseling services will save taxpayers the much higher costs of supporting unproductive drug abusers, either on welfare or in prisons. There is ample evidence by now of the long-term cost savings of effectively run employee assistance programs. . . .

We also believe that it makes good sense to refrain from the proposed drug testing simply as an objective matter of efficient operations and economics, without regard to legal implications. Our position is shared by some of this country's most respected institutions. The American Medical Association in 1987 studied the issue of whether drug tests should be required of civilian airmen. It recommended to the FAA that it would be wiser to test directly for signs of mental or physical impairment by measuring cognitive function. It concluded that the pre-employment drug testing should be reserved only for jobs directly affecting the health and safety of others. Several years later, advances in the technology for cognitive function testing make this option even more practical than it was when the AMA recommended it. Drug testing simply cannot be rationalized as a check on performance impairment—nor does the Postal Service seek to rationalize its proposal on such grounds.

Responding directly to the Postal Service's cost-savings rationale, and putting aside the legal and moral objections, even this rationale does not withstand close examination. The Postal Service has calculated an annual cost savings of about $4 million. Of this figure, $1 million must be subtracted, as the figure attributed to the savings for eliminating the estimated involuntary terminations associated with positive drug tests. By the Agency's own admission, the number of involuntary separations attributable to positive drug tests were neutralized by the number of voluntary terminations associated with negative drug tests.

The selection and training costs that provided the basis for this figure are presumably roughly the same for all new employees. Thus, these costs will be the same regardless of whether termination is voluntary or involuntary.

The estimated $3 million that the Postal Service attributed to the annual absenteeism costs associated with the positive drug test must be weighed, of course, against the cost of the drug tests. Assuming approximately 10,930 new applicants annually, the administrative, medical, and laboratory costs of testing are likely to approach $1.6 million annually.

The remaining asserted savings is not, in our opinion, an excessive price to pay to transform approximately 918 otherwise unemployed and unproductive individuals into useful taxpaying consumers.

We have made no effort to compute the savings in general assistance and other costs saved by removing such individuals from the welfare rolls that presumably would be their only other option.

Practical Reasons to Resist Testing

There are other practical reasons to resist the temptation to institute pre-employment drug tests. All employers—and there is no reason to exclude the Postal Service—pay an enormous price in employee morale for using this draconian policing device.

While some Fortune 500 companies have opted for pre-employment drug testing, the American Management Association found, in a survey that it conducted, that half of those companies presently requiring drug tests felt uncertain about whether it was an effective tool in dealing with workplace substance abuse. It reported, "A surprising number of respondents, representing companies of all sizes, indicated that pre-employment screening was intended as a statement of the firm's commitment to a drug-free workplace."

One corporate vice president and general counsel, L.L. Maltby, has characterized drug testing as "a seductive gimmick that promises instant relief from the awesome responsibilities of management." He concluded that "it just doesn't work. Drug

testing provides inaccurate and irrelevant information and alien-
ates the vast majority of good employees."

Accommodating Veterans Who Are Addicts

Postal office mailhandlers, more often than not, are veterans.
Many of our members, unfortunately, are veterans who are strug-
gling to overcome alcohol and drug addictions, while retaining
employment in an occupation that has been identified as one of
the most stressful. This country cannot turn its back on its veterans. Nor can we afford to turn our backs on the many others who
may be able to salvage their souls if offered the opportunity.

As a federal employer, the Postal Service has both a legal and
moral duty to serve as a model employer by offering employment to alcoholics and drug abusers who can perform their jobs
without endangering others.

As citizens and parents, we are all intensely interested in overcoming this country's current nightmare of drug abuse. But
drug testing is not the answer. It is an easy matter for most determined users to evade detection, while we all pay too high a
price in the loss for mutual respect for each other.

We implore this Committee, the Congress, and the Postal
Service to find the strength to resist the current drug-testing
hysteria, what Justice Antonin Scalia called "a kind of immola-
tion of privacy and human dignity in symbolic opposition to
drug use."

"Random testing is impartial and effective."

Random Drug Testing in the Workplace Is Fair

Robert L. DuPont

Drug use in the workplace has devastating effects on safety, performance, and morale, asserts Robert L. DuPont in the following viewpoint. He believes that random drug testing is the fairest and most effective way to both reduce drug abuse and detect abuse before it causes accidents or injury. DuPont, a clinical professor of psychiatry at Georgetown University Medical School in Washington, D.C., and president of the Institute for Behavior and Health, was director of the National Institute on Drug Abuse from 1973 to 1978.

As you read, consider the following questions:

1. According to DuPont, what is the most important scientific issue separating those who believe there should be random testing for drugs in the workplace and those who object to it?
2. What are the two types of intoxication the author describes? How do they differ in effect?
3. What problems does DuPont see in using neurophysiological tests as a first step in identifying drug-induced impairment?

From Robert L. DuPont, "Never Trust Anyone Under 40." Reprinted with permission from the Spring 1989 issue of *Policy Review*, the flagship publication of the Heritage Foundation, 214 Massachusetts Ave. NE, Washington, DC 20002.

Any organization with employees under the age of 40 should think seriously about testing its personnel for drug abuse. For the past 20 years, millions of Americans who began taking illicit drugs as teenagers have continued their habits as they have entered the work force. Slightly more than 70 percent of all current users of illicit drugs are employed and 69 percent are between the ages of 18 and 34. There is growing evidence that the use of illegal drugs now rivals alcoholism in its devastating effects on workplace safety, performance, and morale. . . .

Within the last decade, however, young people entering the work force have combined alcohol abuse with the use of illicit drugs, especially marijuana and cocaine. Because their effects are longer lasting and less easily recognized, because there is no characteristic odor or other sign of recent use, and because of the criminal aspects of their use and sale, these drugs pose serious problems for workers and employers.

The Costs of Drug Abuse

Drug use in the workplace is accompanied by a host of problems: an increase in health care costs for treatment of both workers and their family members, reduced productivity, increases in theft, drug sales at work, and safety threats both on and off the job.

Drug-using workers, compared with non-using workers, are three to four times as likely to have an accident on the job, four to six times as likely to have an off-the-job accident, two to three times as likely to be absent from work, three times as likely to file medical claims, five times as likely to file a workmen's compensation claim, and 25 percent to 33 percent less productive, according to estimates by the Bureau of National Affairs.

Perhaps the most dramatic example of the workplace effects of drug use was the crash of the Amtrak and Conrail trains on January 4, 1987, in Chase, Maryland, when 16 people were killed, 170 were injured, and an estimated potential liability of $100 million was incurred by the two railroads. The Conrail engineer who was responsible for the accident, Ricky L. Gates, admitted to having smoked marijuana just before driving his engine through three warning lights onto the main, high-speed corridor between Washington, D.C., and New York City. His drug use would not have been detected had it not been for mandatory post-accident drug testing. One serious implication of this accident for all employers is Conrail's potential liability for failure to detect Gates' habitual marijuana and alcohol abuse through testing before the accident.

My own practice is filled with disturbing stories of drug-related problems at work. A physician patient who said he used cocaine only on weekends broke into tears when he told me that for years he had not functioned well on Mondays and Tuesdays, being irritable and impulsive: "I just hope I didn't kill anyone because of my problem." Another patient, a 40-year-old attorney, had embezzled money from trust funds he managed, and depleted his own personal savings, including the money for his daughters' college educations, to pay for his drug habit. He avoided prison only by borrowing money from his mother to repay the funds he had taken, before the loss could be discovered by auditors. . . .

Cocaine is a special problem both in its self-destructiveness and its expense. A person can stay high on marijuana or drunk on alcohol all day for $10 or $20. Cocaine (and heroin and crack) habits run into hundreds of dollars or more a day because they are short-acting drugs to which tolerance develops rapidly, so the user escalates his dose over time. Of the employed cocaine users who call the National Cocaine Hotline (1-800-COCAINE), 70 percent are male, 61 percent white, and 93 percent between the ages of 20 and 40. Seventy-four percent use drugs at work (83 percent use cocaine, 39 percent use alcohol, and 33 percent use marijuana). Sixty-four percent say drugs are easy to obtain at work, and 44 percent say they sell drugs at work. Eighteen percent report having stolen money from coworkers and 20 percent say they have been involved in a drug-related accident at work.

Random Testing: Impartial and Effective

Although drug problems in the workplace are nothing new, drug testing at work is—and it has been met with a great deal of controversy. The technology requires urine, a substance most people are not accustomed to giving their employers, and it detects behavior that may have gone on away from the work site. Drug testing comes in many forms, with most companies starting with pre-employment testing, moving to reasonable cause testing (for example, for apparent intoxication, changed behavior, or accidents on the job) and periodic testing (at the time of annual physicals, when promoted, or when moving to a safety- or security-sensitive job). The least widely used but fairest and most effective drug testing technique in the workplace is random testing, or testing employees without individualized suspicion. With random testing the employee is subject to drug testing at any time while on the job, with no more than a few hours' notice.

When companies conduct pre-employment drug tests, they find between 10 percent and 40 percent test positive for illicit drug use, with about two-thirds of the positives being for marijuana. About one-fifth of all positive tests are positive for cocaine, with the remainder positive for other nonmedical drug use, most commonly amphetamines and tranquilizers. Many positive urine samples demonstrate recent use of more than one drug. Companies that test current employees on a random basis often find that 5 to 15 percent of their initial tests are positive. Once a strong drug abuse prevention program is in effect the positive rate for pre-employment tests often falls below 10 percent and the positive rate for random testing falls to below 5 percent.

Random testing, pioneered in the military, is now being widely adopted by some federal agencies and federally regulated industries including nuclear power plants, public transportation, and defense contractors. Although random testing is impartial and effective as a deterrent and, failing that, in detection, it is uniquely controversial, drawing the fire of the American Civil Liberties Union and many labor organizations.

The single most important scientific issue separating the two camps on random testing is whether trained supervisors can detect drug-caused impairment at work. If they can, then random testing is not needed. If they cannot, then there is no alternative to random testing if drug use at work is to be curtailed. Even after 20 years of clinical experience, and after review of what is, at this point, still preliminary research, I know that I cannot detect drug-caused impairment in my own patients without urine tests. If virtually all drug treatment professionals require, as I do, drug tests for this reason, then how can a supervisor at work detect drug use when he has no reason to suspect a particular employee? . . .

Two Types of Intoxication

There are two types of drug-caused intoxication; both cause impairment in the workplace. Type One impairment, exemplified by alcohol intoxication, produces disturbances in the primitive centers of the brain affecting coordination, balance, speech, and fine movements, and can be readily detected. With training, supervisors and police can even quantify the degree of alcohol intoxication by checking body sway and nystagmus (flicking of the pupils when looking laterally). Type One intoxication may also occur in a new or infrequent user of marijuana, causing uncontrolled, exaggerated laughter and a loss of motor coordination. Other illegal drugs, such as cocaine in high doses, also can produce short-term, discernible Type One impairment.

Type Two intoxication, which typically is produced by cocaine, marijuana, and amphetamine use, lasts much longer and is harder to detect by trained supervisors or even by doctors. It is nonetheless profoundly important at work. Although Type Two intoxication leaves the more basic brain functions of speech and motor coordination relatively unaffected, it impairs the higher functions of judgment, decision-making, memory, and other complex abilities needed to perform work safely and effectively. Type Two intoxication can profoundly affect motivation and is often particularly severe with heavy or frequent use of illicit drugs. . . .

Drug Testing Is Compassionate

Drug testing serves a deterrent purpose. It is not simply designed to catch people who are violating the law. . . . The real purpose is to deter people from using the drugs. . . .

Most drug users follow a progressive pattern of increasing drug use before they become addicted. (The exception may be crack, which seems to be almost instantly addictive.) Most users go through a period of this so-called recreational drug use. By the time you wait until someone is actually using drugs on the job, you have probably waited too long, because the success rate for drug treatment for people who really are addicted is quite low. The best way to cure drug addiction is to prevent it from ever occurring, and that means deterring drug use at the very early stages. Thus, I think drug testing is the compassionate thing for the employer to do, to deter drug use when it is occurring off-duty rather than waiting until it is such a serious drug problem that it shows up on the job.

Richard Willard, *How to Ensure a Drug-Free Congressional Office*, 1990.

Type Two intoxication is particularly insidious in that the affected employee often cannot himself recognize its existence, to say nothing of the impact such intoxication has on his ability to work safely and efficiently. This difficulty becomes more pronounced when the job requires motivation, concentration, quick reaction, and judgment. A properly administered drug screen urinalysis may be able to discover drug use that impacts on an employee's job performance even though such an impact would not be readily apparent to a trained observer or to the affected employee. . . .

Detecting Impairment Without Drug Testing

Some employers, concerned about drug-abuse problems in the workplace but not wanting to subject all employees to urinalysis, have proposed employing direct measures of impairment, such as neurophysiological tests, as a first step toward identification of drug-caused impairment. Once impairment has been identified, then a drug test is indicated. In some ways this is similar to the common practice of highway patrol officers who first smell the driver's breath, and then, if the odor of alcohol is detected, ask him to walk a straight line and complete other simple tests. Only those drivers who fail these tests are subjected to breath tests for alcohol use. Those who fail the breath tests are sent for blood alcohol tests. This experience with alcohol has encouraged the search for complex neurophysiological tests for drug-caused impairment in the workplace.

Measuring Drug-Caused Impairment

There are profound problems, however, with the use of neurobehavioral tests to measure drug-caused impairment without drug testing. First, these tests have not been conducted with illegal drugs, so there is no way to demonstrate that they measure the mental dysfunction caused by marijuana or cocaine use. More fundamentally, there is no way to show that what these tests measure (reaction time, hand-eye coordination, brain wave activity) correlates with the functions that an employer may most want to remain unimpaired (judgment, memory, and the higher cognitive activities).

Second, the necessity of establishing a baseline for each worker against which future neurophysiological test results would be measured introduces virtually insurmountable difficulties. For example, scores curve upwards with practice even under identical psychophysiological conditions because of learning effects. Also, the baseline must be established when the worker is functioning at a "normal" level. A test baseline designed to measure impairment not detectable by a trained supervisor is useful only if it is known that the test-taker is not impaired at the time of the baseline test: this is, by definition, an impossibility without urine or blood testing. Such pre/post testing would permit a drug-using employee to lower his baseline score so that later tests will not show decreases in functioning, even if the employee is using drugs when re-tested.

Third, these neurophysiological tests purport to measure impairment that can be caused by numerous factors. Cognitive impairment of worker performance may be caused by a wide variety of sources including emotional distress, neurological or organic diseases (such as Alzheimer's disease), and poor general physical health. Thus, a "positive" neurophysiological test could result from events unrelated to illegal drug use about which a person might not want to inform his employer (a death in the family, an automobile accident on the way to work, or a neurological disease).

Fourth, neurophysiological tests focus on the general intoxication produced by alcohol, but not on the more subtle (but no less profound and no less work-related) Type Two intoxication. Even in the area of Type One intoxication, however, these tests are far from satisfactory in the work setting. Not only are they not necessarily specific to the tasks of particular workers, but some workers who have not used drugs (and who work effectively) cannot pass the tests and some intoxicated workers can.

Also, any positive biobehavioral test will have to be followed by a drug test to make a final diagnosis. Thus, such tests of impairment only insert an unreliable and often irrelevant step in the process of identification of drug use at work, adding to the complexity and expense of drug abuse prevention without concomitant benefits.

These facts have led most researchers away from the search for tests for work-related behavioral impairments and toward highly specific and direct drug testing to identify the presence of drugs or drug byproducts in the body of the worker. This direct approach to drug testing is far less complex and arbitrary, and establishes a standard that is both easy for the worker to understand (one must be drug-free to work) and relatively easy to administer. Direct drug testing is also amazingly accurate when proper security measures are taken. Urinalysis has been widely used in clinical settings, such as drug treatment programs, for more than 20 years. The technology used now in drug testing is the pinnacle of modern biotechnology and can reliably identify a drug substance at a level of one part per billion—the equivalent of picking out and accurately identifying a single quarter in a string of quarters lined up next to each other from Washington, D.C., to Sydney, Australia.

For-Cause Tests

In highway law enforcement the ultimate standard against which various outcomes, including legal punishments, are judged is the blood alcohol content level or BAC, a specific, objective measure of alcohol level in the body. No driver is punished on the basis of how crooked or how straight the line is he walks for the police officer. Unfortunately, there is no simple measure of concentration of drugs or drug metabolites that corresponds to the measure of alcohol in the blood. . . .

For illegal drugs, the closest equivalent to the BAC is the "cut-off" level used by laboratories doing urine tests. However, unlike BACs, these cut-off levels do not correspond in a simple, direct way to measurable impairment and they are influenced by many extraneous factors, such as how much water the person drank just before being tested. Thus, these tests for illicit drug use are typically interpreted as either being positive or negative for recent drug use, not as a quantitative measure of drug substance in the user's body, much less in his brain.

Because of the absence of easily applied objective criteria to determine the degree of impairment, the only scientifically sound approach is to establish a per se definition of impairment. That is to say, if a urine test indicates recent illegal drug use, then it also indicates that these drugs are present in the user's brain and pose an unacceptable risk of impairment at work.

The best way to enforce this per se standard is random urine testing. While it is attractive to think that a for-cause testing program would provide a strong deterrent to drug use in the workplace—and surely such a drug testing program is far better than none at all—in practice, for-cause drug testing works less well than would be expected. First, drug users deny their drug-caused problems, including impairment at work. They typically assume that they will not appear to be impaired, and so do not change their drug use habits.

In addition, supervisors trained and encouraged to test workers they think are impaired by drug or alcohol use seldom request a drug test of any employee because there are no clear indicators of drug-caused impairment. Many employees suspected of being drug-impaired prove, on testing, to be drug-free. The supervisor quickly learns to stop asking for tests, since by asking for a drug test he is asking for trouble—the suspected employee rarely interprets for-cause testing as a friendly act.

An Ineffective Program

Most important, many supervisors and higher-level managers do not want to find drug problems in their work force, and are therefore reluctant to order for-cause testing. Many companies with thousands of employees conduct only 10 or 20 such for-cause tests a year. As a result, for-cause testing is all too often a paper drug abuse prevention program that has little effect.

Even when companies conduct for-cause testing, and even when it identifies drug use, there is often an appeal by the employee that may reach the level of a labor arbitration or even a court trial. It is common for the supervisor to be unable to substantiate the reason for initial drug testing: either the grounds were flimsy or the employee's attorney was able to show that his client was arbitrarily singled out for testing. In either case, the positive test result may be tossed out and the employee reinstated.

These problems are all solved by random testing, which is fair and impartial. Random testing also does what for-cause testing cannot: deter drug use by making clear to every employee that every day at work he or she may be tested.

"Random or routine urine tests violate the most basic American tenets of freedom."

Random Drug Testing in the Workplace Is Unfair

Eric Neisser

The desire to use drug testing to combat the problems of drug abuse in the workplace is a search for a quick fix, charges Eric Neisser. In the following viewpoint, he argues that random drug testing is unnecessary, ineffective, and an invasion of privacy rights guaranteed by the U.S. Constitution. Neisser, a former legal director of the New Jersey affiliate of the American Civil Liberties Union, is a law professor at Rutgers University Law School in Newark, New Jersey. He is the author of *Recapturing the Spirit: Essays on the Bill of Rights at 200*, from which the following viewpoint is excerpted.

As you read, consider the following questions:

1. Why does Neisser believe the severity of the drug abuse problem does not warrant random drug testing?
2. According to Neisser, what is an employer's only legitimate concern about an employee's possible drug use?
3. How should those in safety-sensitive jobs be tested to assure the public safety, in the author's opinion?

From Eric Neisser, *Recapturing the Spirit: Essays on the Bill of Rights at 200*. Madison, WI: Madison House Publishers, 1991. Reprinted with permission.

The recent proliferation of programs for testing the urine of employees for illicit drugs, despite a documented leveling-off of drug abuse in this country, is a disturbing phenomenon. The desire for a simple answer—a clean test—to a complex and frightening problem is readily understandable. But like any other quick fix, this modern form of loyalty oath must be analyzed closely by everyone concerned with the rule of law and the state of our freedoms. First, I will review the traditional civil liberties concerns: the reversal of the presumption of innocence, the intrusions on personal privacy, and the unfairness of erroneous accusations based upon unreliable test results. I will then address the factors that render these impositions unreasonable: the inability of urine tests to gauge job impairment, which is an employer's only legitimate concern; the discriminatory focus on only one of many causes of poor job performance; and the failure to use less intrusive techniques that do measure ability to perform a job.

Violations of the Fourth Amendment

Random or routine urine tests violate the most basic American tenets of freedom. They presume that all employees are suspect and must prove themselves clean. Like roadblocks, they intrude upon everyone's privacy based not upon evidence of individual criminality or even impairment, but rather upon generalized assumptions about the likelihood of finding some guilty parties in a particular population. As one well-respected federal judge, H. Lee Sarokin, put it, in ruling that the sudden locking of firehouse doors and forced urine testing of all firefighters violated the Fourth Amendment:

> The invidious effect of such mass roundup urinalysis is that it casually sweeps up the innocent with the guilty and willingly sacrifices each individual's Fourth Amendment rights in the name of some larger public interest. The City . . . essentially presumed the guilt of each person tested.

This ruling should have been unsurprising not only to those of us who follow drug-testing litigation, but to all who are familiar with the Fourth Amendment. For what is an across-the-board urine testing program if not a general warrant, the very evil that stirred the colonists to revolt and prompted adoption of the Amendment? As the philosopher Santayana reminded us: "Those who cannot remember the past are condemned to repeat it."

Some would say that the current situation is different, either because the threat to our society posed by drugs is far greater than that posed to eighteenth-century England by colonists' customs violations or because public employees must expect more stringent scrutiny in light of the public trust they have accepted. But surely if the severity of the problem were the test, we would allow general searches of homes for an escaped murderer or missing machine gun cache. But we don't. As for the public trust, we should consider whether we would tolerate routine searches of pockets and handbags as government employees come to work or of lockers and desks while they are on the job. In an age when millions are employed by the government, performing jobs from janitor to general, we cannot simply invoke the public trust to excuse all intrusions regardless of their severity or justification.

Nor is the balance tipped because the intrusions are minor. Urine tests for drugs intrude upon individual privacy in three significant ways. First, they force the individual to perform the most private of bodily functions in front of a stranger. Most people do not perform that function in front of their most intimate friends or lovers, and urinating in public is a criminal offense in most places. Second, to insure accurate testing, the employee is required to disclose all medication, nonprescription as well as prescription, being used. This risks disclosure of a wide variety of physical and mental conditions that are very personal and of no legitimate concern to the employer, but which are often the basis for discriminatory action. Finally, the chemical screening of urine can itself reveal numerous conditions, such as pregnancy, diabetes, or epilepsy, that many would reasonably wish to keep private. Like discarded trash, bodily waste products can reveal a great deal about our lives that we may legitimately wish to keep from others.

Urine Tests Are Unreliable

Arguably the intrusions would be more acceptable if they were reliable indicators of a problem. Unfortunately they often are not. Initial urine tests that are "positive" for illegal drugs may reflect ingestion of lawful substances, including antihistamines and poppy seeds. In one famous instance, a woman who was unable to provide her employer with a sample because she had recently urinated, was offered a drink of bitter-lemon soda. The quinine in the drink produced a "positive" result when she urinated later; even the next day's "negative" did not deter the employer from firing her. Similarly, a supervisor in California taking allergy medication tested "positive" for cocaine. He was forced to spend a month in a hospital treatment program and to submit to regular urine tests thereafter, despite medical findings that he was wholly asymptomatic and that there was no indication of any drug use ever.

Such initial miscarriages of justice have become less frequent because of the development of more accurate confirmatory tests that do not register "positive" for such lawful substances. The most commonly used and reliable one is called GC/MS, or gas chromatography-mass spectroscopy. But even with that test, there is the risk of human error—such as failure to prevent contamination of the sample or failure to clean, calibrate, use, or read the machinery properly. In this regard, we do well to remember an early study by the federal Centers for Disease Control of laboratories doing urine testing for methadone programs. The centers sent the labs various samples for testing, some of which contained only water while others had had traces of illegal drugs inserted. The centers found the different laboratories across the country incorrectly reporting water samples as positive for drugs in 6 to 66 percent of the tests. Likewise the Navy reported that 49 percent of the scientific records and 43 percent of the so-called "chain of custody" records of urine samples were not legally supportable. Similar problems are chronicled in the 1988 House Government Operations Committee report calling for strict federal standards for laboratories performing such tests.

© Joel Pett/Lexington Herald-Leader. Reprinted with permission.

But we need to address the broader issue. Even if all the tests were always accurate, are the reversal of the presumption of innocence and the privacy intrusions justified? As every employer's expert admits, even the most accurately conducted and chemically precise drug test cannot show that the individual was under the influence of the substance or impaired in his or her job performance at the time of the test. Significantly, the test will be negative even though the employee is severely impaired, if the drug was used shortly before the test and thus before the body has had a chance to digest it fully. For example, an airline pilot who snorts cocaine minutes before giving the urine sample and boarding the plane will test negative though she or he is almost certainly impaired. A positive test result also does not show that the individual is drug-dependent, or even a regular user, just as a single abnormal sugar level does not establish diabetes. Indeed, a urine test cannot even show how much of the drug was ingested nor precisely when it was taken. Quite simply, a "true positive" result proves only that the person has ingested some quantity of the substance at some point more than four to six hours before the sample was taken and within the last forty-eight hours (for cocaine) or four weeks (for marijuana).

Job Performance

But an employer's only legitimate concern is with job performance: can the employee do the job safely and efficiently? The employer has the right to demand that the person is on duty for the hours for which paid and that the job gets done. Accordingly the employer may legitimately observe, supervise, and record employee timeliness and work performance. If a person is regularly late for work or falls asleep on the job, a humane employer would seek to determine its cause, whether it is alcohol abuse, drug addiction, too much late night television, fights with a spouse, or an emotional disturbance, and help the employee to resolve it in order to restore him or her to full productivity. There need, similarly, be no special focus on drugs if the employer takes a more traditional disciplinary approach. If the employee cannot perform adequately, she or he should be warned, disciplined, and, if necessary, fired. Conversely, if a person is always on time and is performing the work well, it should not matter to an employer if that employee had six beers or smoked marijuana at a party the prior Saturday night.

The distinction regularly drawn by employers and some courts between off-duty beer and marijuana use is that the former is a legal substance and the latter is illegal. Although this is obviously true, and is relevant to criminal investigations and perhaps to moral judgments, it is simply not a distinction relevant to a job performance analysis. Quite simply, employers are not arms of the law enforcement community, but supervisors of production.

As such, employers should, in fact, be even more concerned with alcohol problems than with drug use. Although drug impairment is a serious problem, it is far from the major source of poor job performance. There are between ten and thirteen mil-

136

lion alcohol-dependent adults in this country, but the latest figures show at most four million drug abusers. In 1989, the National Institute on Drug Abuse reported that, despite the sharp climb in the use of crack cocaine over the last few years, the overall use of illegal drugs has been decreasing for ten years and the decline has accelerated in the last five. From 1985 to 1988, the number of current users (at least once a month) of marijuana and cocaine dropped by 33 and 50 percent, respectively. The number of heroin addicts in this country is the same as fifteen years ago, and daily marijuana use among high school students has declined since 1979. If employers are truly concerned about drug-related job impairment, why don't they regularly require executives returning from lunch to take breathalyzer tests? Unlike urine tests, breathalyzers are very accurate indicators of current levels of alcohol in the system, and thus of current impairment. They are also far less intrusive on privacy and less costly than drug urine tests. The failure to screen for alcohol impairment while investing so heavily in drug tests makes no practical or business sense and is unfairly discriminatory.

Safety-Sensitive Jobs

Some will say—this is all well and good, but what should we do about employees, like pilots and bus drivers, whose work immediately affects the safety of others, thereby denying us the luxury of waiting until after the fact to learn of any inadequacies on the job? With regard to those in safety-sensitive jobs, as with all other employees, the first line of defense is the traditional approach of supervisor and co-worker observation, which has been used for decades to detect alcohol intoxication and other motor impairments.

But for those who work alone or in situations where supervision may not adequately protect us, we now also have available motor coordination and visual acuity tests that can immediately assess current ability to perform the job. For example, there are computer programs that simulate flying or driving and measure the operator's response time and accuracy. Such tests pose no civil liberties problems. There is no privacy intrusion, no presumption of guilt, and no discrimination among differing chemicals and causes of impairment. And they provide far more accurate and relevant information about job impairment. We would all be safer if, instead of giving pilots urine tests (the results of which will not be available until two days after the flight and which would not in any case reveal cocaine snorted in the bathroom just before flight), we required them to pass a flight simulation test immediately before take-off.

In sum, I do not suggest that the drug problem is either minor or under control. Nor do I urge that we ignore either the safety

137

or the productivity impact of employee drug use. Rather I propose that we focus on job performance, establish strict performance standards, employ close and sound supervision, and when indicated by job performance or the unsupervised nature of safety-sensitive work, use only non-intrusive tests directly indicative of job performance, rather than intruding needlessly and focusing narrowly and irrelevantly on the purity of one's urine.

Periodical Bibliography

The following articles have been selected to supplement the diverse views presented in this chapter.

John Coyne — "Drug Testing in the Nineties: Common and Controversial," *Glamour*, July 1991.

John Horgan — "Test Negative: A Look at the 'Evidence' Justifying Illicit-Drug Tests," *Scientific American*, March 1990.

John W. Johnstone Jr. — "The War on Drugs: Saying 'Yes' to Getting Involved," *Vital Speeches of the Day*, March 15, 1989.

Vicki J. Moresi — "Drug Testing and the Fourth Amendment," *Temple Law Review*, Fall 1992. Available from 1719 N. Broad St., Philadelphia, PA 19122.

Pat O'Malley and Stephen Mugford — "Moral Technology: The Political Agenda of Random Drug Testing," *Social Justice*, Winter 1991.

Judith S. Rosen — "*International Brotherhood of Teamsters* v. *Department of Transportation:* The Fourth Amendment, Another Victim of the War on Drugs," *Golden Gate University Law Review*, Spring 1992. Available from 536 Mission St., San Francisco, CA 94105.

Marc A. Schuckit — "Drug Testing: What It Can and Cannot Do," *Drug Abuse and Alcoholism Newsletter*, March 1990. Available from Vista Hill Foundation, 2355 Northside Dr., 3d Fl., San Diego, CA 92108.

Robert M. Stutman — "Can We Stop Drug Abuse in the Workplace?" *USA Today*, July 1990.

Robert Taylor — "Uncle Sam and the Drug Exam," *The Journal of NIH Research*, June 1990. Available from 2000 Pennsylvania Ave. NW, Suite 3700, Washington, DC 20006.

Craig Zwerling, James Ryan, and Endel John Orav — "Costs and Benefits of Preemployment Drug Screening," *Journal of the American Medical Association*, January 1, 1992. Available from 515 N. State St., Chicago, IL 60610.

Craig Zwerling, James Ryan, and Endel John Orav — "The Efficacy of Preemployment Drug Screening for Marijuana and Cocaine in Predicting Employment Outcome," *Journal of the American Medical Association*, November 28, 1990.

How Should Prescription Drugs Be Regulated?

DRUG ABUSE

Chapter Preface

When most people speak of drug abuse, they refer to such illegal drugs as crack, cocaine, and heroin. Yet many Americans abuse legal prescription drugs. Some experts believe that prescription drug abuse has cost $1 billion in unnecessary health care and criminal justice costs. California Congressman Pete Stark concurs that prescription drug abuse is a serious problem. According to Stark, who chairs the congressional subcommittee on health, the United States should regulate doctors and prescription drugs more carefully to reduce both abuse of legal drugs and the fraud and crime that accompany such abuse. Stark states, "A national accountability program for controlled prescriptions easily could save $1,000,000,000 in Medicaid/Medicare costs in addition to preventing pain, suffering, and social and family disruption."

Other experts, including the American Medical Association (AMA), concede that illicit use of licit drugs is a problem and attempts should be made to control prescription drug abuse by monitoring doctors' prescribing practices. The AMA, however, objects to several aspects of Stark's proposed regulations. First, the AMA prefers individual state programs instead of one overarching federal monitoring program. Its policy states, "The AMA believes that it is important for each state to assess its own drug diversion problem and . . . to tailor remedial action to the specific problems of the state involved." The AMA also objects to Stark's proposal that law enforcement agents regulate doctors' prescribing practices. Instead of agents untrained in medicine, the AMA contends that trained medical personnel should monitor prescriptions to see if doctors are overprescribing often-abused drugs. The AMA maintains that this system would both stop the misprescribing of abused drugs and be fair to the doctors required to comply with it.

Even if a strict monitoring system were adopted, only the supply of prescription drugs that individual doctors provide illicitly would be reduced. Those intent on abusing licit and illicit drugs would continue to have other sources. The viewpoints in the following chapter debate the seriousness of prescription drug abuse and how to stop it, as well as other issues surrounding prescription drugs.

"Illegal, fraudulent, and unnecessary prescriptions contribute to an estimated 88,000 hospital . . . admissions per year."

Increased Regulation of Prescription Drugs Is Necessary

Pete Stark

The abuse of prescription drugs is a serious problem in the United States, according to California representative Pete Stark. In the following viewpoint, Stark, who chairs the subcommittee on health, argues that many doctors and pharmacists divert prescription drugs to those who abuse them. Abuse of prescription drugs, Stark contends, is as serious and as profitable as abuse of illicit drugs.

As you read, consider the following questions:

1. How do abusers get prescription drugs, according to Stark?
2. According to the author, what are costs of the diversion of prescription drugs for illegal purposes?
3. What measures does Stark propose to stop the diversion of prescription drugs?

Pete Stark, "U.S. Taxpayers Are Funding Prescription Drug Abuse." Reprinted, with permission, from *USA Today* magazine, July 1991. Copyright 1991 by the Society for the Advancement of Education.

One definite link exists connecting drug abuse, Medicaid fraud, drug company profits, hip fractures in the elderly, and chemical restraints in nursing homes. A simple piece of paper—a prescription—contributes to each of them. A prescription form, legitimate or fraudulent, can "unlock" the medicine cabinet for necessary and effective, but potentially dangerous, pharmaceuticals such as narcotics, tranquilizers, amphetamines, and sedatives.

These drugs must be readily available to treat a broad range of disorders, and the ability of doctors to prescribe needed medication must remain unimpeded. However, illegal, fraudulent, and unnecessary prescriptions contribute to an estimated 88,000 hospital emergency room drug overdose admissions per year, as well as hundreds of millions of dollars in Medicaid fraud and avoidable hospital and nursing home costs. This adds up to crime, drug abuse, and $1,000,000,000 in unnecessary Medicaid/Medicare expenses. This money could be used instead for sadly underfunded health care programs for the elderly and the poor. The simple step of requiring accountable prescriptions for these controlled drugs would prevent many serious crime, drug abuse, and health care problems. An examination of each of these areas clearly will demonstrate the critical role the simple prescription form plays.

Drug Abuse

Controlled drugs are those which are itemized in the Controlled Substances Act and various international treaties as abusable and addictive. They include both illegal and legal pharmaceuticals. The Drug Abuse Warning Network (DAWN) measures hospital emergency visits in which a drug is involved. National projections from DAWN have shown that, between 1985 and 1989, 26-54% of emergency room hospital visits involving a controlled substance were attributable to the use of pharmaceuticals. These drugs, essential for a wide variety of medical conditions, also are widely sought by illicit traffickers. Given an option between a white powder of unknown origin and quality and a pill with a manufacturer's logo, made under U.S. government quality control, the decision for the abuser is easy.

Pharmaceuticals are custom-made central nervous system/mind altering compounds. There are stimulants (uppers), depressants (downers), tranquilizers, and hypnotics which calm jitters, smoothing out the "high" or "bad trip," or the anxiety caused by abusing other drugs. Any success achieved in reducing the supply of illicit substances will increase the pressure on the legitimate drug chain because these items, although popular for abuse, also must be readily available for patients. This means there will continue to be almost 700,000 physicians who can prescribe them and 60,000 pharmacies that can fill the prescriptions. Therefore, accountability for the key to the medicine cabinet—the prescription form—desperately is needed now and will be increasingly important in the future.

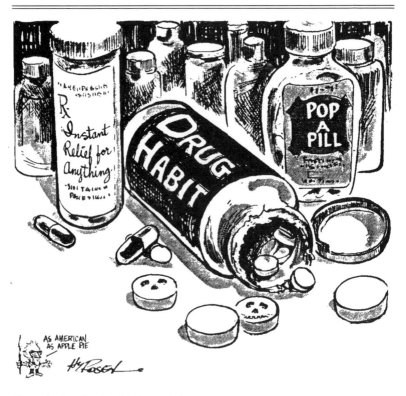

© Rosen/Rothco. Reprinted with permission.

How does the prescription control the abusers' access to drugs? First, prescription forgeries are a major source of pharmaceuticals for abuse. Any printing firm can run off prescription blanks, copying an existing doctor's pad or creating a fictitious physician's identity. A forger or organized group of forgers then visits several pharmacies a day "passing scrip." If the pharmacist even bothers to attempt to call the "doctor" whose telephone number is printed on the prescription, a member of the forgery ring answers "Medical Clinic" and verifies the order. The forger may pay $30 for 30 tablets of a strong narcotic, such as Dilaudid, which can be sold on the street for $60 per tablet—a $1,770 profit.

A second access provided by the prescription form is to "cover" illegal sales by an occasional unscrupulous pharmacy. The pharmacist can sell almost unlimited quantities of drugs to abusers for huge illicit profit. He or she then uses blank forms to create fictitious prescriptions in the names of legitimate physicians and patients from the files. By covering the illegal sales with fake prescriptions for apparently legitimate patients and doctors, the pharmacist makes the sales to drug abusers virtually undetectable by investigators.

The third area in which the prescription provides the key to the medicine cabinet is the outright illegal sale of prescriptions by corrupt doctors, who knowingly supply abusers. The U.S. Drug Enforcement Administration and the various states prosecute or revoke the license of hundreds of physicians each year for illegal drug activities. Recent cases have included doctors selling prescriptions in bars, exchanging prescriptions for sex, or writing 10-15 prescriptions at a time for the same "patient" for up to $150 apiece. One physician set up a "social club" called "Lords and Ladies of the Nile" in which a member received up to 200 controlled drug prescriptions for the $1,000 initiation fee. Another group set up a "stress clinic" in which every "patient" who came in received a prescription for the same popular drug of abuse after a "stress evaluation" and a $125 fee. If these doctors, who are not accountable for their prescriptions, advise the abusers to spread the illegal prescriptions among several pharmacies, the illicit activity is virtually undetectable.

Each of the above examples point out the crime and illegal activity involved in obtaining these pharmaceutical drugs of abuse, but the additional social and health costs cannot be ignored. These drugs resulted in an estimated 88,000 hospital emergency room visits in both 1988 and 1989, compared to 35,000-45,000 for heroin and 4,000 for LSD. Frequently, emergency room visits for overdoses are paid by Medicaid or result in unreimbursed expenses to the hospital.

Medicaid Fraud

The crime and taxpayer expense associated with prescriptions does not stop with the controlled substance. If the abuser has access to a Medicaid card, the opportunities for fraud are almost unlimited. A doctor, medical clinic, or pharmacy willing to sell drugs to abusers usually has no reservations about fraudulently billing the government. The abusers don't care about the false billings as long as they get their fix, especially if they get it for free by allowing kickbacks and phony invoices.

One case in Chicago documented about $19,000,000 in false billings. Several clinics were established solely to sell drugs and defraud Medicaid. Eventually, the conspiracy involved 65 physicians, 22 pharmacies, and two laboratories. Each "patient" had to have a Medicaid card and would receive pre-printed prescriptions for a narcotic cough syrup and Doriden, a hypnotic, known on the street as "juice and beans." The clinic saw as many as 100 drug abusers a day, each of whom paid $25-30 for the unnecessary prescription. Medicaid then was billed by the clinic for up to $200 per "patient" for the office visit and for tests which were not performed. Each "patient" also received between eight and 57 prescriptions for other high-cost items which were not dispensed, but were billed to Medicaid by pharmacies associated with the sham clinics.

In another case, a woman arrived at the doctor's office with the names and Medicaid numbers for 29 people. The physician promptly wrote 29 narcotic prescriptions in the names of those on the list (whom he had never seen for medical treatment) and billed Medicaid about $120 dollars each for an office visit and a medical procedure. Thus, a 15-minute "consultation" resulted in about $3,500 in Medicaid fraud and almost 1,000 pills worth up to $40,000 on the street.

The Office of the Inspector General, Department of Health and Human Services (HHS), reported that, in 1989, Medicaid paid about $525,000,000 for "these prescription drugs favored by 'street' pushers and users." The fraud associated with "office visit bills" to obtain these drugs easily could be two-to-five times the amount spent on the fraudulent prescriptions themselves.

Unnecessary Prescriptions

A 1989 report by the HHS Inspector General noted that mismedication of the elderly has become a critical health care issue and that "overmedication and adverse reactions to drugs are prevalent and have probably become epidemic among the elderly." The report also noted that 2,000,000 of the elderly are addicted or at risk of addiction to minor tranquilizers or sleeping pills because of using them daily for at least one year. The Inspector General cited several studies that report on the "illness-medication spiral" in which the effects of certain drugs create symptoms fitting the physician's stereotype of the elderly (confusion, lethargy, forgetfulness). This leads to the prescribing of more medication to treat symptoms caused by inappropriate drug therapy.

The Public Citizen's Health Research Group's book, *Worst Pills, Best Pills*, notes that, "even though 1,500,000 older adults use minor tranquilizers daily for at least one year continuously, there is no evidence that any of these drugs is effective for more than four months. Drug-induced falls, impairment of memory and thinking, and other adverse effects, especially in older adults, also occur with these drugs that have no proven long-term benefits."

In applying a prescription monitoring program to the group of tranquilizers known as benzodiazepines in 1989, the New York State Department of Health estimated that, prior to the rule:

• 100,000 state residents had been receiving these tranquilizers for seven years or more.

• 3,000 persons were hospitalized each year as a result of accidents attributable to tranquilizer use.

• The seriousness of their injuries required hospital stays that were twice as long as other patients'.

• 600 hip fractures annually among the elderly were attributable to use of benzodiazepines.

• These fractures required 17,000 hospital days plus additional nursing home care.

• Tranquilizers were the most frequently mentioned prescription drugs in deaths due to unnatural causes in the state.

These drugs only are available on the order of a doctor. The volume and frequency of drug-related injuries and resultant health care costs, especially among the elderly, are not due to illegal or fraudulent prescriptions, but the misprescribing and overprescribing by legitimate physicians. Indications are that a vast number of doctors simply are unaware of the need for special attention when prescribing these dangerous substances.

Needed: Accountable Prescription Programs

With such a wide range of problems, what can be done to prevent this illegal, fraudulent, and unnecessary prescribing without interfering with the needs of legitimate patients? The simple solution, proven and tested in several states, is to require a national program of accountable prescriptions for doctors. . . .

Similar programs exist in nine states, which account for almost 40% of the physicians in the U.S. Commonly known as Multiple Copy Prescription Programs (MCPP), they generally require that prescriptions for certain controlled drugs be written on a state-issued pad preprinted with the authorized doctor's name and serially numbered so they will be accountable to the individual prescriber. After completing the diagnosis, the physician simply writes the medication order on a different prescription form. The patient takes it to the pharmacy as with any other prescription. The pharmacist keeps a copy and transmits one (or the prescription information) to the state for monitoring. This simple, unobtrusive program has yielded dramatic results.

Through the MCPP, forgeries and false prescriptions created by pharmacists virtually are eliminated because these blank, serially numbered, controlled prescription forms are not available to patients, forgers, and pharmacists. Doctors engaged in illegal prescribing are deterred because, each time they put pen to paper to write a prescription, they know it is accountable to them and will be monitored by the state. Also, Medicaid fraud from an "office visit" to obtain drugs of abuse is curtailed. The greatest benefit, unlike other monitoring programs, is the preventative aspects—crime, fraud, and abuse are deterred or eliminated before the damage is done. For those abusers, doctors or pharmacists who are *not* deterred, there is a clear, undeniable, accountable trail for law enforcement and health officials to follow, more efficiently and quickly than any other possible investigative technique.

Triplicate Prescription

Nine states already have a drug law known as triplicate prescription, or "trip scrip." Every time a doctor writes a prescription for narcotics, amphetamines or barbiturates, he or she has to file one copy with the state health agency. Variations exist: New York has added benzodiazepines—the class that includes Xanax—to its regulated pharmacopoeia. Under Oklahoma's electronic system, pharmacists report prescriptions just as they report charges on a credit card. . . .

In addition to tracking "scrip doctors," who knowingly prescribe to abusers, trip scrip identifies doctors with bad prescribing habits. According to recent estimates, careless doctors have put 2 million senior citizens in the United States at risk of becoming dependent on tranquilizers. No one knows how many of them are currently hooked.

Cynthia Cotts, *The Nation*, August 31-September 7, 1992.

Finally, the issue of unnecessary or overprescribing is more difficult to address, since the common and logical answer is that we need to educate physicians better, rather than establish new programs. The call for greater education comes from many quarters. However, with all the various issues and medical advances competing for the physician's attention, self-education on the proper prescribing of controlled substances simply doesn't happen. The HHS Inspector General reported a study regarding the prescribing knowledge of physicians who treat the elderly. It found that more than 70% of the doctors tested failed to pass the exam. Thus, another advantage of the accountable program is that it emphasizes to the physician, at the time of prescribing, that the drug requires special attention. It is clear from the experiences of the states with MCPPs that doctors become more attentive to their prescribing practices for these controlled substances.

The nine states (California, New York, Texas, Illinois, Hawaii,

Rhode Island, Idaho, Michigan, and Indiana) have different programs, but each are strong advocates of the system. These programs are not new—California's was initiated in 1940, Illinois' in 1961, and New York's in 1976. The states realized a 35-50% drop in prescriptions and drugs distributed into the state in the first year! Other positive outcomes include:

• In 1984, Illinois added Doriden to the MCPP due to rapidly rising abuse. Deaths and emergency room overdoses in Chicago dropped from 24 to three in the first year and to one overdose by the second year, compared to a 12% increase in deaths and overdoses nationwide.

• In 1980, New York State had one-third of all the hospital emergency room visits for barbiturates in the U.S. By placing these barbiturates on the MCPP, it had a 60% reduction in emergency room visits in one year.

• When Texas established its MCPP in 1982 for major narcotics and amphetamines, there was a 53% reduction in prescriptions for these drugs in the first year, with continued reductions to an over-all drop of 69% by 1989.

• In 1989, New York became the only state to cover the class of tranquilizers known as benzodiazepines (including such trade-name products as Valium, Librium, Xanax, and Tranxene) on the MCPP. The results included a 95% reduction in prescriptions for one group of patients suspected of diverting almost 250,000 prescriptions annually; a 76% reduction in prescriptions for these tranquilizers dispensed by pharmacies previously identified as suspected Medicaid "pill mills"; a 31% decrease in hospital overdose admissions over the first four months of the program; significant reductions in prescriptions for the elderly; and "street price" increases of two to five times, indicating a drying up of illegal supply.

The Only Solution

With crime, drug abuse, and health care costs soaring, we cannot ignore these successful programs. With so many pressures to control health care costs and so many unfunded health initiatives for the elderly, poor, and uninsured, is there any excuse for continuing to fund illegal, fraudulent, and unnecessary prescriptions and associated health care costs? A national accountability program for controlled prescriptions easily could save $1,000,000,000 in Medicaid/Medicare costs in addition to preventing pain, suffering, and social and family disruption.

"The war on drug abuse can and must be fought alongside the war on disease, pain, and suffering; one must not be allowed to impede the other."

Increased Regulation of Prescription Drugs Is Unnecessary

James R. Cooper et al.

In the following viewpoint, James R. Cooper, the associate director of medical affairs for the National Institute on Drug Abuse's Alcohol, Drug Abuse, and Mental Health Administration in Rockville, Maryland, contends that the methods used by drug tracking and enforcement agencies to estimate the abuse of prescription drugs are misleading and inaccurate. In addition, Cooper argues that because accurate studies on the frequency and magnitude of illegal drug use have never been done, no one knows how serious a problem it is. Cooper concludes that measures taken to stop illegal use of prescription drugs could harm those who use prescription drugs legally.

As you read, consider the following questions:

1. What studies do the authors suggest portray prescription drug abuse inaccurately?
2. In the authors' opinion, how could anti-drug measures harm patients who have legitimate uses for prescription drugs?
3. In the authors' opinion, how can accurate information about prescription drug abuse be obtained?

James R. Cooper et al., "Prescription Drug Diversion Control and Medical Practice," *Journal of the American Medical Association* 268 (10): 1306-9 (September 9, 1992). Reprinted with permission.

The nonmedical use of licit psychoactive drugs is a serious public health concern. An estimated 8.5 million people 12 years or older used controlled sedatives, tranquilizers, stimulants, or analgesics for nonmedical reasons at least once during the year preceding the 1990 National Household Survey on Drug Abuse. The degree to which physicians, nurses, and pharmacists contribute to the pool of illicitly used prescription drugs relative to other diversion sources is uncertain. Nevertheless, some federal agencies and state governments have recommended or implemented more restrictive prescription drug diversion control systems. Unlike earlier labor-intensive systems, computerized pharmacy records coupled with electronic data communication now may make it much simpler and less expensive to track drug prescribing and dispensing. For example, Oklahoma began in 1991 using an electronic, computer-based, point-of-sale system that monitors all Schedule II drug prescriptions filled by the state's 900 retail pharmacies. Massachusetts and Hawaii implemented similar systems in 1992.

More comprehensive control programs have obvious potential for reducing diversion. Current widespread concern about drug abuse, as well as soaring health costs, make tighter monitoring of prescribing practices and restriction of drug use to established medical indications appealing to many. However, the possible effects of more restrictions on medical practice and patient care must also be carefully considered.

Prescribed Psychoactive Drug Use

Although several national surveys of the prescribed use of sedative-hypnotic drugs have been conducted, no similar studies of analgesics or stimulants are available. National surveys have consistently yielded the same conclusion: most prescribed use of sedative-hypnotic drugs is conservative, therapeutically appropriate, and limited to short periods (<3 months). In over 95% of the cases, the medication was prescribed by a physician. In addition, there has been a decline in the prevalence of use even by those for whom such use is clearly medically appropriate.

According to the 1990 National Household Survey on Drug Abuse (NHSDA), 1.4% of the general population 12 years of age or older was currently using nonprescribed psychoactive drugs (most commonly, controlled analgesics, followed by stimulants, tranquilizers, and sedatives); 4.1% had used them nonmedically at least once in the previous year. In contrast, 2½ times as many (10.2%) had used marijuana that year, and nearly four times as many (5.1%) were current marijuana users. This survey also found that most people who experiment with nonprescribed therapeutic drugs discontinue their use. For example, although 11.9% of those surveyed had used therapeutic drugs illicitly at some point in their lives, only 1.4% were current users.

The NHSDA included several questions about nonmedical drug use-related problems involving health, work, school, or other people, as well as feelings of depression, isolation, and irritability related to use. Only 0.2% of nonprescribed sedative users and 0.1% of tranquilizer users reported any problem associated with nonmedical use. Two percent of stimulant users had such problems. Problems with analgesic use were too infrequent to yield reliable estimates.

Abuse of Prescription Drugs

The Drug Services Research Survey (DSRS), a NIDA-sponsored national survey of drug treatment facilities, found that the principal drug of abuse in 9.4% of their patients was a "prescription drug." Amphetamines were the fourth most common principal drug, used by 5.9% of patients, following crack/cocaine, heroin, and marijuana/hashish. Benzodiazepines were the principal drugs of abuse of 2.2% of the patients, with barbiturates reported by 1.4%. However, multiple substance abuse was the norm for those entering treatment. While the DSRS classifies these drugs as prescription drugs, it is crucial to recognize that the DSRS makes no distinction as to the source of supply. It is important to emphasize that the source of most amphetamines currently abused is illicit production, not diverted prescribed stimulants.

The Drug Abuse Warning Network (DAWN) monitors drug-related emergency room episodes and provides a crude measure of some consequences associated with drug abuse. There has been a 20% decline in emergency room episodes related to controlled psychotherapeutic drugs since 1985. Despite several important limitations in design and methodology, DAWN data are incorrectly used as prevalence indicators or as a measure of prescription drug abuse consequences. Another critical factor regarding the interpretation of DAWN data is that DAWN-reported episodes are often suicide attempts employing several prescribed medications rather than consequences of drug diversion or abuse. Consequently, estimates of prescription drug abuse based on aggregate DAWN data grossly inflate the magnitude of the problem.

Dramatic isolated examples of prescription drug diversion by the medical profession are frequently cited. Such publicized instances are not necessarily representative of the relative magnitude of this diversion source. Other sources include diversion by means of patient "scams," "doctor shopping," thefts, prescription forgeries, and other sources, such as international drug trafficking and clandestine manufacture. The newest potential source for large-scale diversion involves the increasingly frequent use of the Drug Enforcement Administration physician

152

registration number as a unique identifier by insurance companies. Reliable national figures concerning the extent of diversion or the relative contribution from various sources are lacking. In 1978 the General Accounting Office noted that "the only hard data available on retail diversion are thefts reported by registrants to DEA. . . . Opinions differ on the most likely sources of retail diversion." A later report also stated, "no definitive statistics exist which show the amounts of abused prescription drugs coming from the various points in the legitimate drug distribution chain." There is little evidence that better information currently exists.

Drug Diversion Control Systems

Several federal and state methods used to identify prescription drug diversion are described elsewhere. Evidence of the impact of these systems on medical practice and patient care is also usually anecdotal or, when data-based, difficult to interpret. The recently inaugurated electronic point-of-sale systems in Oklahoma, Massachusetts, and Hawaii are too new to have been systematically evaluated. Most of the limited research in this area involves Multiple Copy Prescription Programs (MCPPs), used in 10 states. These programs usually require that prescriptions for Schedule II drugs be written on special forms, with one copy going to the state. While no patient-level clinical data are currently available, several studies have shown changes in prescription rates that may suggest adverse effects. The earliest of these studies found that Schedule II outpatient drug prescribing in a 1200-bed Texas teaching hospital decreased by 60.4% after regulatory change. Although the therapeutic appropriateness of this change was not studied, house staff physicians felt the new law interfered with medically appropriate prescribing. However, this change in prescribing was attributed to the inconvenience of using the special prescription form rather than increased government surveillance.

More recent studies are primarily based on New York State's multiple-copy prescription program, which was modified in January 1989 to include benzodiazepines. Following this change, the number of benzodiazepine prescriptions decreased dramatically, and alternative drug prescribing increased. The public health implications of these changes in prescription rates remain unclear and controversial.

Few studies document clinical or patient-perceived benefits or hardships of drug diversion control systems. When the medical records of 1200 nursing home residents were reviewed, 62 of the 170 patients receiving benzodiazepines had their medication stopped following the regulatory changes in New York. Administration of these drugs was usually discontinued abruptly, and withdrawal symptoms were noted in nearly one fourth of these patients. More than half were switched to other medications generally regarded as less safe and effective. From a different perspective, patients with narcolepsy have described difficulties in obtaining adequate supplies of stimulant drugs, in locating physicians willing to treat them, in being required to reconfirm well-established diagnoses of narcolepsy, and in encountering pharmacists who were unwilling to dispense stimulants in the quantities needed because of fears of possible censure.

A recent review of the effects of prescription drug diversion control systems on medical practice and patient care concluded that there is no consensus on how to define what constitutes accepted medical practice or the most appropriate design and methodology for evaluating the impact of these systems on medical practice. Thus, most of the studies have had serious weaknesses, asked the wrong questions, or failed to consider alternative factors that might have affected prescribing.

Needed Research

Knowing the relative magnitude of the various diversion sources and weighing the risks and benefits of each diversion control method are essential in developing effective prescription drug abuse prevention strategies that do not have an adverse impact on medical practice or on the quality of patient care. However, the extent to which existing diversion control methods identify and reduce the various diversion sources and the economic, medical, and social costs of each method are unclear and need further study.

Population-based clinical studies are needed that take into account patients' histories, diagnoses, and treatment and the clinical appropriateness or inappropriateness of changes in prescribing practices. While claims of overutilization are frequently made, research suggests that significant underutilization occurs, particularly with regard to the effective use of medications to treat large subpopulations of patients with anxiety disorders or pain. The US Supreme Court decision that the needs of law enforcement to collect prescription data to curtail diversion takes precedence over patients' rights to privacy may make more patients reluctant to seek treatment or to take medications that result in their names being included in a database designed to identify drug abusers. Changes in regulatory systems provide a "natural laboratory" in which "before-and-after" clinical studies can be conducted to determine the extent to which diversion control systems further contribute to underutilization or overutilization of these psychoactive medications.

The risks and benefits of long-term use of psychoactive medications remain controversial. Nonetheless, subpopulations of patients derive continued benefit from the long-term use of tranquilizers, analgesics, and stimulants for illnesses or indications such as anxiety disorders, malignant and nonmalignant pain, obesity, attention deficit disorder with hyperactivity, and treatment-resistant depression. Several medical professional associations have formally acknowledged the appropriateness of long-term use of stimulants and benzodiazepines in subpopulations of patients. Undertreatment of these chronic illnesses is associated with serious morbidity and mortality. Conversely, studies suggest that long-term use of benzodiazepines for the treatment of insomnia is not effective and that, in some patients who have used benzodiazepines on a long-term basis for control of anxiety, drug use can be gradually tapered successfully without adverse sequelae. Therefore, future studies evaluating the impact of diversion control systems on patient care must measure the magnitude of positive and negative consequences resulting from the involuntary discontinuation of long-term therapeutic use of medications.

Cost and Inconvenience

With sufficiently tight controls, a prescription-only system can keep the medical misuse and recreational use of prescribed drugs, and the flow of prescribed or diverted drugs into illicit markets, down to arbitrarily low levels. But the tighter the regulation, the greater the cost and inconvenience imposed on manufacturers, physicians, pharmacists, and patients. Cost and inconvenience will not only annoy those who continue to produce, prescribe, dispense, and use a variety of valuable medications, they will also act as disincentives to production, prescription, dispensing, and use. If there are less abusable equivalents, that may not be a bad result; otherwise, the authors of regulations must balance the risks of misuse and diversion against the loss of therapeutic benefit from underprescription and the dangers of the substitutes.

Mark A. R. Kleiman, *Against Excess*, 1992.

Abuse and addiction risk factors associated with therapeutic use are not well understood. Nonetheless, their association, especially with long-term therapeutic use, is perceived by some to be highly correlated, irrespective of data to the contrary. While long-term use may result in drug dependence, most patients do not escalate dosage or abuse their medication. While there is little overlap between the population taking prescribed psychoactive drugs for therapeutic use and the drug-abusing population, it would be naive to fail to recognize that a minority of those seeking treatment are or will become drug abusers or may be at high risk of escalating dosages or abusing prescribed drugs.

155

Improved means of identifying patient deception, evaluating malingerers, and determining who is at high risk of abusing prescribed drugs are needed to develop more effective prevention and intervention strategies.

Research should also evaluate the effectiveness of alternative approaches to drug diversion control, including innovative approaches to educating physicians with respect to the prescribing of drugs having a potential for abuse and heightening their awareness of patients likely to abuse drugs. While a number of variables have been identified that influence prescribing behavior, no systematic studies have evaluated the relative impact of regulatory controls on physicians' prescribing. Studies of factors influencing prescribing decisions are needed to develop more effective physician education programs.

Current Systems

Some states will undoubtedly establish comprehensive drug-monitoring systems before the research results are available. Computerized prescription data systems are currently widespread, are frequently utilized for third-party reimbursement, and are able to readily identify physicians and patients who prescribe or consume large quantities of drugs. While statistical norms based on a mechanical analysis of "average" prescribing patterns can detect statistically deviant prescribing, such methods do not take into account the complexities of actual medical practice. Separating those physicians who frequently prescribe larger quantities of drugs inappropriately or illicitly from those who prescribe similar quantities for legitimate medical purposes will require more precision, time, and expense.

Several desirable attributes of a prescription drug diversion control program emerge from our limited knowledge. While competent medical peer review is clearly essential, it must be predicated on established practice parameters incorporating a wide range of responsible professional opinion with respect to appropriate treatment. A suitable algorithm derived from these practice parameters must then be developed to screen statistically nonconforming practitioners while minimizing the burden of having to peer review each exception. The practice parameters and the algorithm will need periodic updating as new medications are introduced, as prescribing behaviors change, or as the nature of the patient population changes in response to emerging demographic trends. The medical peer review must include physicians knowledgeable about the various diagnoses and associated pharmacotherapeutic complexities often encountered in treatment-resistant or chronically ill subpopulations. The impact on medical practice will likely depend on the flexibility of the practice parameters and the composition of the peer review board.

In developing practice parameters, it is critical to recognize that psychoactive drugs are sometimes prescribed for unapproved indications, in higher doses, and for longer durations than those appearing in drug labeling approved by the Food and Drug Administration (FDA). Current federal health policy recognizes this use of approved drugs for unapproved indications as medically desirable, leaving decisions regarding the appropriateness and duration of treatment to local medical standards. Unapproved uses of psychoactive medications often appear in the research literature, and their therapeutic benefit is recognized for some subpopulations. For example, while the use of stimulants for treatment-resistant depression is not approved by the FDA, for some patients there is evidence that they are effective. Nonetheless, such flexibility is progressively being restricted. Some legislators, health care administrators, third-party payers, medical licensing boards, physicians, and federal law enforcement officials favor limiting psychoactive drug prescribing to well-defined therapeutic indications and to doses, frequencies, and durations of treatment sanctioned by FDA-approved labeling. South Carolina already has such restrictions for all state-controlled substances. Other states have either limited the indications for use of one drug class (opioids) or have prohibited some FDA-approved indications for use of a specific drug (eg, amphetamines). . . .

Restrictive Policies

The simplicity of these restrictive policies reduces the burden of having to consider and evaluate the complexities of medical practice. It may also lower health care costs by reducing the amount of drugs prescribed and may limit the risk of abuse by restricting availability. If practice parameters are developed that limit prescribing to only approved indications or to certain dosage units or durations of treatment, this will undoubtedly affect the quality of patients' lives, particularly those with treatment-resistant or chronic illnesses.

The attitudes and biases of some peer-review physicians regarding therapeutic use and abuse of psychoactive drugs are an important but often unrecognized variable. Simply having a drug diversion control system located in a state health department and having peer review performed by physicians do not guarantee that medical practice and patient care will not be adversely affected. The attitudes and biases of physicians vary sharply regarding these issues. Some deny or minimize the benefit from long-term therapeutic use or believe that the potential risks and consequences of prescription drug abuse and diversion outweigh the benefits to the patient in need of medication for long-term therapeutic use. For example, some prominent physicians in both the United States and Europe support or promote drug-control policies derived from liberal interpretation of international, federal, or state drug abuse control laws or regulations that limit the use of some psychoactive medications to their own definition of therapeutic usefulness. The more that similar attitudes and beliefs influence or represent the majority of peer reviewers, the more likely accepted medical use will be narrowly defined. The time and expense required to justify exceptional prescribing behavior will likely be inversely proportional to many physicians' willingness to continue treating such patients. Physicians who fail to justify exceptional prescribing behavior may risk having their patients labeled as drug abusers and themselves investigated for suspected drug diversion.

Balancing the need to make psychotropic medications readily available for therapeutic use while minimizing the risk of their diversion for abuse has been the avowed intent of federal law for the last 30 years. In this equation must be factored the evidence that existing control methods to severely restrict the medical use of drugs such as heroin and amphetamines have had little impact on their availability for abuse purposes. Thus, it is important to determine the nature and magnitude of prescription drug diversion, the role of prescribers in diversion, and the most suitable control systems for reducing this problem without adversely affecting legitimate medical practice or patient welfare. The actual contributions of the various sources of drug diversion are by no means clear. Thus, changes in the drug diversion control system may be fostered as much by the perception that a problem exists as by its actual dimensions. In the absence of hard data, reliance is often placed on anecdotal and impressionistic information to justify or oppose many policies developed to control diversion. Perceptions in this area as well as definitions of drug abuse are, however, profoundly affected by the vantage point of those involved. Law enforcement officials are likely to perceive that significant numbers of physicians and pharmacists contribute to drug diversion but may be unaware of or minimize the impact of diversion control systems on medical care. On the other hand, the primary concern of many health professionals is that diversion control systems may have a chilling effect on medically appropriate prescription drug utilization. As was noted in the American Medical Association's 1990 recommendations for drug policy control: "The war on drug abuse can and must be fought alongside the war on disease, pain, and suffering; one must not be allowed to impede the other." Here, as in medicine more generally, the medical precept "First do no harm" surely applies.

"It would be foolish to forgo the benefits of . . . advertising because of a misplaced fear of deception when the benefits are improved health and reduced costs for drugs."

Advertising Prescription Drugs Is Beneficial

Paul H. Rubin

Advertising prescription drugs directly to consumers would lower costs, would inform patients of new treatments, and might alert patients to unknown conditions, according to Paul H. Rubin. In the following viewpoint, Rubin argues that current restrictions on advertising are unnecessary and prevent consumers from having valuable information about new and improved drugs. Rubin is a former senior advertising economist at the Federal Trade Commission. He is currently the vice president of Glassman-Oliver Economic Consultants, Inc. in Washington, D.C.

As you read, consider the following questions:

1. Why does Rubin believe that advertising prescription drugs will not deceive consumers?
2. In what two situations does the author believe advertising a new remedy would be beneficial?
3. According to Rubin, how would advertising make prescription drugs more affordable?

Paul H. Rubin, "What the FDA Doesn't Want You to Know," *The American Enterprise*, May/June 1991. Copyright © 1991, *The American Enterprise*. Distributed by The New York Times/Special Features.

The commissioner of the Food and Drug Administration, David A. Kessler, has indicated in interviews that he plans to increase FDA regulation of direct-to-consumer ads for prescription drugs. He has appointed new people to run the FDA's advertising division and is doubling the staff devoted to advertising regulation.

Excessive Regulation

There is already excessive and inefficient regulation of drug advertising, so imposing further restrictions or increasing enforcement would be a move in the wrong direction. Dr. Kessler advocates stronger enforcement because he fears deceptive advertising, but his fears are misplaced in the prescription drug market. Further, several health benefits from direct advertising are already apparent, and this advertising also will reduce prices of drugs. Thus, with no identifiable benefits, but with some certain costs for consumers and manufacturers, stricter regulations would be a mistake.

There is no evidence that any deception has occurred in the ads. More important, deception is highly unlikely in this market. Because approval by a physician is required for purchase of a prescription drug, there is less chance of deception in this area than in almost any other consumer market. A consumer will of necessity have a second, informed opinion before acting on an ad.

Moreover, consumers are not mere pawns. They are aware of the source of information and treat it with appropriate skepticism. Sidney Wolfe of Public Citizen Health Research Group, a Ralph Nader organization, has criticized ads for prescription drugs because "they encourage patients to pound on the doctor's door and demand the new miracle treatment." Wolfe apparently views the abilities of consumers to make rational judgments with some disdain.

Current Policy

Although direct advertising of prescription drugs is now allowed, there are severe restrictions. One is known as the "brief summary" and it is required on some direct-to-consumer advertisements. It is hardly "brief" given that it is usually the equivalent of one or two typewritten pages. It often appears in small print, and it lists the side effects and contraindications associated with the prescription drug. This information may be useful for physicians, for whom it was originally intended, but the lengthy statement is virtually worthless to most consumers because it is written in technical language and is probably read by only a very small number of them. Moreover, since a prescription will be needed for the drug in any case, a consumer buying the product will perforce consult with a physician who will be able to tell him the same information contained in the brief summary. There is little benefit from ensuring that both the consumer and the physician have the same information. Because an informed intermediary, a physician, must be contacted before a prescription drug can be purchased, information is probably better in the pharmaceutical market than in almost any other consumer market, and requiring a complex disclosure statement provides no benefits.

Benefits of Drug Ads

Analysis indicates that there are several health benefits from direct advertising of Rx drugs. This is because consumers have information about their own health status which may not be easily accessible to physicians (for example, that a consumer has ceased taking some medication because of undesirable side effects). Advertising can provide product specific information (that a new remedy without the side effects is available) which can be combined with this consumer information to lead to improved health among consumers. Direct advertising can also reduce prices paid by consumers for drugs by increasing competition. Finally, since consumers must consult with a physician in order to acquire an Rx drug, there is less reason to fear deception in this market than in any other area, and so less reason to regulate advertising to consumers.

Paul H. Rubin, *Journal of Regulation and Social Costs*, November 1991.

When must an ad contain the brief summary? The regulations make no objective sense. If an ad mentions a health condition and gives the name of a drug that can be used for that condition—or even indicates that a drug exists for that condition—then the ad must also contain the brief summary. For example, if an ad says that there is a new medication to help a consumer stop smoking, or if it states that Nicorette gum, specifically, will help some people quit, then the ad must contain the brief summary.

Other ads need not print the brief summary. If an advertisement mentions only that one should "See your physician" for unspecified treatment for smoking, or if an ad mentions the price of a product ("Nicorette is on sale!") but not what the product is used for, then the brief summary is not required. The FDA enforces these distinctions with a bureaucratic assiduousness verging on the absurd.

The regulations governing direct-to-consumer ads may actually reduce or even deny information to consumers. The regulations prevent prescription drug advertising on television. They increase the cost of print ads when the brief summary is required and thereby reduce the number of such ads. And, finally, ads that do not carry the brief summary are less informative. Thus, the regulations, in effect, cause consumers of pharmaceuticals to be less well informed than would be the case with more sensible requirements.

Even though the existing rules overregulate and have perverse effects, Dr. Kessler is considering imposing even stricter ones. Any increase in regulation could easily eliminate direct-to-consumer advertising altogether. It would be foolish to forgo the benefits of this advertising because of a misplaced fear of deception when the benefits are improved health and reduced costs for drugs.

Health Benefits

Several types of health benefits accrue from prescription-drug advertising. Consider that a consumer may not be aware that a treatment exists for a particular condition. Two prominent examples are Minoxidil, a treatment for some types of baldness, and Nicorette gum, a substitute for cigarette smoking for those who are trying to quit. In both cases, advertising is an efficient mechanism for informing consumers that prescription remedies exist for these conditions. Nicorette is a particularly interesting case. Cigarettes (which are not regulated by the FDA) can be advertised with only a one-line mention of the health risks of smoking, but advertising a remedy for smoking requires a lengthy discussion of side effects and other contraindications.

One benefit of promoting prescription drugs through advertising is wider consumer awareness. A consumer may suffer from some condition (for instance, excessive thirst) without realizing that it can be a symptom of a disease (diabetes, for one), so he will not consult a physician and therefore not learn as soon as possible that he has a treatable disease. An ad can induce the consumer to contact a physician.

A consumer may have previously been diagnosed as having some then-untreatable disease (or condition) for which a new treatment has since become available. Since he believes that the disease is not treatable, he is not likely to contact a physician and therefore will not learn about the new therapy. Advertisements can inform him and lead him to treatment. A similar analysis applies to the creation of a new vaccine for a condition to which some may know themselves to be susceptible—such as a vaccine for hepatitis B.

New Remedies

When a new remedy with fewer side effects becomes available, advertising can provide benefits in two cases. Those who do not know that symptoms they are experiencing are side effects and so would not ask a physician about them may learn from ads that there are alternative remedies without these side effects. Those who have ceased treatment because of side effects and so are not seeing a physician may begin treatment again if they learn of therapies that do not have the same side effects.

For instance, antihypertensives may cause impotence as a side effect. Some patients may not know that this condition is related to the medication they are taking for high blood pressure and may be unwilling to discuss the problem with a physician; others may have stopped taking it because of the condition. Either group can benefit from ads indicating that a treatment with reduced side effects is available. New drugs to lower cholesterol levels that need not be taken as often or are less unpleasant than the older drugs would also be candidates for advertising.

Price Effects

Price is currently less effective as a competitive tool in pharmaceuticals than it is in many other areas of commerce because the physician chooses the product but does not pay for it directly and therefore has little incentive to pay attention to price. Thus, providing information that would enable consumers to compare prices more easily should have a larger-than-average effect. There is evidence from many markets that increased advertising leads to lower prices, and this information has been used by the Supreme Court in overturning some state bans on various types of advertising. In pharmaceuticals, there should be an even greater reduction in price from increased advertising.

There are several mechanisms through which advertising can lead to lower prices. Advertising can inform consumers that two brands of the same drug are in fact equivalent and that one is cheaper. They can then ask physicians to prescribe the lower-priced drug. Increased competition brought about by advertising can lead manufacturers to reduce prices.

Increased information can also make competition by retailers more effective. Some drug stores now compete by advertising the names of drugs and the prices they charge for them. For those consumers who are not actively aware of the name of the drug they are taking, this information is useful. However, since the purpose of the drug cannot be included in the ad without triggering the brief summary, consumers who know that they are taking a drug for hypertension but do not know its name would not be able to benefit from this information about low prices. Elimination of the requirement for the brief summary could lead to increased price competition at the retail level and reduced prices for many consumers.

There would be definite advantages to advertising simultaneously the name and function of a drug without including the brief summary. Firms would be more likely to advertise if they could mention their own brand name because general advertisements would benefit their competitors but increased sales of their own brand would help them recoup the costs of advertising. Advertising the name and function of a drug can increase pressure to lower prices across the industry. Ads containing both the brand name and the uses of a drug convey more information and thus help provide all of the beneficial functions mentioned above.

The FDA reduces information in some over-the-counter markets as well. Particularly noteworthy is the continuing prohibition on advertising the benefits of aspirin in reducing the chances of heart attack. One major study has shown that aspirin could reduce the chance of a first heart attack in middle-aged men by almost 50 percent. The FDA has been unwilling to allow advertising of this information even to physicians. The FDA does allow physicians to receive information about the beneficial effect of aspirin in reducing second heart attacks, but not consumers. Even though these restrictions are "voluntary," manufacturers are unwilling to oppose the FDA, which has considerable power over them. It is likely that several thousand heart attacks could be prevented annually if full dissemination of this information were allowed.

In sum, a major weakness of the current regulatory system for pharmaceuticals is the limitations on direct-to-consumer advertising. This advertising would provide health benefits and lead to price reductions. The FDA imposed an absolute ban on direct advertising from 1983 to 1985. It then sensibly relaxed this ban. It is now time to take the next step and eliminate the costly and pointless requirement for a "brief summary" in ads that name the product and its use. A return to a system that severely limits direct advertising of prescription drugs would make for poorer and less healthy consumers and should not be a goal of sound public policy.

*"Direct-to-the-public advertisement of
prescription medication is a bad idea."*

Prescription Drug Advertising Is Harmful

Eric P. Cohen

Eric P. Cohen is assistant professor of medicine at the Medical
College of Wisconsin in Milwaukee. In the following viewpoint,
Cohen asserts that drug companies advertising prescription
drugs directly to consumers might help patients learn about
new drugs. Unfortunately, he states, these consumers are unlikely to learn enough about a particular drug from the advertisements to make informed treatment decisions. This could
harm the relationship between doctor and patient by placing
more pressure on doctors to justify their prescription choices
and by misleading patients about the effectiveness of the drugs
they wish to take. For these reasons, Cohen concludes that such
advertising should be prohibited.

As you read, consider the following questions:

1. Why is the prescription drug market unlike that of any other
   industry, according to Cohen?
2. According to Cohen, why have previous efforts to market
   drugs directly to the public been stopped?
3. How does the author rebut the idea that advertising will
   reduce the price of prescription drugs?

Eric P. Cohen, "Are Pharmaceutical Ads Good Medicine?" *Business and Society Review*,
Spring 1990. Reprinted with permission.

Prescription medication has been under the purview of doctors and pharmacist-apothecaries since the Middle Ages, with most prescriptions written only after individual and private encounters between patient and physician. In our time, advertising has so far played only a supporting role by means of physician-directed advertisements. These are regulated in the United States by the Food and Drug Administration (FDA), with obligatory mention of side effects, toxicities, and contraindications. So-called fair balance is thus ensured, with concomitant mention of the good and bad of a drug. Direct-to-the-public ads for prescription medication may alter this balance and change the doctor-patient encounter. The possibility of the widespread use of such ads is now quite real and to many in medicine, a clear and distinct concern.

Marketing Prescription Drugs

Like any business, the pharmaceutical companies advertise their products to bolster market share and company profit. But the prescription market is different than the market for ordinary consumer goods. While no special expertise is required to understand and use hairspray or lawn mowers, four years of medical school and often as many more in postgraduate training are required for the practice of medicine and, by implication, the wise and reasoned prescription of medication. Federal legislators have recognized the need for regulation of prescription drug advertisements and have mandated mention of all side effects, toxicities, and contraindications in such ads, thereby effectively keeping these ads from the lay media. The "small print" that accompanies prescription drug ads in professional journals would simply be too expensive to show on network TV or in popular magazines. These rules do not guarantee that deception will not occur, but they have, so far, helped to limit the impact of any outrageous claims that prescription drug ads might contain. Physicians can be influenced by advertising, otherwise the drug companies would not be spending $400 million a year on ads in medical media. But at least physicians have the background necessary to adequately interpret the ads—the lay public simply does not.

Fair Balance

These advertising rules have been challenged, and changes in the practice of prescription drug advertising may soon be upon us, with unbalanced ads for prescription drugs appearing on TV and print media, devoid of small print, just like so many other commercial pitches. The possibility of direct ads was actually first publicly mooted in 1983 by Dr. Arthur Hull Hayes, then Food and Drug Administration commissioner. He urged caution, and indeed enforced a temporary moratorium on any such ads, to allow careful assessment before any precipitate action. Subsequent studies by the FDA and others have shown that such direct ads would not easily satisfy the requirements of fair balance. During this mid-1980s assessment period, opposition to direct ads was formulated and published by many organizations, including the American Medical Association, the American College of Physicians, the American Society for Clinical Pharmacology and Therapeutics, the American Society of Hospital Pharmacists and the American Association of Retired People. State medical organizations in Minnesota, Wisconsin, Illinois, and Ohio have also affirmed their formal opposition to any moves to advertise prescription drugs directly to the public. Furthermore, as of 1984, the great majority of pharmaceutical companies agreed with congressional sentiment that such ads would be ill-advised and said so in letters to Rep. John Dingell (D-Mich.), whose oversight committee had been concerned with such ads. But because of the potential for advertisement earnings, this caution has not lasted. A coalition of interests in the pharmaceutical and advertising industry was formed in 1988 with the express purpose of weakening the FDA rules so that direct-to-consumer ads could appear in the lay media without the inconvenient mention of side effects, toxicities, and contraindications. The Prescription Drug Advertising Coalition (PDAC) has thus far not convinced Representatives Dingell, Henry Waxman, and Edward Markey, who remain opposed to such direct ads. But the PDAC efforts continue, along with scattered actual attempts at direct ads in the public media.

Direct Ads

The direct ads that have appeared so far have included arthritis medicine, allergy medicine, and a salve for hair growth. The first of these, for the drug ibuprofen (Rufen), was shown on cable TV in Florida in 1983. Lack of fair balance was among the reasons that these ads ran only briefly. Excessive claims were the reason that the ads for clemastine (Tavist) were pulled from the newspapers in 1987. Finally, the ads for topical minoxidil (Rogaine) have proven too expensive, and are no longer prominent. But the ad makers have seen failure before and will surely not rest so soon. If the past several years are any guide, further direct ads seem certain to appear. We may see print or TV ads for antihypertensives, seizure medicines, or even cancer medication in formats not unlike those for beer, cars, or laundry detergent. If fair balance is dispensed with, the ad makers will make the same shrill sorts of claims for prescription drugs that we are accustomed to seeing for over-the-counter cold medicines. Deception, not quiet reason, will prevail along with a commercial hucksterism more suited to county fair snake-oil sales than to prescription medication.

Nevertheless, some beneficial effects of direct ads have been suggested. It has been said that direct ads would provide information to the consumer, and that direct ads would only do harm if factual information was lacking. But short TV ad spots and slick glossy magazine spreads are not designed to educate. They are designed to persuade, if need be, through misinformation. Advertising, like propaganda, seeks to win adherents. Indeed the principles of advertising—salesmanship in print—are incompatible with factual education. Ad agency founder David Ogilvy summarized his review of car advertisements, stating that these ads were full of "fatuous slogans and flatulent generalities," hardly the making of education. The "facts" that advertisers use in promotional campaigns are hardly better. Ogilvy pointed out that "when we (Ogilvy and Mather) advertise brand X gasoline, we give the consumer facts, many of which the other gasoline makers could give but don't. When we advertise brand Y airlines, we tell travelers about the safety precautions which all airlines take but fail to mention in their advertisements."

© Lee Schertz. Reprinted with permission.

It is true that adverse effects of medication might be better known if publicly advertised. It is, however, hard to imagine drug companies boldly advertising adverse side effects. An additional argument disproving the potential educational role of drug advertisements is provided by a 1985 study conducted by L.R. Krupka and A.M. Vener. They found that "great investment in advertising is necessary in order to achieve high levels of sales for drugs such as Valium (diazepam) which do not have a clear-cut ameliorative effect [and] that saturation advertising would not significantly enhance sales of such drugs as Dyazide R (triamterene and hydrochlorothiazide) because of its well-established therapeutic value." In other words, drugs with known benefits would not need much advertising, whereas those with less sturdy therapeutic indications might need much more advertising. This phenomenon, which I first discussed in *The New England Journal of Medicine* in 1988, further supports the premise that the intent of advertising is to increase sales, not knowledge.

Competitive advertising may help to lower prices for eyeglasses or automobile tires and, claim its devotees, might do the same for prescription drugs. The cheapest drugs on the market today, however, are generics that are not advertised at all. As exemplified by the Rogaine campaign and the "talking stomach" ads for ulcer medication before that, the costs of the ads may force retail prices up, not down. Finally, advertised over-the-counter medicines cost more than the generic varieties, thus associating advertisement even more closely with higher, not lower prices.

Despite these early failures and their costs, some drug companies have already stated that they would advertise direct-to-consumers if their competitors did. This surge in marketing efforts would increase costs, further increasing the already high advertisement-to-sales ratio in the prescription drug market. And, to preserve profits, these marketing costs would trickle down to the consumer, tending to lead to higher, not lower, retail prices.

Ads and Costs

Even if competitive ads would result in lower unit costs for a given drug, as proponents argue, pharmaceutical companies would require higher overall sales to maintain profit margins. Higher sales, however, mean greater per capita use of prescription medication. All this would be unfortunate, as I pointed out in *The New England Journal*, because much of the time it is better to be using less rather than more medication.

A more insidious effect of direct ads would be their potential to influence editorial policies of the media carrying them. Such influence has clearly occurred in the case of cigarette ads. The latter are a source of revenue whose magnitude has restrained the expression of media disapproval of tobacco. A similar phenomenon might occur with direct ads for prescription drugs. Media criticism, either of prescription medication or of its makers, might be muted because of the potential loss in revenue that could result from such commentary. The same free speech "right to advertise" claimed by the ad makers could thus have quite the opposite effect on the organs of free speech, the print and broadcast media.

A Bad Idea

On balance, then, direct-to-the-public advertisement of prescription medication is a bad idea. It has the potential to accelerate already rapidly rising drug prices, to raise unwarranted expectations by unrealistic promotion, and to subject the public to barrages of advertisements, at best unnecessary and at worse contraindicated. Such ads would be at variance, too, with the notion that our pharmaceutical companies have a privileged role in providing high-quality medication to the sick, whose interests and vulnerability should not be betrayed by the flashing lights of commercialism.

It is worth noting that one adman recently spoke in approval of direct ads saying, "If we can turn patients on to a drug . . ." I remember such phrases in the 1960s and 1970s as part of the hippie drug culture. Is that really what we want on the airwaves and in the newspapers of America?

"The recession scarcely bothers an industry that is the most profitable in the country and has a relatively captive market."

Drug Companies' Profits Are Excessive

Viveca Novak

In the following viewpoint, Viveca Novak opposes the idea that drug companies need extremely high profits in order to continue to develop new drugs. She maintains that drug companies could still profit if they made less money. Novak also maintains that if drug companies continue to raise their prices, many people will no longer be able to afford the drugs and the companies will lose money. Novak is a senior staff writer for *Common Cause* magazine, the quarterly journal of Common Cause, a citizens' lobbying group that works to improve the way federal and state governments operate.

As you read, consider the following questions:

1. Why does the drug industry spend so much money lobbying Congress, according to Novak?
2. Why does Novak conclude that the drug industry's high profits are unjustified?
3. According to the author, what has the government done to counter consumers' perceptions that drug prices are too high?

From Viveca Novak, "The Other Drug Lords," *Common Cause*, Fall 1992. Copyright 1992 by Common Cause, Washington, D.C. Reprinted with permission.

The scene was right out of middle America's worst nightmare about what goes on under the Capitol dome. Special interest lobbyists prowled the halls buttonholing lawmakers. Debating in the chamber, senators parroted industry-supplied talking points and attacked the legislation at hand as a threat to the American way of life. Senators trotted out charts and graphs, the snazziest of them provided by industry.

At the end of the wearying eight-hour debate in March 1992, Sen. David Pryor's (D-Ark.) amendment to restrict a tax break enjoyed by U.S. pharmaceutical makers with factories in Puerto Rico went down by a margin of almost two-to-one.

Chalk up another one for the drug industry, a lobby that ranks among the most muscular in town, adept at deploying plenty of both PAC [political action committee] money and lobbyists—many of them former congressional aides—to make its arguments and usually carry the day.

"I believe that the drug industry is more feared than respected by Congress," says Pryor, a perpetual foe.

The Drug Lobby

A look at how this industry operates in Washington gives a glimpse of how tough it will be to enact any meaningful national health care reform. At even the hint that Congress might curb the skyrocketing price of prescription drugs, the drug lobby enters with guns blazing:

• When Congress tried to control drug prices for the Medicaid program, the industry persuaded minority leaders to warn of "second-class medicine" for the poor.

• When legislators sought to limit profits on drugs for rare diseases, the industry divided the disease victims' advocacy community.

• When lawmakers were debating a landmark Medicare bill to cover catastrophic illness, the drug industry helped whip up senior citizens, ultimately bringing the law crashing down—because it included a prescription drug benefit that might have led to cost controls.

• When Pryor and others tried to cut the industry's Puerto Rico tax subsidy, the industry wailed about the threat to the free market system—even though the subsidy is a basic government giveaway.

Pharmaceutical firms, in short, want it both ways—to preserve their freedom to charge what they want for drugs while still holding on to various government blessings such as tax breaks and generous patent protection. Unlike physicians and hospitals, drug makers have so far fended off virtually all government attempts to control prices.

It's the public that pays, through inflated health care costs and medications that are often priced beyond the reach of many who need them. In 1990 Americans spent more than $67 billion for prescription drugs. While drugs are less than a tenth of the nation's health care budget, their prices shot up at three times the rate of inflation in the 1980s—a startling 152 percent, far outpacing even the rise in other health care costs. Pharmaceutical companies are the darlings of Wall Street. The recession scarcely bothers an industry that is the most profitable in the country and has a relatively captive market.

As the population ages, the industry's future can only get rosier. More than half of all Americans over age 45 regularly take prescription drugs. Among those 65 and older, the rate is 76 percent. Surveys show that prescription drugs are the largest out-of-pocket expense for three out of four seniors. Sixty-four-year-old Mary Mitchell of Atlantic Beach, N.C., for example, spends more than $100 per month—from a Social Security income of $398—on four medications to treat a skin condition, high blood pressure and asthma. "I think the drug industry is going overboard," Mitchell says.

Prescription Drug Costs

Americans spend $67 billion yearly on prescription drugs. Although drugs constitute only 7 percent of the nation's total health care bill, they represent the fastest growing portion of health costs, rising 20 percent faster than overall medical costs and 250 percent faster than the Consumer Price Index from 1985 to 1991.

The reason for these skyrocketing increases? Drug companies can get away with them. Each company has a monopoly on most of the drugs it produces and can extract whatever price it likes from consumers, who have little choice but to pay.

Harvey F. Wachsman, *The New York Times*, January 16, 1993.

Or consider the growing population of AIDS patients, who on average spend $4,000 a year on medications—with some spending more than $10,000 a month.

Since 1981, 29 drug industry political action committees (PACs) have handed out more than $8.5 million in contributions to House and Senate candidates. . . .

"From my experience, the pharmaceutical manufacturers are one of the best lobbies out there," says a Senate staffer.

But the sheer chutzpah of the drug industry is starting to stir public and congressional resentment. Sensitive to this, the Pharmaceutical Manufacturers Association (PMA), which represents name-brand drug makers, launched a $7 million advertising campaign that portrays the industry as vibrant, visionary and even thrifty. Drugs are expensive, they say, because research and development is costly—and besides, drugs often help prevent even higher-priced treatment like surgery.

Critics on and off Capitol Hill counter with compelling arguments of their own. Of course drug makers spend a lot on R&D, they argue—new drugs bring lucrative patent protections and unlimited pricing freedom. Besides, they say, the industry spends at least as much on marketing as on research. And while drugs may be cheaper than other choices, they add, that's little comfort if people can't afford to buy them.

Tax Haven

Pryor's longtime efforts to get a handle on drug prices took a new turn in 1991 when he proposed cutting a tax break for manufacturers with factories in Puerto Rico. His bill stalled, but he offered virtually the same measure—slicing the tax break by 20 percent for each percentage point over inflation that a drug company raised its prices—as an amendment to the pending tax bill.

Section 936 of the tax code, designed to create jobs in Puerto Rico, is no small write-off. Drug companies save an average of $70,000 in taxes for every Puerto Rican worker they employ, according to the General Accounting Office (GAO). From 1980 through 1990, the industry's tax savings topped $10 billion. . . .

Major Markups

Industry's critics say it bought its own bad image by boosting drug prices to an extreme. Particularly hard-to-swallow examples aren't hard to find. ABC's "PrimeTime Live" recently reported that Johnson & Johnson markets identical drugs for sheep, at a cost of 6 cents a pill, and for humans, at $6 a pill. (A company spokesperson denied the preparations are the same.) The price of the controversial tranquilizer Halcion, made by Upjohn, went up more than 75 percent between 1986 and 1991. Even Orrin Hatch has warned drug companies against gouging consumers.

It doesn't have to be like this. In Europe, where most countries regulate drug costs, consumers pay 54 percent less for pharmaceuticals than Americans. In Canada a review panel can shorten a drug's patent period if drug prices are too far out of whack with the inflation rate.

Drug firms defend high prices, saying that it takes hundreds of millions of dollars to bring a new drug to market and that drug makers lead all domestic industries in R&D investment. The business also entails costly risks—Abbott recently had to pull its new antibiotic, Omniflox, from the market after several deaths and other adverse reactions.

But critics point to weaknesses in the industry's claims. For one, it may or may not cost an average $231 million—the figure repeated ad nauseam in debate over Pryor's tax measure—to develop new drugs. A draft study by the Office of Technology Assessment called the figure "an arbitrary number with no intrinsic meaning."

Also, drug firms' R&D budgets are often equaled or exceeded by what they spend on pushing their products. Drug companies are famous for spending lavishly to wine and dine doctors and send them on conference junkets. Some firms plan to invest millions in a new venture by Whittle Communications to bring doctors a daily broadcast of medical news laced with drug ads.

The drug makers' refrain of heavy costs is further undercut by the fact that some of their work is done—for free—by federal scientists. Taxol, for instance, a promising new treatment for ovarian cancer derived from the bark of the Pacific Yew tree, was developed through research by the National Cancer Institute. In 1991, the government agreed to give its research exclusively to Bristol-Myers, which will bring taxol to market—and get the profits.

AZT, the AIDS drug, also was developed in large part by the government. Burroughs-Wellcome initially priced AZT at $10,000 for a year's supply. Pressure from AIDS activists helped bring the price down, but it still costs about $2,400 a year.

For the elderly, drug costs—which are not covered by Medicare—are a significant hardship. A recent survey by AARP [American Association of Retired Persons], which is pushing for a Medicare drug benefit, estimated that eight million people skimp on necessities like food and heating fuel to pay for their prescriptions.

Drug coverage was included in the landmark, but short-lived, 1988 Medicare catastrophic insurance law. The law would have paid for prescriptions but favored cheaper generic brands. Pharmaceutical companies, which saw the provision as the first step toward cost controls, fought back with video news releases and professionally orchestrated grassroots opposition. When a weaker version became law, the industry played a role, along with various seniors' groups, in stirring up the revolt among the elderly that shocked lawmakers—who thought they had done something clearly positive for once—into repealing it.

"It was a very negative, cynical effort that was not appreciated by members of Congress," says one Senate aide. But it worked.

Improbable Allies

In 1990 the drug makers suffered a rare, if partial, loss in Congress. But the battle left a bitter residue of racial politics, which had been used to weaken the reform measure. And since the cost-containment bill became law, the industry has struck back to recover its losses.

The chief mover of the bill was once again Pryor, though the White House's Office of Management and Budget made a similar proposal. Their goal: Get drug makers to cut their prices to Medicaid, the federal-state health program for the very poor. Since Medicaid pays for close to 15 percent of all prescriptions sold—about $5.5 billion in 1991—why not use that market clout to bring down drug prices and save the government money?

Inflation of Prescription Drug Prices

DRUG	TO TREAT	MAKER	1992 Sales (millions) U.S.	WORLD
Zantac	Ulcers	Glaxo	$1,785	$3,435
Vasotec	Heart disease	Merck	835	1,985
Mevacor	High cholesterol	Merck	1,040	1,285
Prozac	Depression	Eli Lilly	785	1,070
Procardia XL	Heart disease	Pfizer	1,062	1,062

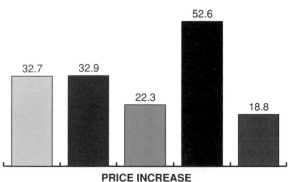

PRICE INCREASE
Percentage change, 1988-1992

Sources: Prime Institute, University of Minnesota; Capital Institutional Services Research; Bureau of Labor Statistics; company and industry reports.

The industry made its usual pitch. But this fight took an especially depressing turn when, as some critics saw it, PMA played the race card.

The trade group hired civil rights veteran Vernon Jordan, former president of the National Urban League and partner with the law and lobbying firm Akin Gump Hauer & Feld, to help make its case. Jordan urged minority groups to oppose the proposal; they did, saying its provisions would mean "second-class medicine" for poor blacks. One letter from the National Black Caucus of State Legislators to another group characterized the Medicaid proposals as coming from "mean-spirited bigots [who] want to strike at the black underclass"—Pryor's strong civil rights record notwithstanding. . . .

But Pryor's aides point out that the bill contained an override allowing doctors to prescribe any drug they deemed "medically necessary." Many third-party payers and hospitals nationwide use rules similar to those the bill would have imposed, they maintain.

Although it was reported that some of the bill's opponents had longstanding financial and other ties to the drug industry, and the bill had many supporters—AARP, the American Public Welfare Association, the National Governors Association, the National Caucus and Center on the Black Aged, and others—the damage had been done.

As a result, the bill that eventually passed, while still a win for Medicaid, was watered down. It requires manufacturers to charge Medicaid the "best price" they give other bulk purchasers, a formula that should lead to discounts of at least 15 percent. Stripped from the legislation were measures that could have encouraged use of less expensive drugs.

Getting Rich Off Old People

And, after a year-and-a-half under the law, the industry has recovered part of its loss. Many firms raised their "best prices" to other bulk purchasers, so the scale for establishing the Medicaid price was ratcheted up. Within a year, the Department of Veterans Affairs, for example, was hit with drug price increases averaging 21 percent, but in some cases much more, costing it an estimated extra $90 million in 1991. One 76-year-old disabled veteran, Ralph Beckwith, wrote Rep. Mike Synar (D-Okla.) about price hikes on his eye medicine—which he has to pay for, along with his other medications, out of a $400 monthly income. "Must I go blind now," Beckwith wrote, "so some pharmaceutical company can get rich off of the old people?"

PMA's Gerald Mossinghoff says the industry can't afford to pass along the same deep discounts it once gave the veterans to the much larger Medicaid market, so it's natural that all prices would rise. Several bills to address the problem have been proposed, but the PMA's arguments have a familiar ring. For the government to step in again, Mossinghoff testified, "would cause an unwarranted and unprecedented disruption of the U.S. free-market system—at a time when free-market principles are sweeping the world."

Drug firms, of course, don't operate in a pure free-market environment, and one of the more generous government-granted benefits is called orphan drug status. While many feel it's been exploited, fixing it is harder than it seems.

The nine-year-old Orphan Drug Act gives pharmaceutical makers research tax breaks and a seven-year monopoly for new drugs developed to treat patients with rare diseases—small and normally unprofitable markets that drug companies might otherwise ignore. It's worked: More than 60 orphan drugs are on the market, and without the law important breakthroughs might not have occurred.

Two problems, though. One is that some of the drugs are priced beyond the reach of those who need them—"ransom" for a captive market, says Sen. Howard Metzenbaum (D-Ohio). A year's supply of Genzyme's Ceredase, for example, developed to treat Gaucher's disease, can cost more than $300,000.

And while a drug may be developed for one malady, other uses sometimes develop; while its market burgeons, it is still protected by orphan drug status and the manufacturer can raise prices substantially. Fujisawa USA's aerosol pentamidine was developed to treat a rare form of pneumonia that affects just a few hundred people in this country. Then it turned out that AIDS victims often get the same sickness. The drug's sales have soared—and so has its cost.

Pending before the Senate is a bill cosponsored by Metzenbaum and Sen. Nancy Kassebaum (R-Kan.) to trim exclusive marketing rights for orphan drugs to two years; the monopoly can continue for up to nine years if a drug's sales don't top $200 million. Industry lobbying helped convince President Bush to veto more modest changes to the law in 1990.

"What's happened is more and more companies have abused and violated the intent of the act," says Abbey Meyers, executive director of the National Organization for Rare Disorders, which supports the changes. Senate staffers say the industry has at least one lobbyist covering each member of the Senate Labor and Human Resources Committee. One of the best-credentialed: Former committee member Paula Hawkins (R-Fla.). Hawkins, who lost her Senate seat in 1986, earns $120,000 annually as a consultant for Genentech and rents a limo when she comes to town, according to lobbying disclosure reports. . . .

Do Not Pass Go

The drug industry also cares deeply about hanging on to its monopoly rights for larger market drugs. Normally drug patents last 17 years, but industry argues that the Food and Drug Administration (FDA) is so slow in approving products that few years are left before competitors can enter the scene. With more than 30 of the 100 leading drugs scheduled to lose their patents by 1995, drug companies have begun pushing the House and Senate Judiciary committees for valuable patent extensions.

"We definitely see more lobbying on this issue these days," says Dennis Burke, a Senate Judiciary staffer.

Congress last granted a patent extension in 1988, when a reprieve for a Warner-Lambert drug was quietly attached to a big trade bill. But in June 1992, Rep. William Hughes (D-N.J.) and the judiciary subpanel he chairs approved three extensions—including one to American Home Products that had not been the subject of hearings or debate. That company's CEO, joined by veteran drug industry lobbyist J.D. Williams, called on virtually every member of the House and Senate Judiciary committees, Hill staffers say. Hughes denied he was influenced by lobbyists.

The bill, which passed the full committee, paradoxically toughens standards for future extensions while not applying those criteria for the three it approves. An attempt to rush it through on the House floor without debate in early August was slowed when Rep. Pete Stark (D-Calif.) demanded a roll call vote, questioning "whether billions of dollars should be given away to three of the largest, most profitable pharmaceutical manufacturers in this country who already enjoy generous" government support. Even so, it passed. A similar bill is pending in the Senate.

A Drug Industry Wish List

The drug industry also complained about the FDA to Vice President Dan Quayle's Council on Competitiveness. In November 1991, after meetings with the PMA, the Industrial Biotechnology Association, the Association of Biotechnology Companies and representatives of Eli Lilly (based in Quayle's home state of Indiana), the council announced several recommendations for speeding up the drug approval process, some of which closely resembled a drug industry wish list. . . .

Under increasing attack, some drug companies have begun subsidizing heart and AIDS treatments for the poor and elderly, providing rebates on drugs given out by federally financed public health programs, and giving away experimental drugs to patients with life-threatening diseases. Several firms have vowed to limit price hikes, for now, to the inflation rate.

But underestimating the drug lobby is a proven mistake. Nothing is expected to dampen the zeal of the drug firms for fighting every perceived threat to their surprisingly free rein, and industry analysts still expect drug company earnings to climb.

"If we are to produce new drugs that benefit society, we must maintain our profitability."

Drug Companies' High Profits Are Justified

Richard J. Kogan

Richard J. Kogan is the president and chief operating officer of Schering-Plough Corporation, a pharmaceutical manufacturing company in Madison, New Jersey. He was the 1990-91 president of the Pharmaceutical Manufacturers Association. In the following viewpoint, Kogan contends that companies that make prescription drugs need high profits. To develop potentially lifesaving drugs, drug companies have to spend more money to research and develop new products than companies in other industries, according to the author. Kogan maintains that the numerous ways in which prescription drugs benefit society warrant the expense of these drugs.

As you read, consider the following questions:

1. According to the author, how has the American public benefited from the prescription drug industry?
2. Why is the research and development involved in new products so costly, according to Kogan?
3. In addition to research and development, what other reasons does Kogan give for the high price of drugs and the companies' high profits?

Richard J. Kogan, "Life, Death, and Money," a speech delivered at the annual meeting of the Pharmaceutical Manufacturers Association, Boca Raton, Florida, April 2, 1990. Reprinted with permission.

At the beginning of the 20th century, the average life expectancy of a newborn American child was only 49 years. By 1940, life expectancy had improved by 30 percent to 64 years. Today, a newborn American can expect to live 75 years, a 17 percent increase over the 1940 level and an improvement of 53 percent from 1900.

Increased Life Expectancy

The dramatic increases in life expectancy over the past 90 years reflect the even more dramatic decreases in the annual U.S. death rate per thousand that you see here. In 1900, a little more than 16 people out of a thousand died from diseases and accidents.

Forty years later, the death rate had decreased by about 35 percent to between 10 and 11 people. And today, it stands at 5.4 people, down a whopping 49 percent from 1940 and an even more impressive 66 percent from the very high rate in 1900.

Obviously, many factors were and still are involved in those life and death numbers and the way they have changed over the course of this century.

Those factors include what can be broadly called the health environment—everything from where we live and work to educational levels. Another major factor affecting health is the behavior of individuals—negative behavior such as drinking and smoking and positive behavior such as dieting and exercising. And we know that heredity is also a significant factor in the general health of individuals and the age at which they die.

Chances are good that some combination of those three factors—environment, behavior and heredity—was largely responsible for the sharp drop in the death rate between 1900 and 1940. But thereafter, another factor—health care services—has played an increasingly important role in improving the health of Americans and producing the decreases in the death rate and increases in average life expectancy we have examined.

Impact of Pharmaceuticals

Out of the whole spectrum of health care services, major progress in preventing and treating disease has resulted from the use of pharmaceuticals and advanced surgical techniques—techniques which themselves are often made possible by pharmaceuticals. Indeed, pharmaceuticals used directly for treatment and for enhancing the positive outcome of advanced surgical techniques, make it possible for many Americans to live long and prosperous lives. . . .

Today, antibiotics and vaccines have virtually eliminated a number of infectious diseases that took such a toll of life 50 years ago and have brought others under control. Pharmaceuticals are also playing a major role in improving the survival rate for patients with various chronic diseases.

And many surgeries, such as transplants, are safer today because of the antibiotics used to prevent post-operative infections. Other surgical procedures, including open heart surgeries, have, in fact, been made possible largely through new pharmaceuticals.

Drugs and Money

Having looked at some aspects of life and death, it's time to turn to money. Disease involves not only the tragic human cost of pain and suffering; it also burdens our society with enormous economic costs as the result of productivity lost through premature deaths or disabilities.

A study currently underway is attempting to identify cost savings that have resulted when premature deaths and disabilities were avoided due to pharmaceuticals at various points over the past 50 years. In the case of tuberculosis, for example, it is estimated that as many as 90,000 deaths have been avoided with accompanying cost savings that may be as much as $11 billion.

The study also indicates that we have avoided close to a million cases of polio, of which some 400,000 would have resulted in severe disabilities. The costs associated with those polio cases could total as much as $31 billion.

In the case of coronary heart disease, it's conservatively estimated that more than 600,000 lives were saved, representing about $80 billion in avoided costs.

The data on cerebrovascular disease, excluding the impact of life style factors and non-pharmaceutical treatment, indicate that close to a half million deaths were avoided for a combined cost savings of about $16 billion, and as many as six million nonfatal strokes were also prevented.

In the cost figures I cited, an estimated 1.6 million lives were affected and close to $141 billion were saved. To be sure, the pharmaceutical industry was not solely responsible—but what's important to remember is that *pharmaceutical products* achieved those dramatic results.

Cost of Health Care

The role of modern pharmaceuticals in helping contain the total cost of health care was recognized by the U.S. Department of Commerce in these words: "Drugs shorten hospital confinement by speeding up recovery and by eliminating the need for surgery in many instances. They also curtail visits to physicians [and] reduce the number of days away from work."

That recognition is nice, but it understates our contribution. The fact is: modern pharmaceuticals are a proven value. Today, less than seven cents out of the total health care dollar buys pharmaceuticals that are far more effective than the medication, which, 50 years ago, accounted for more than 16 cents of that dollar.

Research and Development Expenditures

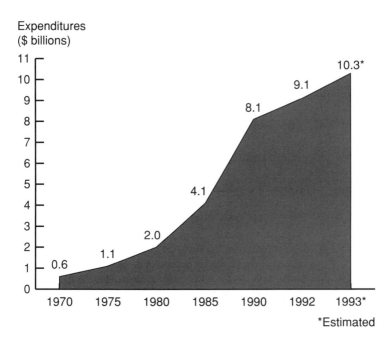

In 1993, the research-based pharmaceutical companies will invest a record $10.3 billion in research and development. This research commitment has been growing at a rate of more than 10 percent a year. The industry's research investment has doubled every five years since 1970.

Source: Pharmaceutical Manufacturers Association, *Good Medicine*, 1991.

An even more telling fact is that this small industry—an industry with U.S. prescription product sales that, in total, are only about one-quarter the size of General Motors, approximately half the size of IBM—now annually invests more than 16 percent of its sales revenue in research and development. By comparison, R&D investment as a percentage of sales averages only 3.4 percent among all other major U.S. companies.

The billions of dollars we commit every year to develop new products—a record $7.3 billion in 1989 and $8.2 billion in

1990—is one of, and maybe *the*, riskiest investment made in American business. It costs the industry more than $200 million to bring a single new pharmaceutical to market.

And bringing new products to market is not only an expensive, but also a slow and arduous process that takes on the average close to 10 years in the United States. The development of every new compound involves a lot of trial and error, with many false starts and blind alleyways.

Risky Business

Society must be fully aware of the time-consuming, risky and costly task that the industry faces in developing new pharmaceuticals. If we are to produce new drugs that benefit society, we must maintain our profitability. Without strong profits and cash flows, we won't be able to continue investing in R&D at current levels; we won't be able to attract needed capital; and we won't be able to employ the highly skilled people who are vital to the tasks of inventing, developing and commercializing important new medicines.

And we are making these medicines available at prices which—after adjustment for inflation—are actually lower than 1967 prices. Furthermore, we are selling at those prices during a period of accelerating competition from generic products and the impact of market-driven factors such as intensive competition, managed health care, third-party reimbursement, and restrictive formularies.

But despite this competitive environment, I think the outlook in the 1990s remains positive. That confidence is based on the fact that this industry has prospered, has increased its return on equity and cash flow, and has strengthened its research capability. As we embark on this new decade, we are in a strong position to provide unique and vital benefits to society. Who else will assist the medical profession in unraveling the mysteries of AIDS, cancer, and Alzheimer's disease?

The demographics of an aging American population require special research on an urgent basis to tackle the degenerative and chronic diseases associated with old age. Our industry is reacting to this urgent need. Today, 16 drugs are being clinically tested for Alzheimer's, 5 for Parkinson's disease, and 15 for osteoporosis, while 11 are being studied for the treatment of osteoarthritis.

Genetic Engineering

More than half of the genetically engineered drugs in the human testing stage are being evaluated for treatment of various kinds of cancer—which, along with cardiovascular disease, is a leading killer of people over 65. Overall, 92 cancer pharmaceuticals are being tested—26 for colon cancers, 21 for breast cancer,

184

21 for lung cancer, 14 for skin cancers, and 12 for prostate cancers. All of these malignancies primarily affect our older citizens.

On the cardiovascular front; 39 pharmaceuticals are being clinically tested for hypertension, 23 for congestive heart failure, and 11 for arrhythmia. Concurrently, 13 pharmaceuticals are being studied for treatment of coronary artery disease.

During 1990, the industry will spend approximately one-half of its planned annual $8.2 billion R&D investment on diseases of the aging.

As our life expectancy moves out toward 80 years and beyond, the new pharmaceuticals now in development will not only help avoid premature deaths but will also improve the quality of our lives. They'll also hold down overall health care costs by enabling elderly people to avoid expensive surgeries and hospitalization. . . .

Drugs Benefit Society

As you can tell, I'm bullish about our ability to continue to provide substantial benefits to society. More than 400 new pharmaceuticals are under development and there are more to come. This new decade, however, holds significant challenges and will require substantial resources. Extrapolating from the 1990 projection of $8.2 billion for R&D investment to the balance of the decade, we're going to be looking at a total 10-year R&D tab of more than $130 billion. For perspective on this figure—putting a man on the moon cost this country $25 billion.

Truly, this is an expensive and extensive effort and, of course, everyone wants better pharmaceuticals. But we also must be willing to pay for them.

One of the ironies of the pharmaceutical industry's many achievements in prolonging and improving life is that our senior citizens are among our most vocal critics. You've heard the gripes about pharmacy bills from your family members, and I've heard them from mine. If you tell them that novel therapies are giving them more good years to attack the industry, they don't always smile.

But it's a fact—with pharmaceutical innovation, we're often dealing with life and death issues, not merely the price of a new palliative. Someone who *is* smiling, because he stands a good chance of enjoying his senior years, is a Long Island computer specialist named Alan Rosenbaum. Diagnosed in the 1980s as having incurable hairy cell leukemia, he today is a healthy family man with a wife and two young daughters—thanks to a product of biotechnology, alpha interferon.

Alan had only a few months or even weeks to live. He'd already exhausted the avenues of splenectomy and chemotherapy. His red blood cell and platelet counts were low, he was receiving bi-weekly transfusions, and he was having a tough time warding off infections. Yet, just six weeks after beginning interferon therapy, he returned to work, and to his family outings at the Bronx Zoo and beach picnics on the Sound. As a patient, Alan is now indistinguishable to a physician from any other normal individual.

High Costs Are Justified

Convincing our older family members is one thing. Convincing the critics who see what they term "exorbitant pharmaceutical prices and excessive profits" is quite another. Too often, the industry is getting polemics instead of understanding from some politicians. It is simply easier for them to criticize pharmaceutical prices as too high rather than to do the homework necessary to make judgments that are in the interest of our society.

Government and third-party insurers feel compelled to push back against rapidly escalating health care costs, and targeting our industry is an easy way, a simplistic way, and a politically expedient way of doing that.

But society cannot afford to allow our Washington Beltway critics to impose artificial constraints on our industry. Taxing and restraining innovation is not acceptable. The life-saving benefits and the cost savings our products provide to society as a whole can only be achieved if the industry has the freedom of action and financial strength to continue and expand our research efforts and capabilities.

Today, many countries in the world are busily discovering what we have known all along in the United States.

The free-market, profit-driven, private enterprise system works. Centralized government planning doesn't work. It's a resounding failure as a social, political, and economic system. Ask Mikhail Gorbachev, ask the people in the Eastern Bloc. They know from bitter experience that centralized planning and bloated bureaucracies are not the answer.

Consider the performance of the Internal Revenue Service in answering taxpayer questions over the telephone. In 1989, IRS agents gave wrong answers to four out of every 10 questions. Almost half the time, the agency couldn't give accurate information on its own laws and regulations.

Some of you may have read the article in a January 1990 issue of *The Economist* that said, "If (drug) companies are to risk the losses that such abortive quests entail, they must be allowed to make money—and in amounts that seem large by the standards of less risky businesses—when they get it right."

Having noted that drug prices weren't the problem, the article then pointed out that providing medication and other treatment to AIDS sufferers or others too poor to afford it is something the government should pay for as a matter of social policy. The article ended on this note, "A thoughtless assault on drug company profits is beside the point, and all too likely to leave those unlucky enough to need treatments yet to be invented worse off."

Part of the Solution

Life, death, and money: three concerns at the core of our national debate. Our industry has proven that our products save lives, avoid premature deaths, and save billions of dollars in costs resulting from disease. The pharmaceutical industry is not part of the health care cost problem in America, but instead is a vital part of the solution.

Periodical Bibliography

The following articles have been selected to supplement the diverse views presented in this chapter.

Reed Abelson	"Drug Wars," *Forbes*, February 3, 1992.
Carla Atkinson	"Not What the Doctor Ordered," *Public Citizen*, January/February 1992.
Carla Atkinson and John Geiger	"Just Say No?: When Drug Companies Make Offers Doctors Can't Refuse," *Public Citizen*, March/April 1991.
John Carey	"How Many Times Must a Patient Pay?" *Business Week*, February 1, 1993.
Cynthia Cotts	"The Pushers in the Suites," *The Nation*, August 31-September 7, 1992.
CQ Researcher	"Prescription Drug Prices," entire issue, July 17, 1992.
Christine Gorman	"Can Drug Firms Be Trusted?" *Time*, February 10, 1992.
Mary Graham	"The Quiet Drug Revolution," *The Atlantic*, January 1991.
David A. Kessler and Wayne L. Pines	"The Federal Regulation of Prescription Drug Advertising and Promotion," *Journal of the American Medical Association*, November 14, 1990.
Elizabeth Larson	"Unequal Treatments," *Reason*, April 1992.
Ralph Nader	"High Cost of Rx Drugs," *Liberal Opinion*, June 8, 1992. Available from Cedar Valley Times Inc., 108 E. Fifth St., Vinton, IA 52349.
Brian O'Reilly	"Drug Makers," *Fortune*, July 29, 1991.
Doug Podolsky with Richard J. Newman	"Good Drugs, Bad Effects," *U.S. News & World Report*, October 28, 1991.
Andrew Purvis	"Cheaper Can Be Better," *Time*, March 18, 1991.
Elizabeth Stone	"Low Anxiety," *Mademoiselle*, January 1993.
William Styron	"Prozac Days, Halcion Nights," *The Nation*, January 4-11, 1993.
Catherine Toups	"Bitter Pill for the Maker of Prozac," *Insight*, April 29, 1991
P. Roy Vagelos	"Are Prescription Drug Prices High?" *Science*, May 24, 1991.
Harvey F. Wachsman	"Regulate the Drug Monopolies," *The New York Times*, January 16, 1993.

How Can Drug Abuse Be Reduced?

DRUG ABUSE

Chapter Preface

Efforts to reduce drug abuse aim at two targets: The criminal justice system attacks supply, and educators and public health researchers take on demand.

Both approaches, however, have drawbacks. While federal, state, and local governments have been successful in seizing many tons of heroin, marijuana, and cocaine; breaking up powerful international drug rings; uncovering lucrative money laundering schemes; and arresting and jailing dealers and buyers, the problem still exists. Indeed, many experts argue that no matter how many tons of drugs are seized or how many drug dealers are arrested, the enormous potential for profit—as much as $100 billion per year—ensures that there will always be new supplies of drugs available and new smugglers and dealers ready to replace those arrested. Sam Staley, author of *Drug Policy and the Decline of American Cities*, concurs: "Supply-side strategies aimed at cutting off the inflow of drugs into domestic markets are, ultimately, doomed to failure. In essence, there are too many alternatives available to importers and traffickers to significantly affect long-run availability."

The problems associated with reducing the demand for drugs are equally complex. Massive education programs seem to have persuaded a few—especially children—to avoid drugs or to stop using them before they become dependent. For others already addicted, James Q. Wilson of the American Enterprise Institute maintains, "Drug treatment can work, but its reach is limited both because there are too few treatment slots available (a fact everyone discusses) and because too few people feel that treatment is preferable to indulgence (a fact hardly anyone discusses)." Even for those who choose treatment and find a program, few successfully escape addiction. One analysis, the *Treatment Outcome Prospective Study*, found that fewer than half of those entering programs complete three months of treatment, the minimum most experts believe necessary to change addicts' habits. Even when cocaine addicts complete treatment, the study found, at least half of them relapse within one year. As Mathea Falco, author of *The Making of a Drug-Free America*, observes, "There's nothing tougher than an intensive drug-treatment program, as anyone who has participated in one will tell you, because it involves a really profound change in your attitudes and your behavior."

Neither reducing demand nor cutting supply seems able to completely abolish illegal drug use—a goal that few people believe a free society can achieve. The authors of the following viewpoints debate how far society should go to reduce illegal drug use and the most effective ways to achieve that goal.

"Evidence suggests that legalization may well be the optimal strategy for tackling the drug problem."

Legalization Would Reduce the Drug Problem

Ethan A. Nadelmann

Ethan A. Nadelmann is assistant professor of politics and public affairs at the Woodrow Wilson School of Public and International Affairs at Princeton University in Princeton, New Jersey. In the following viewpoint, Nadelmann challenges the idea that drug abuse is a serious problem. Instead, Nadelmann argues that the American public inaccurately perceives drug use as abusive and very harmful. Drug laws, not drug abuse, are the real cause of drug-related crime and other social ills, Nadelmann states. He concludes that the solution to these problems is to legalize drugs.

As you read, consider the following questions:

1. According to the author, how have drug laws increased the number of murders and crimes committed?
2. How does abuse of illegal drugs such as cocaine and heroin compare to abuse of legal drugs such as alcohol and tobacco, according to Nadelmann?
3. In what specific ways would legalizing drugs benefit the United States, according to the author?

From Ethan A. Nadelmann, "The Case for Legalization." In *The Drug Legalization Debate*, edited by James A. Inciardi. Copyright 1991 by Sage Publications, Inc. Reprinted by permission of Sage Publications, Inc.

What can be done about the "drug problem"? Despite frequent proclamations of war and dramatic increases in government funding and resources in recent years, there are many indications that the problem is not going away and may even be growing worse. In 1990 alone, more than 30 million Americans violated the drug laws on literally billions of occasions. Drug-treatment programs in many cities are turning people away for lack of space and funding. In Washington, D.C., drug-related killings, largely of one drug dealer by another, are held responsible for a doubling in the homicide rate in 1990. In New York and elsewhere, courts and prisons are clogged with a virtually limitless supply of drug-law violators. In large cities and small towns alike, corruption of policemen and other criminal-justice officials by drug traffickers is rampant. . . .

A New Strategy

If there were a serious public debate on this issue, far more attention would be given to one policy option that has just begun to be seriously considered, but which may well prove more successful than anything currently being implemented or proposed: legalization. Politicians and public officials remain hesitant even to mention the word, except to dismiss it contemptuously as a capitulation to the drug traffickers. Most Americans perceive drug legalization as an invitation to drug-infested anarchy. Even the civil-liberties groups shy away from the issue, limiting their input primarily to the drug-testing debate. The minority communities in the ghetto, for whom repealing the drug laws would promise the greatest benefits, fail to recognize the costs of our drug-prohibition policies. And typical middle-class Americans, who hope only that their children will not succumb to drug abuse, tend to favor any measures that they believe will make illegal drugs less accessible. Yet when one seriously compares the advantages and disadvantages of the legalization strategy with those of current and planned policies, abundant evidence suggests that legalization may well be the optimal strategy for tackling the drug problem. . . .

There is, of course, no single legalization strategy. At one extreme is the libertarian vision of virtually no government restraints on the production and sale of drugs or any psychoactive substances, except perhaps around the fringes, such as prohibiting sales to children. At the other extreme is total government control over the production and sale of these goods. In between lies a strategy that may prove more successful than anything yet tried in stemming the problems of drug abuse and drug-related violence, corruption, sickness, and suffering. It is one in which government makes most of the substances that are now banned legally available to competent adults, exercises strong regulatory powers over all large-scale production and sale of drugs, makes drug-treatment programs available to all who need them, and offers honest drug-education programs to children. This strategy, it is worth noting, would also result in a net benefit to public treasuries of at least $10 billion a year, and perhaps much more.

Reasons to Consider Legalization

There are three reasons why it is important to think about legalization scenarios, even though most Americans remain hostile to the idea. First, current drug-control policies have failed, are failing, and will continue to fail, in good part because they are fundamentally flawed. Second, many drug-control efforts are not only failing, but also proving highly costly and counter-productive; indeed, many of the drug-related evils that Americans identify as part and parcel of the "drug problem" are in fact caused by our drug-prohibition policies. Third, there is good reason to believe that repealing many of the drug laws would not lead, as many people fear, to a dramatic rise in drug abuse. . . .

Today, Americans are faced with a dilemma similar to that confronted by our forebears 60 years ago. Demand for illicit drugs shows some signs of abating, but no signs of declining significantly. Moreover, there are substantial reasons to doubt that tougher laws and policing have played an important role in reducing consumption. Supply, meanwhile, has not abated at all. Availability of illicit drugs, except for marijuana in some locales, remains high. Prices are dropping, even as potency increases. And the number of drug producers, smugglers, and dealers remains sizable, even as jails and prisons fill to overflowing. As was the case during Prohibition, the principal beneficiaries of current drug policies are the new and old organized-crime gangs. The principal victims, on the other hand, are not the drug dealers, but the tens of millions of Americans who are worse off in one way or another as a consequence of the existence and failure of the drug-prohibition laws. . . .

The Benefits of Legalization

Repealing the drug-prohibition laws promises tremendous advantages. Between reduced government expenditures on enforcing drug laws and new tax revenue from legal drug production and sales, public treasuries would enjoy a net benefit of at least $10 billion a year, and possibly much more. The quality of urban life would rise significantly. Homicide rates would decline. So would robbery and burglary rates. Organized criminal groups, particularly the newer ones that have yet to diversify out of drugs, would be dealt a devastating setback. The police, prosecutors, and courts would focus their resources on combating the types of crimes that people cannot walk away from. More ghetto residents would turn their backs on criminal careers and seek out legitimate opportunities instead. And the health and quality of life of many drug users—and even drug abusers—would improve significantly.

All the benefits of legalization would be for naught, however, if millions more Americans were to become drug abusers. Our experience with alcohol and tobacco provides ample warnings. Today, alcohol is consumed by 140 million Americans and tobacco by 50 million. All of the health costs associated with abuse of the illicit drugs pale in comparison with those resulting from tobacco and alcohol abuse. In 1986, for example, alcohol was identified as a contributing factor in 10% of work-related injuries, 40% of suicide attempts, and about 40% of the approximately 46,000 annual traffic deaths in 1983. An estimated 18 million Americans are reported to be either alcoholics or alcohol abusers. The total cost of alcohol abuse to American society is estimated at more than $100 billion annually. Alcohol has been identified as the direct cause of 80,000 to 100,000 deaths annually, and as a contributing factor in an additional 100,000 deaths. The health costs of tobacco use are of similar magnitude. . . .

Legalization Less Destructive

The problems, hurts, and difficulties that will definitely result from legalized drugs will be far, far less numerous and less destructive to the whole society than the theft, bribery, violence, murder, mayhem, and self-degradation that are daily bread in the United States today. U.S. citizens must have the integrity and the painful honesty to keep in the forefront of their minds that they are *not* preventing addiction to crack or any other drug at this time. The current methods are not working.

John Clifton Marquis, *U.S. Catholic*, May 1990.

Most Americans are just beginning to recognize the extensive costs of alcohol and tobacco abuse. At the same time, they seem to believe that there is something fundamentally different about alcohol and tobacco that supports the legal distinction between those two substances, on the one hand, and the illicit ones, on the other. The most common distinction is based on the assumption that the illicit drugs are more dangerous than the licit ones. Cocaine, heroin, the various hallucinogens, and (to a lesser extent) marijuana are widely perceived as, in the words of the President's Commission on Organized Crime, "inherently destructive to mind and body." They are also believed to be more addictive and more likely to cause dangerous and violent behavior than alcohol and tobacco. All use of illicit drugs is therefore thought to be abusive; in other words, the distinction between use and abuse of psychoactive substances that most people recognize with respect to alcohol is not acknowledged with respect to the illicit substances.

Most Americans make the fallacious assumption that the government would not criminalize certain psychoactive substances if they were not in fact dangerous. They then jump to the conclusion that any use of those substances is a form of abuse. The government, in its effort to discourage people from using illicit drugs, has encouraged and perpetuated these misconceptions—not only in its rhetoric but also in its purportedly educational materials. Only by reading between the lines can one discern the fact that the vast majority of Americans who have used illicit drugs have done so in moderation, that relatively few have suffered negative short-term consequences, and that few are likely to suffer long-term harm. . . .

Dealing with Drugs' Dangers

The dangers associated with cocaine, heroin, the hallucinogens, and other illicit substances are greater than those posed by marijuana, but not nearly so great as many people seem to think. Consider the case of cocaine. In 1986 NIDA [National Institute on Drug Abuse] reported that more than 20 million Americans had tried cocaine, that 12.2 million had consumed it at least once during 1985, and that nearly 5.8 million had used it within the past month. Among those between the ages of 18 and 25, 8.2 million had tried cocaine, 5.3 million had used it within the past year, 2.5 million had used it within the past month, and 250,000 had used it weekly. Extrapolation might suggest that a quarter of a million young Americans are potential problem users. But one could also conclude that only 3% of those between the ages of 18 and 25 who had ever tried the drug fell into that category, and that only 10% of those who had used cocaine monthly were at risk. (The NIDA survey did not, it should be noted, include people residing in military or student dormitories, prison inmates, or the homeless.)

All of this is not to deny that cocaine is a potentially dangerous drug, especially when it is injected, smoked in the form of crack, or consumed in tandem with other powerful substances. Clearly, tens of thousands of Americans have suffered severely from their abuse of cocaine, and a tiny fraction have died. But there is also overwhelming evidence that most users of cocaine do not get into trouble with the drug. So much of the media attention has focused on the small percentage of cocaine users who become addicted that the popular perception of how most people use cocaine has become badly distorted. In one survey of high school seniors' drug use, the researchers questioned recent cocaine users, asking whether they had ever tried to stop using cocaine and found that they couldn't. Only 3.8% responded affirmatively, in contrast to the almost 7% of marijuana smokers who said they had tried to stop and found they couldn't, and the 18% of cigarette smokers who answered similarly. Although a similar survey of adult users would probably reveal a higher proportion of cocaine addicts, evidence such as this suggests that only a small percentage of people who use cocaine end up having a problem with it. In this respect, most people differ from monkeys, who have demonstrated in experiments that they will starve themselves to death if provided with unlimited cocaine.

With respect to the hallucinogens such as LSD and psilocybic mushrooms, their potential for addiction is virtually nil. The dangers arise primarily from using them irresponsibly on individual occasions. Although many of those who have used one or another of the hallucinogens have experienced "bad trips," others have reported positive experiences, and very few have suffered any long-term harm. . . .

Can Legalization Work?

It is thus impossible to predict whether legalization would lead to much greater levels of drug abuse, and exact costs comparable to those of alcohol and tobacco abuse. The lessons that can be drawn from other societies are mixed. China's experience with the British opium pushers of the nineteenth century, when millions became addicted to the drug, offers one worst-case scenario. The devastation of many native American tribes by alcohol presents another. On the other hand, the legal availability of opium and cannabis in many Asian societies did not result in large addict populations until recently. Indeed, in many countries U.S.-inspired opium bans imposed during the past few decades have paradoxically contributed to dramatic increases in heroin consumption among Asian youth. Within the United States, the decriminalization of marijuana by about a dozen states during the 1970s did not lead to increases in marijuana consumption. In the Netherlands, which went even further in decriminalizing cannabis during the 1970s, consumption has actually declined significantly. The policy has succeeded, as the government intended, in making drug use boring. Finally, late nineteenth-century America was a society in which there were almost no drug laws or even drug regulations—but levels of drug use then were about what they are today. Drug abuse was considered a serious problem, but the criminal-justice system was not regarded as part of the solution.

There are, however, reasons to believe that none of the currently illicit substances would become as popular as alcohol or tobacco, even if they were legalized. Alcohol has long been the principal intoxicant in most societies, including many in which other substances have been legally available. Presumably, its diverse properties account for its popularity—it quenches thirst, goes well with food, and promotes appetite as well as sociability. The popularity of tobacco probably stems not just from its powerful addictive qualities, but from the fact that its psychoactive effects are sufficiently subtle that cigarettes can be integrated with most other human activities. The illicit substances do not share these qualities to the same extent, nor is it likely that they would acquire them if they were legalized. Moreover, none of the illicit substances can compete with alcohol's special place in American culture and history.

Drug Prohibition

Most of the serious problems that the public tends to associate with illegal drug use in reality are caused directly or indirectly by drug prohibition. Let's assume the war on drugs was given up as the misguided enterprise it is. What would happen? The day after legalization went into effect, the streets of America would be safer. The drug dealers would be gone. The shootouts between drug dealers would end. Innocent bystanders no longer would be murdered. Hundreds of thousands of drug "addicts" would stop roaming the streets, shoplifting, mugging, breaking into homes in the middle of the night to steal, and dealing violently with those who happened to wake up. One year after prohibition was repealed, 1,600 innocent people who otherwise would have been dead at the hands of drug criminals would be alive.

Within days of prohibition repeal, thousands of judges, prosecutors, and police would be freed to catch, try, and imprison violent career criminals who commit 50 to 100 serious crimes per year when on the loose, including robbery, rape, and murder. For the first time in years, our overcrowded prisons would have room for them. Ultimately, repeal of prohibition would open up 75,000 jail cells. The day after repeal, organized crime would get a big pay cut—$80,000,000,000 a year.

James Ostrowski, *USA Today*, May 1990.

An additional advantage of the illicit drugs is that none of them appears to be as insidious as either alcohol or tobacco. Consumed in their more benign forms, few of the illicit substances are as damaging to the human body over the long term as alcohol and tobacco, and none is as strongly linked with violent behavior as alcohol. On the other hand, much of the damage caused today by illegal drugs stems from their consumption in particularly dangerous ways. There is good reason to doubt that many Americans would inject cocaine or heroin into their veins even if given the chance to do so legally. And just as the dramatic growth in the heroin-consuming population during the 1960s leveled off for reasons apparently having little to do with law enforcement, so we can expect a leveling-off—which may already have begun—in the number of people smoking crack. The logic of legalization thus depends upon two assumptions: that most illegal drugs are not so dangerous as is commonly believed, and that the drugs and methods of consumption that are most risky are unlikely to prove appealing to many people, precisely because they are so obviously dangerous.

Perhaps the most reassuring reason for believing that repeal of the drug-prohibition laws will not lead to tremendous increases in drug-abuse levels is the fact that we have learned something from our past experiences with alcohol and tobacco abuse. We now know, for instance, that consumption taxes are an effective method of limiting consumption rates. We also know that restrictions and bans on advertising, as well as a campaign of negative advertising, can make a difference. The same is true of other government measures, including restrictions on time and place of sale, prohibition of consumption in public places, packaging requirements, mandated adjustments in insurance policies, crackdowns on driving while under the influence, and laws holding bartenders and hosts responsible for the drinking of customers and guests. There is even some evidence that government-sponsored education programs about the dangers of cigarette smoking have deterred many children from beginning to smoke.

Clearly it is possible to avoid repeating the mistakes of the past in designing an effective plan for legalization. We know more about the illegal drugs now than we knew about alcohol when Prohibition was repealed, or about tobacco when the anti-tobacco laws were repealed by many states in the early years of this century. Moreover, we can and must avoid having effective drug-control policies undermined by powerful lobbies like those that now protect the interests of alcohol and tobacco producers. We are also in a far better position than we were 60 years ago to prevent organized criminals from finding and creating new opportunities when their most lucrative source of income dries up.

Rights of Americans

It is important to stress what legalization is not. It is not a capitulation to the drug dealers—but rather a means to put them out of business. It is not an endorsement of drug use—but rather a recognition of the rights of adult Americans to make

198

their own choices free of the fear of criminal sanctions. It is not a repudiation of the "just say no" approach—but rather an appeal to government to provide assistance and positive inducements, not criminal penalties and more repressive measures, in support of that approach. It is not even a call for the elimination of the criminal-justice system from drug regulation—but rather a proposal for the redirection of its efforts and attention.

There is no question that legalization is a risky policy, since it may lead to an increase in the number of people who abuse drugs. But that is a risk—not a certainty. At the same time, current drug-control policies are failing, and new proposals promise only to be more costly and more repressive. We know that repealing the drug-prohibition laws would eliminate or greatly reduce many of the ills that people commonly identify as part and parcel of the "drug problem." Yet legalization is repeatedly and vociferously dismissed, without any attempt to evaluate it openly and objectively. The past 20 years have demonstrated that a drug policy shaped by exaggerated rhetoric designed to arouse fear has only led to our current disaster. Unless we are willing to honestly evaluate our options, including various legalization strategies, we will run a still greater risk: we may never find the best solution for our drug problems.

"Legalization is plainly no panacea."

Legalization Would Not Reduce the Drug Problem

Mitchell S. Rosenthal

In the following viewpoint, Mitchell S. Rosenthal argues against the legalization of drugs. Rosenthal contends that the social problems associated with drugs—high crime, poverty, and poor education—are not simply the result of the prohibition of the drugs but instead are a result of the abuse of the drugs. Thus, Rosenthal concludes that legalization will not reduce either these social problems or drug abuse. Rosenthal, a medical doctor, is the president of the Phoenix House Foundation, a national organization that provides a variety of short- and long-term treatment programs to drug abusers.

As you read, consider the following questions:

1. With what aspects of the legalization argument does Rosenthal agree? Why?
2. According to the author, why would drug crime continue to be a problem even if drugs were legalized?
3. Why would drug abuse increase if drugs were legalized, according to Rosenthal?

From Mitchell S. Rosenthal, "Panacea or Chaos? The Legalization of Drugs in America," a speech delivered at the North Shore University Hospital, Long Island, New York, January 15, 1993. Reprinted with permission.

Legalization of drugs is not a subject that has lent itself to dispassionate discourse. Much of the debate has been characterized by acrimony, a scramble for moral "high ground," and little willingness to grant the good will of those who hold contrary opinions.

To some degree, this is changing, and there are signs of greater flexibility in the legalization camp. Nevertheless, in my own encounters with advocates of legalization, I have found few areas of agreement, for we view quite differently both the use of illicit drugs and the problems that derive from illicit drug use. We have, in addition to different perspectives, different priorities and different concerns.

So, while we track the same developments, study the same phenomena, and analyze the same data, we emerge with quite different findings. In some ways, we resemble the blind men examining the elephant, each describing the beast in terms of whatever piece he's grabbed onto, whether it's a leg, the trunk, or the tail.

Understanding Drug Abusers

In describing the problem of drug abuse, the piece of the beast in the grasp of my team, drug treatment professionals, is the drug *abuser*. So, *our* view of the problem and *our* expectations of legalization are based, in large measure, on our understanding of people who abuse drugs.

The proponents of legalization have grabbed hold of other pieces of the problem, different from ours and often quite different from each other's, for there is no single, unified, "legalization" position, although certain basic assumptions are shared by most of the legalization lobby, people like William Buckley, economist Milton Friedman, Princeton's Ethan Nadelmann, and Baltimore Mayor Kurt Schmoke.

Their bottom-line concerns are drug-related crime and the costs, both economic and social, of enforcing drug laws. Their fundamental conviction is that drug prohibitions are relatively ineffective, increasingly costly, and counterproductive. As Nadelmann puts it, "Many of the drug-related evils that most people identify as part and parcel of the drug problem, are, in fact, the costs of prohibition policies." Legalization, they maintain, would curb these "drug-related evils."

Now, doing away with *all* drug laws, which no legalization scenario actually proposes, would plainly eliminate all drug law offenses. But, beyond that, say legalization advocates, the availability of legal and affordable drugs would further reduce crime by eliminating the need for addicts to steal, mug, or burgle in order to pay inflated "street level" prices. Moreover, they contend that drug gangs, with no profits to protect, would cease battling for control of the illicit market and spare inner city communities the carnage of inter-gang conflict. Faced with this not-unreasonable-sounding proposition, it seems most important to know just how legalization would work.

Although a number of scenarios were proposed when the legalization notion reappeared a few years ago, advocates today are generally reluctant to spell out the specifics of drug distribution in the post-prohibition era. This is understandable, for implementation has proven to be one of the weakest points of the legalization proposition. Opponents were quick to point out just how difficult it would be, as a practical matter, to eliminate illicit drug traffic. For example, unless *all* presently illicit substances including heroin, crack, pcp, and the latest in designer drugs were legally and readily available, and at discount prices, *some* illicit traffic was bound to survive. And, since no legalization scenario anticipates sales to minors—that is, anyone under the legal drinking age of 21—this major consumer group would likely continue to secure drugs as they now do.

THE DAY THEY LEGALIZED DRUGS

Henry Payne. Reprinted by permission of UFS, Inc.

Advocates rarely dwell on implementation these days and have become somewhat more willing to seek common ground with those who find the legalization position less than totally convincing. Nadelmann, who, more than anyone, is responsible for the rebirth of the legalization notion, is quick to admit that "legalization is no panacea." He now maintains that the benefits of what he calls "a free market"—by which he means the open and legal sale of drugs—are most likely to be realized by narrowing the differences between those on his side of the issue, whom he considers "progressive legalizers," and those on the other side who merit his designation of "progressive prohibitionists."

There has also come to be something of a middle ground. Harvard's Marc Kleiman, who writes extensively, and wisely, on drug abuse policy and is clearly unwilling to embrace legalization, nevertheless believes that we need to explore the broad range of regulatory options that lie between the extremes of prohibition and legalization. Under the rubric of "grudging toleration," he suggests we might tighten restrictions on alcohol and tobacco, while loosening them on substances like marijuana. . . .

While Kleiman's position is prompted by concerns about individual liberty, what worries Peter Reuter at the Rand Corporation's Drug Policy Research Center, is what he perceives to be "the evils of enforcement." Reuter, who considers himself neither a drug-war hawk nor a legalization dove, contends that there is a "punitive trend in American drug abuse policy" evidenced by the rapid rise in state and local arrests for drug offenses, which nearly doubled between 1980 and 1990 to well over one million.

Drug Abuse and Crime

To me and most of my treatment colleagues enforcement is not—by definition—evil, nor is drug policy necessarily seen as punitive. This does not mean that we are indifferent to the growing number of offenders now in prison because of harsh, mandatory sentences for drug offenses or to the overall growth of the nation's prison population, now close to a million and made up mostly of drug abusers. But we view the relationship between drug abuse and crime quite differently than do the advocates of legalization.

Understand, that the majority of drug abusers in prison today are not there for violating *drug* laws, and legalizers would have it that they wouldn't be there at all if they didn't have to rob and steal to meet the high prices set by greedy drug lords. But the relationship between crime and drug use is far more complex.

Even when provided with *free* drugs, we cannot assume that drug-abusing criminals will cease their lawless ways, for drug abusers do not commit crimes *only* to buy drugs. A British study of addicts receiving heroin from a government clinic during the mid-seventies found that fully half were convicted of a crime while enrolled in the clinic program and receiving *huge* amounts of free heroin.

The reality is that the criminal involvement of most drug abusers is less the result of drug laws and drug prices than a manifestation of their generally disordered behavior. And it is often difficult to tell if criminality *preceded* drug abuse or, as is often the case, evolved *from* it. Nor is this an important distinction, for the root causes of *both* their criminality and their drug abuse are much the same. So, we cannot say that drug abusers commit crimes *in order* to use drugs. They commit crimes *because* they use drugs.

Although much expansion of the prison populations may be due to stiffer penalties for drug offenses, a good share of it can be accounted for by a general increase in *criminality*. Paralleling the rise in drug abuse during the past two decades has been an extraordinary growth in the number of men and women who commit crimes, serious crimes, that are in no way drug-related.

While the focus of legalization advocates is on the costs of crime or the costs of punishment, treatment professionals view criminality within a broader context. And, although the criminal involvement of drug abusers remains a major concern, it is overshadowed now by other manifestations of drug-related disordered behavior.

One would be hard-pressed these days to ignore the degree to which drug abuse now drives our natin's most intractable social problems—not only crime, but a long and troubling list that starts with homelessness and chronic mental illness and includes domestic violence, child abuse, and the spread of AIDS. . . .

Impact of Drug Abuse on Health

We cannot hope to meet the health care needs of our inner cities without recognizing and responding to the fact that the physical ills of many patients there are directly attributable to their substance abuse. This is no small number. New York City's Lincoln Hospital Center estimates that 51 percent, more than half of the adults admitted to inpatient units, are substance abusers.

Drug abuse takes a tremendous physical toll and exposes abusers to a wide range of disorders. Yet hospitals will ignore the abuse while they deal with the consequences—seizures and blackouts, unlikely infections, and impaired liver function. They will repeatedly treat the chronic bronchitis of crack addicts without ever addressing their use of crack.

As do many physicians, legalization advocates tend to minimize the impact of drug abuse on health and health care costs. David C. Lewis, who is professor of medicine and community health at Brown and favors a "cease-fire in the war on drugs" and gradual decriminalization of drug use, makes the minimalist case this way. "No more than 10,000 deaths occur annually from all illegal drug use," he explains, "while the toxicity and medical complications of alcoholism account for over 100 thousand deaths annually, and the medical complications of chronic cigarette smoking for 400 thousand."

Now, it seems to me that this formulation somehow misses the full range of drug-related morbidity and mortality, which would include the disabilities of drug-impaired infants and children and drug-related HIV infection that extends well beyond the effects of needle sharing. Heterosexual contact, most often involving drug abusers, is now the fastest growing vector for the spread of AIDS. And studies now underway at Phoenix House indicate that irresponsible sexual behavior among crack abusers may be responsible for levels of HIV infection similar to those found among IV drug users. . . .

The perception of drug abuse as altering pathologically the nature and character of abusers is hard for proponents of legalization to swallow. It flies in the face of an assumption basic to the legalization proposition—that drug abusers are otherwise normal people who just happen to use drugs. On this point is pinned the presumption that drug prohibitions exist primarily to protect individuals from the consequences of their own actions or to impose moral constraints on their freedom of choice.

There is a far more practical basis for drug prohibitions. They are meant, not to protect otherwise normal folks from themselves, but to protect society from folks who can easily lose the ability to function normally.

Legalization Will Not Work

Legalization is not the answer to America's drug problems. The unprecedented emphasis on law enforcement in recent years has polarized popular thinking about drug policy. Most Americans support even tougher criminal sanctions while a vocal minority argue for abolishing all penalties.

Mathea Falco, *The Making of a Drug-Free America*, 1992.

Now, the treatment community does not contend that society is at risk from the behavior of *all* drug abusers or even the great majority of them. The case for prohibition rests on the substantial number of abusers who cross the line from permissible self-destruction to become "driven" people, who are "out of control" and put others in danger of their risk-taking, violence, abuse, or HIV infection. As much a part of the drug abuse syndrome as chemical dependency are changes in attitudes and values that lower self-esteem, erode character, and prompt behavior that is characteristically anti-social, often violent, and manifests an almost absolute indifference to the welfare of others.

What we see today, in the key role that drug abuse has come to play in the spread of social disorder, is a greater proportion of "out-of control" individuals in the drug abusing population. As overall levels of drug use have declined, heavy and high-risk use of the most disabling illicit drugs has persisted. And it has proved most persistent and most pernicious within the nation's most vulnerable populations—the poor, the unemployed, the emotionally fragile, and the troubled young. In many ways, the legalizers are right. The problem is worse than ever. But they are wrong to assume that nothing can be done —that everything has failed—and we need resort to legalization as a strategy of last resort.

"Everything" has *not* failed. Much has succeeded. But what must now be done has yet to be tried.

What's needed today is a far bolder and more aggressive strategy of demand reduction, targeting heavy, high-risk use and concentrating on those populations and those communities most affected by drug-driven social disorder.

Reducing the Demand for Drugs

Demand reduction, I should explain, is the opposite of the supply-side strategies that proponents of legalization attack, with some justification, as wasteful and ineffective. Rather than attempting to stem the flow of drugs to the street market, demand reduction seeks to shrink the market through prevention, treatment, and local, street-level enforcement. Together they work. And there is solid evidence of this.

It's hard to ignore the impact of recent prevention efforts in schools, communities, and national media campaigns. Overall levels of drug use *are* falling, although they aren't falling fast enough and they aren't falling much at all where drug abuse is rampant.

Here, the burden of demand reduction will fall most heavily on treatment. And let me state now . . . that predictably effective treatment regimens have been developed over the past 25 years, capable of enabling disordered drug abusers not only to overcome chemical dependency but also to change the attitudes and values that prompt self-destructive and anti-social behavior. There is now a substantial body of research documenting both *that* these treatment regimens work and *how* they work. But I should note here that not all drug abusers *need* treatment. Many require only a compelling reason to quit, and the majority can be helped by interventions that are only moderately intrusive.

Successful treatment, however, demands both the active participation of the patient and prolonged involvement in the treatment process. It is these requirements that make treatment difficult, for drug abuse is unlike other disorders, and the men, women, and children who abuse drugs, no matter how disordered their behavior, rarely *seek* treatment and almost invariably resist it.

They enter treatment only when compelled to do so or confronted by far less desirable alternatives. Although motivation is needed to overcome dependency, few abusers bring much with them to the treatment setting, and generating motivation is the first goal of the treatment process.

It is external pressure that generally brings abusers into treatment, and this pressure tends to reflect societal attitudes. When there is widespread tolerance for drug use, the level of pressure on drug abusers is low. When tolerance declines, pressure rises. Families, friends, or employers most often exert this pressure. But so does the criminal justice system. When police crack down, when they make it more difficult or dangerous to buy drugs or to sell them, then a substantial number of users are prompted to quit or to get the help they need in order to quit.

When the courts allow drug abusing offenders the option of treatment, they open a door that many would never open for themselves. Indeed, the most dysfunctional drug abusers, who lead lives of extraordinary danger and disorder, and are, for those reasons, most in need of treatment, are unlikely to come to treatment by any route *other* than the criminal justice system.

So, the enforcement of drug laws serves as a potent adjunct to treatment. And I am not convinced that the removal of drug laws would bring any compensating benefits, not even a reduction in crime. . . .

Effects of Legalization

What I and many other treatment professionals would expect to see in a drug-legalized America is a sharp rise in the amount of drug-related crime that is *not* committed for gain—homicide, assault, rape, and child abuse. Along with this, an increase in social disorder, due to rising levels of drug consumption and a growing number of drug abusers, while the social problems that plague us today would become even less likely to be resolved.

It is hard to imagine that making drugs both affordable and legal will not produce significantly higher levels of use. Price and access plainly influence the incidence of drug use. Heroin consumption rose rapidly at the start of the Seventies, when supplies were plentiful. But this "epidemic" ended between 1973 and 1975, as supplies shortened, prices climbed, and there was an abrupt decline in levels of purity. By increasing access, removing disincentives, and, in effect, sanctioning or "normalizing" drug use, we would be eliminating all the impediments that, no matter how imperfectly, now limit its spread.

Not only would the treatment community expect to see the number of drug users increase following legalization, we would also anticipate a higher proportion of drug use to be heavy and high risk. Absent disincentives and high prices, it would be extraordinarily difficult for many users to control the amounts they consume. Cocaine abusers in treatment at Phoenix House almost uniformly report that cost alone limited their intake.

Opposition to legalization does not mean that I or my treatment colleagues believe in punitive enforcement or harsh mandatory sentences for drug offenses. Draconian measures don't work very well, not because some of the minimally culpable receive punishment of undue severity, but because, if sufficiently severe, the mandatory sentence becomes the felon's best defense. And juries that would readily see a defendant sent off for a year or two are reluctant to convict when conviction means an automatic eight to ten years.

For drug laws to truly discourage drug traffic, dealers at all levels must fear not the severity of the sentence but the certainty of arrest, conviction, and imprisonment or an appropriate alternative. Better that 40 dealers each do six months than one does 20 years while 39 range free.

But while I believe strongly in disincentives to drug use, I do not believe that abusers must be imprisoned simply because they break the law in order to use drugs.

I agree with those advocates of legalization who contend that drug abuse is more a matter of public health than public safety. And where I fault the law is in not allowing us to respond to drug abuse as the public health menace it is and denying us a public health solution.

Such a solution would bring the most disordered and dysfunctional drug abusers into treatment by a more certain and compassionate route than the criminal justice system, for it would allow us to impose treatment on those drug abusers for whom treatment is most necessary.

Mandatory treatment is a legitimate public health strategy, and one that we are hearing more about these days, now that TB [tuberculosis] has reappeared, and we are threatened by the irresponsible behavior of patients—most of them drug abusers—who are infected with new and highly resistant strains.

Now, I am not suggesting that civil commitment and mandatory treatment are appropriate means of dealing with *all* drug abusers or even very many of them. But this route plainly provides the most humane means our society has to deal with the most troubled and troublesome among them. And it would also serve as a bottom line disincentive, an inducement to other drug abusers to enter treatment voluntarily.

Legalization is plainly no panacea. Even its proponents do not contend that it is. The debate is over just how chaotic would be the outcome were the legalization proposition to be realized. The folks on my side of the elephant believe it would be devastating.

"There's not a shortage of beds, there's a shortage of beds for the poor."

Increasing Federal Funding for Treatment Programs Will Reduce Drug Abuse

George M. Anderson

The federal government should supply more money for education and treatment to stop drug abuse, according to George M. Anderson. In the following viewpoint, Anderson, a Roman Catholic priest on the staff of St. Aloysius Church in Washington, D.C., contends that treatment programs are either underfunded or overpriced. For this reason, many poor and middle-class addicts must wait months to get treatment and many, especially pregnant addicts, never receive treatment at all.

As you read, consider the following questions:

1. Why is private insurance coverage inadequate, according to Anderson?
2. What does the author mean by stating that some addicts need habilitation?
3. What keeps the government from properly funding drug treatment programs, according to Anderson?

George M. Anderson, "Drug Treatment and the Poor," *America*, July 13, 1991. Reprinted with permission of Fr. George M. Anderson and of America Press, Inc., 106 W. 56th St., New York, NY 10019, © 1993. All Rights reserved.

Low-income Americans who are substance abusers face serious and sometimes insuperable obstacles in obtaining needed care. Waiting lists in urban areas like Los Angeles, New York and Miami extend to weeks and even months. Lengthy time-lags of this kind can mean the difference between recovery and deeper dependency on illicit drugs.

Substandard Treatment for the Poor

According to a 1990 study by the National Academy of Science's Institute of Medicine, an estimated 5.5 million people are in need of treatment. Less than half this number receive it, however, because of a lack of slots or beds in outpatient and inpatient facilities. Entitled "Treating Drug Problems," the study attributes this lack to our two-tiered system for providing treatment, one for the poor and one for the non-poor. The latter are those who, through private insurance, have ready access to care. The former are the indigent for whom resources for adequate treatment are not available.

Douglas Chiapetta, director of the national office of the non-profit Therapeutic Communities of America, put the matter this way: "There's not a shortage of beds, there's a shortage of beds for the poor. It's a critical distinction."

Mr. Chiapetta, whose organization includes as members such well-known residential programs as Phoenix House and Daytop Village, went on to say that while there have been some incremental increases in Federal funding as a result of the Anti-Drug Abuse Acts of 1986 and 1988, the drug strategy remains centered on law enforcement rather than on therapy.

"Seventy percent of the budget is on the supply side of the drug problem," he said, 'whereas what we should have is a heavier focus on reducing the demand side through education and treatment—but it's this side that's grossly underfunded."

At present, funds for public-tier treatment do not, in fact, come primarily from Federal sources. Two-thirds are from state, local and private sources. The situation used to be otherwise, but as noted by the Institute of Medicine's study, between 1975 and 1986 Federal support dwindled, resulting in what it now calls a hollowing out of programs through resource attrition. Unable to fill the gap, state and local governments have been pressed still further by the fiscal constraints of 1990-91. In the District of Columbia, for instance, Mayor Sharon Pratt Dixon's 1991 budget cut funds for drug treatment programs by almost a third. And yet a 1990 report by the majority staffs of the Senate Judiciary Committee and the International Narcotics Control Caucus, "The President's Drug Strategy: One Year Later," stated that the District has the highest rate of hard-core cocaine addicts of any jurisdiction in the nation.

Because much insurance is limited, even middle income people can find themselves with no option but a search for help in the already crowded public-tier system. At the National Association of State Alcohol and Drug Abuse Directors (NASADAD), Diane Canova said that some private facilities charge as much as $35,000 for in-patient care.

"But most insurance coverage is only for 28 days," she observed, "so if the insurance runs out before treatment is completed, the public system becomes a dumping ground for the middle class too."

Along with others in the field of drug abuse treatment, Ms. Canova, who is NASADAD's public policy director, expressed concern about the 28-day inpatient model set by the insurance industry.

"The same model tends to be true of the public system too," she said. "Especially if you're living on the streets, four weeks aren't enough. Urban drug abusers should have a longer period because of their greater need for support and stability."

For those whose impoverished backgrounds lack the stabilizing elements of basic education, job skills and a home, therapy entails not just rehabilitation, but what some call habilitation, the teaching of primary life skills that were never acquired early in life. For this reason, drug-free therapeutic communities like Phoenix House involve stays ranging from six months to two years.

"We're less expensive than private residential programs, around $15,000 a year," Mr. Chiapetta said, "and our track record is good, so the government assists us financially; but we're still grossly underfunded.". . .

Incomplete Surveys

In the past few years, awareness of the therapeutic needs of addicted adolescents has grown through an emphasis in schools on prevention. As a result, many more adolescents are being identified as in need of treatment.

"But ironically," observed Ms. Canova, "when youngsters in school identify their peers as needing help, teachers discover to their dismay that treatment services are not available."

A further irony concerns a recent Federally sponsored survey of high school seniors that contends that by 1990 the use of cocaine and crack by this segment of the population had begun to drop. But the survey, which is periodic, does not take into account high school dropouts who, particularly in large urban centers, tend to be at greater risk for substance abuse than those who continue to their final year of school.

Similarly, the National Household Survey, which is conducted every two or three years, has also claimed a drop in illicit drug use in the population at large. But with this survey, too, critics (including Mr. Rangel, who is Representative for residents of Harlem) have charged undercounting, because it assumes that men and women who abuse controlled substances will reply truthfully to interviewers' questions. The National Household Survey, moreover, does not take into account the homeless and the incarcerated; the latter alone now number over a million. Both groups have high percentages of substance abusers. . . .

Benefits of Drug Treatment

Virtually all economic measures show that the burden of crime and other economic consequences of drug abuse are lower after treatment than before.

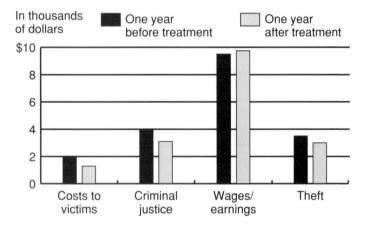

Source: "Drug Abuse Treatment: A National Study of Effectiveness" by Robert L. Hubard et-al.

Neither in the nation's capital nor in other large cities is quick access to treatment readily available for female addicts. The brief detoxification program at Washington's hospital for the indigent, D.C. General, can entail a three-week wait; admission to the city's four-week program at St. Elizabeth's Hospital can take up to two months. Even for those who are admitted, addictions specialist Ms. Barbara Pearson echoed the opinion of Ms. Canova in declaring that a 28-day period is too brief to reach the core of many addiction problems, especially for women. She pointed out that the treatment needs of women are often complicated because of backgrounds that may include incest, rape, prostitution and other kinds of abuse that result in extremely low self-esteem—a lack of self-worth that makes it all the more difficult to break away from addicted male companions who take advantage of them.

"A lot of the women have been used by men to sell drugs on the street, and they went along with it because they feel there's something wrong with them if they don't have a man," she said.

Pregnancy greatly compounds the dangers of permanent harm to the addicted woman and her unborn child. The Senate Judiciary Committee's report asserts that 375,000 drug-injured babies are born every year, and that only seven of every 100 pregnant addicts receive treatment—"a national scandal," to use the report's own words. A 1990 New York City survey found that only one in ten drug facilities would admit pregnant females at all. This reluctance on the part of treatment centers arises from what are perceived to be the special risks associated with the pregnancy of addicted females. Although maternal substance abuse programs have been targeted by the Federal Government as a priority, the number of available treatment slots remains low.

At Mount Carmel House's companion facility, Mount Carmel Place in Washington, D.C.—a transitional residence for addicts who are pregnant—the director, Sister Nancy Conley, said that as of the spring of 1991 less than 50 beds were available for pregnant addicts in the District. Only a dozen of these are partly funded through public sources; the rest are privately funded.

"We get calls every day asking if we have room, but we seldom do," Sister Conley said. "The lack of space means that many women have to stay in shelters till delivery.". . .

The First to Go

At facilities like Mount Carmel Place, the emphasis is on job preparation, the search for permanent housing, and on developing a sense of responsibility, trust and self-esteem—all part of the life skills needed to bridge the gulf between addiction and freedom from substance abuse. For women and men alike, these same life skills are generally lacking among addicts who are incarcerated. A White House report issued early in 1991 on the Administration's drug control strategy states that 80 percent of the current prison population has a history of drug and alcohol abuse.

The report goes on to claim that the Administration's national strategy places a high priority on serving this group's treatment needs. But the claim has not been borne out in practice. Indeed, the Senate Judiciary Committee's report asserts that the criminal justice system provides treatment for only one in seven of the incarcerated population. NASADAD strongly supports drug treatment for the imprisoned.

"But with penal facilities continuing to overcrowd and strip off services considered non-essential," Ms. Canova said, "drug treatment becomes one of the first to go, which in turn contributes to prisons being the revolving doors they are."

With no therapy inside and none on the streets for those who are released, addicted men and women can be expected to return to prison within a relatively short time. Several promising programs do exist, including in-prison residential communities like Stay N Out in New York, X-Cell in Delaware and Cornerstone in Oregon. As Ms. Canova pointed out, however, these are, for the most part, demonstration projects whose usefulness is limited if there are no funds to replicate them. Yet the Institute of Medicine's study notes that projects like these, when linked to community-based aftercare, have been shown to reduce significantly the treated groups' rate of rearrest.

Erosion of Support

The challenge in regard to the indigent—whether institutionalized or on the streets—therefore becomes one of attempting to reverse the past decade's erosion of support which, with the increased demand for treatment, has meant that only 10 percent of the people who seek treatment in the public sector now receive it. While some effort has been made by the Federal Government to alter this situation, some unexpected side effects have served only to highlight its gravity. One such effort concerns waiting lists, a subject commented on by Mr. Chiapetta.

"A few years ago Congress decided to do something about the backlog in treatment services for the poor, so it authorized funds for a waiting list reduction program," he said. "At first it had a positive effect, but then word got around in the street that treatment was available, and more addicts came in than ever before, which meant that soon the waiting lists became still longer, up to five months."

In February 1991, President George Bush called for an increase in spending for the war against drugs. But once again the bulk of the funds was to be earmarked for law enforcement rather than for treatment, which would receive only $100 million. In the opinion of advocates like Ms. Canova and Mr. Chiapetta, an increment of this size is merely scratching the surface.

According to the Institute of Medicine, the funds needed to upgrade and expand public-tier treatment—residential and outpatient alike—would involve $2.2 billion in annual operating costs for a comprehensive plan, plus $1.1 billion in one-time costs. As large as these sums are, they are not out of proportion to needs which, if left unaddressed, are sure to increase the overall costs of health care for the poor, for homelessness, for drug-related crime and other societal ills. Nor do the sums appear so staggering if one remembers that on a single day in March 1991, Congress appropriated $42 billion for another war, the war in Iraq.

But in the current period of local budget crises and diminished Federal support of social programs in general, the major hope may lie in a move toward restructuring the 70-30 allocation of available drug-war funds, so that more could be made available for treatment. As long as a majority of the public and elected officials continue to regard addiction to illicit drugs as a criminal-justice issue rather than a public-health issue, however, the hope is a fragile one, with the addicted poor at risk of remaining underserved for years to come.

"There is actually little evidence that drug treatment, federally subsidized or otherwise, ever can be more than a Band-Aid on America's drug crisis."

Increasing Federal Funding for Treatment Programs Will Not Reduce Drug Abuse

Jeffrey A. Eisenach and Andrew J. Cowin

In the following viewpoint, Jeffrey A. Eisenach and Andrew J. Cowin argue that federal funding for drug treatment programs increased dramatically under the Bush administration. This funding, the authors maintain, was unnecessary and a waste of taxpayers' money because most drug treatment programs do not reduce drug abuse. Eisenach is a visiting fellow and Cowin is a research associate at the Heritage Foundation, a well-known conservative think tank in Washington, D.C.

As you read, consider the following questions:

1. What evidence do the authors use to conclude that treatment programs fail to keep addicts off drugs?
2. According to the authors, increasing federal funding for treatment programs was unnecessary. Why?
3. On what would Eisenach and Cowin prefer the funding to be spent?

From Jeffrey A. Eisenach and Andrew J. Cowin, "The Case Against More Funds for Drug Treatment," *Backgrounder*, May 17, 1991. Reprinted with permission of the Heritage Foundation, Washington, D.C.

Subsidies for drug treatment are by far the fastest-growing major component of federal spending on drug abuse. Advanced by many policy makers as the key to curbing drug use, federal expenditures for drug treatment have risen by 341 percent since 1986—20 percent faster than the total drug budget, 30 percent faster than spending for drug law enforcement and 700 percent faster than overall federal spending. . . .

Explosive Growth in Spending

Despite this explosive growth in spending, there is actually little evidence that drug treatment, federally subsidized or otherwise, ever can be more than a Band-Aid on America's drug crisis. To the contrary, the evidence shows that treatment programs generally fail to get and keep people off drugs. The evidence available on federally subsidized treatment programs, moreover, suggests that they are often poorly run, fail to follow standard treatment practices, and function as "revolving doors" for addicts seeking respite from the criminal justice system or other problems.

In some cases, drug treatment can help individuals escape drug addiction and return to productive lives. And even for the majority for whom treatment is not completely successful, it may reduce drug use and the pathologies with which it is associated. For pregnant women, treatment may make the difference between life and death for their unborn children. Thus for humanitarian as well as utilitarian reasons, some public commitment to treatment appears justified.

What is not justified by the evidence is the explosive growth of federal spending on drug treatment in recent years. It is particularly not justified when such spending siphons away resources from more pressing needs in drug law enforcement and corrections. There is no excuse for continued funding of programs that ignore sound treatment practices, waste taxpayer dollars and contribute little, if anything, to winning the war on drugs.

The Burgeoning Drug Treatment Industry

In 1987, the last date for which comprehensive data are available, there were 5,100 facilities providing drug treatment in the United States. These were treating 263,000 people, at an annual cost of approximately $1.3 billion. While the recent explosion in drug treatment funding no doubt has increased all these figures, the major methods of treatment and the general distribution of funding almost surely have not changed significantly.

There are three major types of drug treatment programs currently operating in the United States: 1) outpatient (non-methadone) treatment and counseling programs; 2) outpatient methadone maintenance programs; and 3) residential programs.

Outpatient Treatment. Outpatient treatment and counseling is the dominant form of drug treatment in America, in terms of number of patients, number of providers and spending. In 1987 there were 2,765 outpatient drug treatment facilities in America, serving 144,000 people at an average cost of $2,400 per patient per year. Nearly twice as many patients were treated in outpatient clinics in 1987 as in 1982.

These programs vary widely in approach, quality and success rates. At one end of the spectrum are programs consisting of little more than rap sessions, in which former addicts discuss drug abuse with current users, offer assistance with daily problems and serve as points of entry for other types of social services. At the other end of the spectrum are rigorous outpatient programs that maintain regular contact with patients, encourage (or require) participation in self-help groups such as Narcotics Anonymous and insist on abstinence from drugs, policed by regular urinalysis. In most cases, these outpatient programs treat patients who abuse several types of drugs; cocaine, heroin, marijuana, amphetamines, sedatives and alcohol are among the most prevalent.

Methadone Maintenance

Methadone Maintenance. Originating in the late 1960s, these programs require heroin patients to show up daily at clinics to receive an orally administered dose of methadone, a synthetic narcotic drug. Methadone produces little if any high, yet relieves temporarily the addict's withdrawal symptoms and cravings for heroin. It also prevents addicts from feeling the effects of heroin should they take the drug while on methadone. Like heroin, methadone is addictive, although withdrawal is said to be less painful than withdrawal from heroin. Most methadone clinics mainly treat heroin addiction, although most patients also abuse other drugs.

The 330 methadone maintenance programs operating in 1987 treated about 80,000 heroin addicts, or nearly one-third of the total drug treatment population, at a cost of roughly $2,500 per patient per year. The methadone maintenance population has remained nearly unchanged since the mid-1970s.

Residential Treatment. Various residential treatment programs range from very expensive private programs (like The Hazelden Foundation in Minnesota and the Betty Ford Clinic in California) to publicly funded programs like Phoenix House in New York City and similar programs operated by many urban hospitals. The widely varying treatment methods include short-term detoxification programs (helping addicts withdraw from drugs), "chemical dependency" approaches (three-to-six-week programs using the twelve-step Alcoholics Anonymous model) and "thera-

218

peutic community" approaches (involving six-to-fifteen months of residence, communal living, peer pressure and extensive counseling). These programs treat all types of drug abuse, although many specialize.

There were about 2,000 residential programs in 1987, treating approximately 37,000 resident patients. Annual costs of these programs vary widely, from as little as $15,000 per patient-year to as much as $30,000 for a hospital stay of just a few weeks.

Public vs. Private Drug Treatment

The growth of drug use among the middle- and upper-middle classes during the 1970s and 1980s was followed, not surprisingly, by the expansion of private-sector drug treatment programs designed to treat those who could afford to pay. As of 1987, nearly 1,300 of the 5,100 drug treatment facilities in the U.S. were privately operated and financed primarily by insurance reimbursements and direct client payments. Of these, 801 were hospital-based programs; more than 331 were outpatient programs; 76 were non-hospital residential programs; and 67 were methadone-based. Client and insurance payments for drug treatment rose from $79 million in 1982 to $505 million in 1987, equal to 38 percent of all drug treatment revenues.

The cost of outpatient treatment is virtually identical in the private and public sector programs. The average for all patients, however, is higher in private programs ($2,450 per admission versus $1,240 for public sector programs), owing in large measure to the higher proportion of private patients in hospital-based residential programs, which is the most expensive type of treatment.

The Disheartening Realities of Drug Treatment

Press and congressional advocates of more federal spending on drug treatment extol its benefits. The *New York Times* editorialized in November 1990 that "vastly" expanding funding for drug treatment would "shrink crime rates, save hundreds of millions in prison costs and rescue lives by the thousands." Senator Joseph Biden, the Delaware Democrat, proposing to double current spending on drug treatment, is equally insistent, stating that "the nation will mark the time until we provide treatment on demand in cocaine-damaged babies, abused children, crime, violence and human tragedy."

This enthusiasm for drug treatment finds some support among drug policy experts. The authors of the most recent and extensive study of drug treatment programs ever conducted, the Treatment Outcome Prospective Study (TOPS), for example, conclude "that publicly-funded treatment programs are effective in reducing drug abuse and that long-term treatment helps addicts to become more productive members of society" and that "treatment can and does work."

Yet an objective analysis of the evidence on drug treatment is far less encouraging than those rosy assessments would suggest. While drug treatment certainly helps some people some of the time, the majority of those who enter treatment drop out, and the majority who stay in treatment later relapse into drug use. An examination of the most extensive data base on drug treatment effectiveness (which forms the basis for the TOPS study) exposes very disheartening realities about drug treatment programs.

Reality No. 1: People in the final stages of drug abuse are not receptive to easy cures.

A Minor Contribution

Liberals and conservatives agree that drug use and abuse is a serious national problem. For liberals, the answer to this mainly seems to be increased federal funding for drug treatment. But drug treatment will make only a minor contribution to curing America's drug ills. There is, moreover, virtually no credible evidence that there is a pervasive shortage of drug treatment, even in major cities where the problem is said to be most acute.

Jeffrey A. Eisenach and Andrew J. Cowin, *The Heritage Foundation Backgrounder*, May 17, 1991.

Perhaps the most striking aspect of the TOPS data lies in the characteristics of the patients entering treatment:

• Seventy percent of the patients in the outpatient programs and 81 percent of the patients in residential programs abused more than one drug.

• Thirty-three percent of those in outpatient programs and 75 percent of those in methadone maintenance programs had been in treatment before.

• Eleven percent of those in residential programs and 24 percent of those in methadone maintenance received most of their income from public assistance.

• Forty-one percent of all patients (60 percent in residential treatment programs) admitted to having engaged in predatory criminal activity during the previous year. Indeed, approximately as many patients reported crime as their primary source of income as reported full-time work.

Terrible Social Costs

More than anything else, these statistics paint a picture of the terrible social costs of drug abuse. Those seeking treatment represent the end of a drug abuse pipeline, which takes in healthy, productive (or potentially productive) individuals and spits out people who are largely incapable of participating in mainstream society, prey regularly on law-abiding citizens and are unlikely ever to recover fully. The terrible plight of those who enter drug treatment is a powerful argument for efforts to deter people from ever using drugs, or if they have started, to stop before they reach the end of the drug abuse pipeline.

Reality No. 2: Most people who enter drug treatment programs do not complete them.

Virtually all experts agree that the longer individuals stay in treatment, the more likely the program will succeed. The amount of time in treatment is so important to success that the TOPS study does not even discuss outcomes for those who are treated for less than three months. Analysis of the TOPS data base suggests that the critical threshold for successful treatment may be six months to a year.

High Dropout Rate

The trouble is that the vast majority of patients do not stay in treatment for six months, or even for three months. In fact, only 36 percent of those entering outpatient programs and 45 percent of those entering residential programs complete three months of treatment. Even among those who stay three months, only 50 percent in outpatient programs and 38 percent in residential programs actually complete treatment.

Reality No. 3: Most people who complete treatment relapse into drug use and associated behaviors.

The most daunting reality of drug treatment is that most individuals who participate in treatment programs, even for three months or longer, do not stop using drugs.

The TOPS data base contains information on post-treatment drug use of the same drugs used regularly before treatment. For psychotherapeutic drugs (like sedatives and amphetamines) and heroin, the data show that slightly more than half of all regular users who spent three months or more in treatment return to drug use within one year. For cocaine, the relapse rate within one year is between 53 percent and 60 percent, depending on type of treatment. For marijuana, the success rate is even lower: More than 80 percent of all regular marijuana users return to marijuana use within a year of leaving treatment. . . .

The Benefits of Drug Treatment

There are, of course, some benefits from drug treatment. There is strong evidence that drug use and its associated behavior declines significantly for patients while they are being treated and that treatment often results in reduced drug use, even if it does not lead to abstinence.

It appears, moreover, that some forms of treatment produce much better results than others. A growing body of research suggests that treatment works best when it includes drug testing, the threat of criminal penalties for relapse and when the twelve-step Alcoholics Anonymous method is used. . . .

The Importance of the "AA" Approach

So-called "twelve-step" programs, based on the now-famous Alcoholics Anonymous (AA) model, are an essential component of successful drug treatment programs. There is, of course, almost no systematic research on the benefits of these programs because the participants are anonymous. The one study available, however, shows dramatic results. This study examines the post-treatment drug use of over 1,000 patients at fifty different residential treatment locations. It finds that the strongest single determinant of long-term success is regular attendance in self-help groups modeled on AA. In these, nearly 80 percent of regular attendees recover, compared with only 49 percent for those not attending such groups.

Robert DuPont, former Director of the National Institute on Drug Abuse and currently a drug treatment practitioner in Maryland, calls AA and related programs a "modern miracle" and attributes to them much of the success of other forms of drug treatment. Writes DuPont:

> Today these [residential] programs that do work educate and link individuals and families to the twelve-step programs. . . . People get well and stay well by going to meetings that are free to everyone, rich and poor alike.
>
> My richest chemically dependent clients in Montgomery County, Maryland, who often want to buy recovery, find that it is not for sale at any price. They cannot send their assistants. They cannot hire therapists to cure them. They do not get well from chemical dependence unless they go to twelve-step programs in a community of recovering people, day after day after day.

The most effective drug treatment programs in America, in other words, are not run by government, and do not receive public or private money.

Treatment Availability

Calling in late 1990 for another $40 million for drug treatment programs, Representative Henry Waxman, the California Democrat who chairs the Health and Environment Subcommittee of the House Energy and Commerce Committee, argued:

> Every day there are thousands of people in this country who come to terms with their drug addiction and decide to seek treatment, but cannot get it . . . Because when they finally get to the clinic doors, they are turned away; they are told there

222

are no slots; they are told to come back in six weeks or six months, or maybe a year.

The facts show otherwise. Indeed, the best available evidence suggests that there is no shortage of treatment facilities in America. On the contrary, there may well be a surplus.

A 1990 report by the General Accounting Office (GAO), for example, shows that in New York, one of the states most often said to lack adequate treatment capacity, there is no wait for treatment at all. The study, which focuses on treatment availability for intravenous drug users at methadone clinics, finds that while some treatment programs are filled, these programs regularly refer applicants to other programs that offer similar services but are operating below capacity.

The GAO also surveyed treatment programs in California and Oregon, finding that although the centers in these states usually do not follow New York's referral practices, intravenous drug users are seldom turned away because of a lack of space. Moreover, high-priority patients (like pregnant women and HIV-infected addicts) are admitted promptly.

Shaky Claims

According to the most recent nationwide survey of drug treatment programs, conducted before the huge increases in federal drug treatment funding in 1989, 1990 and 1991, publicly funded methadone programs in 1987 were operating at 95 percent of capacity. Publicly funded programs in general, however, were operating at only 84 percent of capacity, and private programs were operating at 66 percent of capacity. Indeed, the study finds that private programs have additional capacity available equal to 40 percent to 80 percent of current caseloads.

Why, then, the constant drumbeat for more funding? For two reasons:

Low Demand. First, some of the evidence used to argue for greater treatment capacity is based on counting all the drug abusers with serious drug problems who are presumed to need treatment. No attempt is made to differentiate between those who need treatment and those who do not want treatment. In fact, recent research shows that very few addicts demand treatment. Instead, roughly 90 percent go into treatment only after significant pressure from family, the law, an employer or a combination of the three.

Second, waiting lists are typically the basis upon which the claims of Waxman and others often rest. Such lists are a poor measure of the demand for drug treatment. Advises Mitchell S. Rosenthal, director of Phoenix House: "Waiting lists are soft. You've got one guy on four lists for two weeks and he's not waiting anymore anyway. Addicts by nature call for help one moment and an hour later they're far away, emotionally or geographically. It's a motivation built on sand."

The main benefits of drug treatment may be political. Demanding federally subsidized drug treatment allows politicians to appear to be doing something about drug use. Extra federal funds spent on drug treatment facilities in the home state or district then allow the politician to bring home pork. Since 1986, Congress has, with the full cooperation of the Reagan and Bush Administrations, more than quadrupled spending on drug treatment programs.

The available evidence nevertheless casts considerable doubt on the wisdom of this vast commitment of federal dollars, for several reasons.

First, while drug treatment may help a small number of Americans to end their dependence on drugs, it cannot stop others from following them down the same path. By contrast, a greater emphasis on law enforcement, prevention and education approaches would deter drug use before it started or encourage people to stop drug abuse before reaching its final, terribly destructive stages.

Ignoring Success Level. Second, there is virtually no evidence that government-funded treatment programs observe the principles of effective treatment such as drug testing and the twelve-step method. One reason for this is that Administration efforts to insist on increased accountability for drug treatment programs have been rejected by Congress, apparently on the grounds that such a requirement would be too burdensome. In fact, there is no requirement today for federally subsidized treatment programs to demonstrate any level of success, let alone require drug testing or any other approach shown to succeed.

Third, there is no convincing evidence that the demand for drug treatment exceeds the supply. There is excess supply in virtually every segment of the drug treatment industry. And allegations of shortages and long waiting lists in some specific areas do not appear to hold up under careful examination.

For these reasons, further increases in federal funding for drug treatment should be strongly opposed. Indeed, federal spending on drug treatment should be reduced, with the savings in the anti-drug budget used for more effective anti-drug strategies, such as law enforcement, teaching students to avoid drug use and increased use of drug testing in the criminal justice system and elsewhere. Better use should be made of the funding that remains.

"[Community] coalitions are making a major difference in many cities, and bring more informed, better funded strategies to bear on local drug problems."

Community Involvement Can Reduce Drug Abuse

Mathea Falco

In the following viewpoint, Mathea Falco describes some of the successful community-based coalitions that are fighting drug abuse around the country. Falco contends that these organizations can draw in many diverse groups of citizens, from neighborhood residents, to businesses, to local governments. Together, she maintains, these coalitions can increase funding and provide a wider range of services to prevent and reduce drug abuse than either the federal government or private individuals. Falco is a visiting fellow at New York Hospital-Cornell Medical Center in Ithaca, New York, and was assistant secretary of state for international narcotics matters from 1977 to 1981.

As you read, consider the following questions:

1. What drug abuse projects have various community groups successfully implemented, according to the author?
2. According to Falco, how did some of the community-based coalitions start?
3. Why have some small community drug abuse programs had trouble reducing the drug problem, according to Falco?

To live with hope is to believe in the possibility of change. Hope is not simply willpower; we need to work together and find our common ground. This is the beginning of a national movement that can carry the day against substance abuse. This is the chance to mobilize the resources for a better America. This is a gathering of people of hope who want to repair their fractured communities with care and tenderness and devotion.

With this stirring invocation, the Reverend Edward Malloy, president of the University of Notre Dame, convened the first national meeting of community coalitions in Washington, D.C., in November 1990. More than 450 people attended from 172 cities. This new movement had started only two years earlier, when citizens came together in communities across the country to create their own strategies to combat substance abuse.

A Community Responds

Edward Foote, president of the University of Miami and chairman of the Miami Coalition for a Drug-Free Community, describes the experience of many cities in the late 1980s. "We heard the hopelessness of people in Miami—we were known as the cocaine capital of the country," he recalls. "We realized that solutions wouldn't come from Washington. Building more prisons and sending more ships to the Caribbean weren't making a difference. Instead, we needed to develop a long-term comprehensive response that involved the entire community. We knew we couldn't wait and hope someone else would do it for us. We had to take ownership of the problem."

These local antidrug coalitions harness the many different talents within a community. Volunteers from all walks in life participate directly in community action, often for the first time, and provide the impetus for many of the most creative programs. "People want to do something, but don't know what to do, so they sit around, wringing their hands. The Coalition channels this energy and helps people feel they can be part of the solution," says Marilyn Wagner Culp, executive director of the Miami Coalition, which now has more than 1,500 volunteer members. "Everyone can make a difference, by raising the level of awareness at the office, in church, in social clubs. And they can work on Coalition task forces that target specific community drug problems."

Because they are broad and diverse, community coalitions bridge the divisions that usually separate private and public, city and county drug programs. Francisca Neumann, director of Day One, Pasadena's coalition, blames bureaucratic rivalries for the weakness of earlier campaigns against alcohol and drugs. "When we put Day One together, all the different groups sat down around the table and pledged to work together. The problem was so big we realized we all had to be on the same side," Neumann says. "Day One gives us a larger perspective, so we can think as a community instead of individual programs and agencies."

Effective Antidrug Coalitions

The most effective antidrug coalitions draw on the strength of powerful local foundations, businesses, churches, and universities. For example, Kansas City's Metropolitan Task Force on Alcohol and Drug Abuse builds on the success of STAR, the comprehensive community prevention program which engages the city's schools, media, and civic leadership. STAR provides financial and technical support for the task force.

Gregory Dixon, deputy director of Fighting Back, the Robert Wood Johnson Foundation's nationwide initiative to encourage community coalitions, believes that STAR may be unique. "STAR is very well staffed and privately funded, and it may not be easily replicable. Most cities don't have a benefactor like Ewing M. Kauffman (founder of Marion Labs in Kansas City), who has donated millions of dollars to do remarkable things," Dixon says. "That kind of philanthropy is rare, particularly in the area of substance abuse, and it means that STAR doesn't have to rely on government bureaucracies or local fund-raising for its existence."

Community Activism

The key is community. Drugs have generated the most sustained burst of community activism in America since the 1960s. From Miami to Seattle, tens of thousands of Americans have taken to the streets, seeking to win them back from the drug trade. Initially, this activism took the form of crime-patrol groups that worked with the police to push out dealers. Over time, though, these groups have evolved into highly versatile organizations concerned with basic quality-of-life issues. Taken together, these groups constitute a vibrant national network that may be able to attack the drug trade at its roots—if they receive the proper support from Washington.

Michael Massing, *Dissent*, Spring 1991.

But if STAR and other models continue to show good results, philanthropists in other cities may be willing to support additional efforts. When Eugene Lang first announced his "I Have A Dream" program in 1981, promising to pay the college tuition for all the children who graduated that year from P.S. 121 in Harlem, few believed that others would follow his lead. Yet today, there are 150 "I Have A Dream" type projects in forty-three cities across the country, helping more than ten thousand children.

The Miami Coalition, one of the largest and best organized antidrug coalitions in the country, grew out of an informal dinner meeting of business and professional leaders in April 1988. Alvah Chapman, vice chairman of the Miami Coalition and former chief executive officer of Knight-Ridder Inc., describes the Coalition's beginnings: "Since the early 1970s, a group of forty of us have been getting together for dinner once a month to talk about what we can do to make things work better in our city. I was co-chair of this 'nongroup,' as we call ourselves, and Tad Foote kept bringing up the drug problem, but no one wanted to focus on it. Finally, I scheduled a whole evening on the subject, and we invited in drug experts and federal and city officials.

Starting Out

"Before the meeting, we visited treatment centers and went out with the cops on a drug sting. At our dinner, one of the enforcement officials made an impassioned plea that the problem was too big for them to handle and that the private sector had to get involved. That convinced a lot of us who were still on the fence. So I appointed a steering committee which met intensively. By the fall, we were ready to form the Coalition, name a board, and hire an executive with $1 million we raised from local corporations."

Pasadena's coalition began in March 1987 when half a dozen civic and church leaders became concerned about drug abuse resources for local youth. The group hired Francisca Neumann, who was working at the Pasadena Boys and Girls Club, to conduct a community survey which documented Pasadena's drug and alcohol problems. Using the survey as a springboard, a larger group including the mayor and key city officials decided to create a community coalition to combat substance abuse.

Day One was incorporated in 1988 with funding from Kaiser Permanente Medical Group and the City of Pasadena. Francisca Neumann explains the coalition's name as "divine inspiration." "We wanted to capture the idea that we must be anchored in the present, and work together with whatever we have to combat alcohol and drug abuse," she remembers. "Like the Alcoholics Anonymous motto that recovery is 'one day at a time,' we believe that each of us can take charge of our lives and take care of our communities beginning right now."

In the Kansas City, Miami, and Pasadena coalitions, the strong endorsement of a critical mass of local leadership—a major foundation, academic and business organizations, civic and religious groups—has been indispensable. While local government officials may play a role, these coalitions are largely volunteer efforts.

Since 1989, the Robert Wood Johnson Foundation has spent $26 million on its Fighting Back programs, money which is earmarked for encouraging the growth of citizen coalitions. Funds have been provided to thirteen cities for five-year community prevention programs. "We are trying to stimulate comprehensive responses to alcohol and drug abuse involving prevention, treatment, and the criminal justice system which can be models for other communities," explains Gregory Dixon. "Ordinary citizens, local bureaucrats, and learned professionals are, perhaps for the first time, all on the same side when it comes to substance abuse. The toll has grown so great that many of us have set aside our differences, our biases, and our pet projects to work for the greater good of the whole society. That is the essence of Fighting Back."

Stimulating Federal Support

Fighting Back has also stimulated the federal government to provide support for community coalitions. Since 1990, the Office of Substance Abuse Prevention (OSAP) has provided $243 million to support 252 coalitions working on substance abuse prevention, including Pasadena's Day One and the Miami Coalition.

The new coalitions have agendas that reflect the particular problems of their communities. . . . A new coalition of tribal and civic leaders has taken on alcohol marketing aimed at Native Americans, and plans to deglamorize drinking through a campaign of public education and stricter enforcement of the liquor laws. In Santa Barbara, California, the Citizens' Task Force is chaired by the publisher of the local newspaper. It aims to overcome pervasive denial of substance abuse problems, which account for 80 percent of local crime, as well as educate elderly residents about the dangers of prescription drug abuse. In San Antonio, Texas, former governor Dolph Briscoe, Jr., chairs the Citizens' Task Force, which works to provide comprehensive treatment services to the city's predominantly black and Hispanic East Side, the area's major marketplace for drugs.

Because drug and alcohol abuse are closely related, most coalitions also try to change local practices which encourage drinking. In Pasadena, Day One conducted a study of alcohol-related crime to shine what Francisca Neumann calls "a flashlight in a dark place which everyone knows is a terrible problem but no one really wants to see." To try to limit public drinking, Day One members pushed successfully to prevent sales of single cold cans of beer and to convince convenience store owners that they should discourage loitering. "One way of reducing alcohol-related violence is to get people to defer their drinking until they're away from crowds of other drinkers," Neumann explains. "But we also have to create positive alternatives, so that there are well-lighted, attractive parks and recreation areas in Pasadena where abstinence is the norm."

In Kansas City, STAR works with local residents to discourage drinking and drug use, particularly among young people. In 1988 a STAR survey found that the highest levels of drinking occurred in schools located closest to convenience stores which sold beer. STAR recruited these store owners to attend its two-day "baseline" training for parents, community leaders, and other concerned citizens. The groups explore their own attitudes toward drugs and alcohol and study ways that individuals can make a contribution to substance abuse prevention in the community. After the training, the store owners agreed to enforce the drinking-age laws more rigorously. As a result, drinking in nearby schools has dropped significantly.

Cal Cormack, STAR's director, explains the theory behind this group training: "We are convinced we can draw community out of people, connect them to each other, and empower them to deal with problems like substance abuse. Once they see they can make a difference, they are usually willing to take the necessary steps, even if it means giving up something."

Changing Political Priorities

Community coalitions become advocates for changing the priorities of state and local governments, although many encounter political resistance to new initiatives. In Florida, twenty-seven community coalitions have created a statewide alliance to lobby state legislators to increase funding for prevention and treatment.

"Politicians often think about substance abuse right before elections, and then they pour more money into prisons because it looks like they're doing something," says Miami's Marilyn Culp. "Florida needs to make demand reduction a top priority instead of an afterthought, and our communities should be able to rely on dedicated funding sources, like beer taxes, to support drug treatment."

Florida's group was instrumental in getting alcohol taxes raised, but the state legislature allocated the increased proceeds to the general revenue fund rather than designating it for drug treatment. "We'll have a new strategy each year until we prevail," declares Culp. "Treatment is too important to be left to the whims of the political process."

In Washington, D.C., the Corporation Against Drug Abuse (CADA) was created in late 1988 by a group of the city's professional, corporate, and civic leadership. CADA's first step was to commission independent studies to assess Washington's substance abuse problems and devise effective strategies to address them. CADA found that Washington schools do not have comprehensive drug prevention programs but rely on general health curricula, while nearby Maryland and Virginia schools use a number of different prevention programs. CADA concluded that effective community prevention programs were urgently needed and that Kansas City's STAR should be introduced into all junior high schools in the greater metropolitan area. Thus far, however, progress has been slow. STAR is currently operating in only fifteen schools in the District of Columbia.

Progress Against Drugs

This is the real value of neighborhood groups: they provide a vehicle for involving inner-city residents in their communities. Only when this happens can we hope for progress in the fight against drugs.

Michael Massing, *Dissent*, Spring 1991.

"The sad thing is that our public schools will not embrace prevention," says Connie Bush, CADA's community prevention program director. "The research is right there on STAR's results. The Kauffman Foundation provided the initial training, which CADA is now supporting. But systems don't like change. Principals and teachers see this as one more thing they have to do, even though it means our kids are missing out." By 1993 CADA hopes to extend STAR to an additional twenty schools in Washington. The coalition will continue to campaign for comprehensive community prevention programs in all area junior high schools.

Coalitions are often able to appeal effectively for community support for a wide range of new programs. In northwest Pasadena, Sheila Clark, a counselor at the Jackie Robinson Community Center, works with pregnant drug abusers in nearby public housing projects, urging them to seek treatment. She immediately ran into a roadblock: The only residential program in the area refused to provide space for the women's children. Clark brought the issue to Day One, and Francisca Neumann persuaded the Junior League to support a new center where women could stay with their children. "Day One has mustered the support of the entire city," Clark observes. "Fran hooks up different places and people to get things done."

Three thousand miles away, the Miami Coalition also helps generate political support for new approaches, like the Dade County Drug Court which diverts first-time drug offenders from the criminal justice system into closely supervised treatment.

"Without the Coalition, we would never have been able to get all the different agencies to agree to the Drug Court," says Judge Herbert Klein. "It takes real clout to overcome ingrained bureaucratic resistance to new ways of operating, and the Drug Court looks revolutionary!" In order to finance the $1.3 million annual cost of the new program, Chief Judge Gerald Wetherington raised Miami traffic-school fees by $10 and negotiated successfully with the county government to direct the majority of the additional revenues to the Drug Court.

Drugs in the Workplace

Getting drugs out of the workplace is a central focus for many coalitions, reflecting business concerns about employee absenteeism, productivity, safety, and higher health insurance rates. The Miami Coalition's Business Against Narcotics and Drugs (BAND) has recruited over 375 companies, which employ a third of the local work force, to set up model drug programs. BAND has also published a drug policy manual in Spanish as well as English for small businesses.

In Washington, D.C., CADA offers free assistance to employers to help them establish drug-free programs and is working with small businesses to develop affordable employee assistance programs. In Pasadena, Day One cooperates with the local Chamber of Commerce to convince local businesses that they will save money and improve performance by adopting strong antidrug policies. It also publishes a manual of prevention and treatment resources within Pasadena and holds four seminars a year to educate employers on how to reduce drug abuse in the workplace.

Coalitions often enlist local media to expand community awareness of drug and alcohol problems as well as to build public support for their efforts. Newspaper publishers, advertising agencies, and heads of TV and radio stations are valuable coalition members, who can arrange for contributions of free radio, television, and print media spots. Some coalitions have been particularly successful. The Miami Coalition, which enlisted media involvement at the outset, raised over $3.5 million in donated air time and print space in its first year. In 1989 BAND carried out an intensive two-month media campaign to let Miami residents know that "We're banding together—the business community against narcotics and drugs," and giving out a telephone number to call to join the effort. Within a year, the number of companies participating in BAND jumped from 55 to 276.

The Coalition has also used the media to enlist direct public participation in making sure that drugs are not sold near schools, effectively turning the larger community into citizen patrols. "Very few people knew about our 1987 law prohibiting drugs within one thousand feet of a school," Marilyn Culp recalls. "So we got the PTA to post big signs inside all the schools warning that drugs were off-limits, and the Chamber of Commerce to put up similar signs outside. Then we did media spots educating people about the law and asking anyone who saw any suspicious activity near a school to call a special police number. The police let the schools know if an arrest is made so the schools can track the case through the courts."

Today coalitions are making a major difference in many cities, and bring more informed, better funded strategies to bear on local drug problems. As T. Willard Fair, director of Miami's Urban League, points out, "The Coalition lifted the issue of drug abuse to a point of urgency in the larger community, and made many people aware that they have responsibilities. When the power brokers of the community bring together corporate resources to bear on the problem, clearly you're going to get some changes." Surveys conducted in 1990 by independent Miami researchers indicate the Coalition is making progress—many citizens believe the drug problem is getting better and report fewer cases of drug abuse in schools and workplaces.

The deep concern many Americans feel about substance abuse is a powerful catalyst for community action. Coalitions are channeling that concern into programs that require active citizen participation, connecting people to each other and their communities in entirely new ways. These efforts generate enormous human energy, as coalition members discover that they can make a difference, even against seemingly intractable problems like substance abuse. This sense of empowerment is critically important in overcoming the hopelessness and apathy that often prevent communities from taking action.

The coalitions, like all volunteer initiatives, depend on the commitment of their members as well as on the leadership of a few highly dedicated individuals. Sustaining that commitment over time is a difficult challenge. Many coalitions have responded by creating small professional staffs to share the administrative burden. But the uniqueness of these efforts lies in their ability to engage many different parts of the community in a common campaign to drive out drugs, led largely by volunteers who care deeply about the future of their cities.

James Burke, chairman of the Partnership for a Drug Free America, believes the coalitions are providing vital new answers to America's drug problems: "We elect people to go solve our problems, but the federal government can't and won't solve this one. The people who know how to are those who are closest to it—parents, police, teachers, local businessmen, and media. This is old-fashioned democracy at work, where communities forge their own solutions."

"The core of the military program—testing and harsh consequences for persons proved without any doubt to be abusers—should be adopted by . . . our society."

Methods Used by the Military Could Reduce Drug Abuse

Lester David

The U.S. military has effectively reduced drug abuse through preventative education, random urine testing for drugs, rehabilitation for abusers, and the discharging of repeat offenders. In the following viewpoint, Lester David argues that the military can serve as an example for schools and private businesses. Such methods, the author believes, will decrease the demand for drugs and thus reduce drug abuse. David is a free-lance writer and frequent contributor to *The American Legion*, a monthly magazine for veterans.

As you read, consider the following questions:

1. What are some of the harsh penalties used by the military to punish drug offenders, according to the author?
2. What does David say is the goal of the military's rehabilitation program?
3. According to the author, how have courts helped reduce drug abuse?

From Lester David, "A Drug War We've Won," *The American Legion Magazine*, February 1992. Reprinted by permission of *The American Legion Magazine*, © 1992.

In the 1980s, the American military was confronting a massive drug problem, as bad as the one gripping the civilian population and in some installations even worse.

The top brass, including the commander-in-chief himself, were astounded to learn that more than one in every four persons in uniform was gulping amphetamines and speed, popping barbiturates, smoking marijuana and hashish, snorting cocaine and even shooting heroin. In some outfits and overseas bases, the number of drug abusers topped 35 percent. In a few places, the scourge had engulfed half of the personnel.

By 1980, the services knew they had a serious situation on their hands but weren't sure how extensive it was. Reports were being received from duty stations worldwide that soldiers, sailors and Marines were reporting for duty ill because of drug-taking. Some were hung over, red-eyed and wobbly, others nauseated at their posts, and increasing numbers, unable to work at all, were being sent home or to hospitals.

The True Extent of the Problem

Alarmed at what was happening, the Department of Defense (DoD) launched a global survey of alcohol and non-medical drug use among military personnel. The true extent of the problem became clear.

The DoD study, involving 17,300 persons, was conducted by the Research Triangle Institute of North Carolina. It revealed that 27 percent of the military was using some kind of illicit drug such as stimulants, sedatives, hallucinogens or opium derivatives.

Broken down by services, the rates of illegal drug use were 29 percent of the Army, 33 percent of the Navy, 37 percent of the Marine Corps and 14 percent of the Air Force. According to Dr. William Mayer, former assistant Secretary of Defense for Health Affairs, the survey disclosed that abuse "involved fairly large segments of people," particularly very young enlisted personnel.

The military, facing the hard realities, decided a "get tough" program to stop the menace was needed. After all, what could be more crucial than a drug-free military service?

Spearheaded by DoD officials, special programs were put in place on an urgent basis. Now, more than 10 years later, the results have been almost sensational. Three more studies have been conducted since the initial disclosure of the problem.

• In 1982, two years into the programs, the percentage of abusers in all services fell from 27 percent to 10 percent, indicating the new policies were beginning to take hold.

• By 1985, the number of abusers had dropped to 9 percent.

• And the newest poll has shown that 5.8 percent, or just one in 17 members of the Armed Forces, is abusing drugs.

According to Army Maj. John Algner, a drug and alcohol policies officer, only six years ago 8.3 percent of Army personnel—one in 12—suffered "negative effects" from drug use.

This meant that the offenders were denied promotion, got letters of reprimand, and received punishment ranging from extra duty to dismissal from the service with a less-than-honorable discharge.

Since the tough policy went into effect, that figure has dropped to one in 20. The other services had equally satisfying results. The programs of the Army, Navy and Air Force differ in some minor respects, but all have the same basic principles. Let's examine how the Army is winning the drug war within its ranks.

As described by the Pentagon in Army Regulation 600-65, the plan consists of three lines of assault:

Drug Education. Almost as soon as a recruit dons his uniform, he is given an intense course in the physical and mental havoc illicit drugs inflict on his body, his job and the safety of his fellow soldiers. These courses are incorporated into all basic training programs and are stressed as heavily as venereal diseases were in World War II. Will any WWII veteran ever forget the "Mickey Mouse" movies? The education continues throughout an individual's military career. After recruits are assigned to posts, classes are held periodically at the company and battalion levels.

Education and Rehabilitation

Every time a person has a change of assignment, every time he is transferred to a special service training school or has any kind of military career change, the risks of drug abuse are hammered home. Along with this continuing education is a constant reiteration of the rule that illicit drug use is incompatible with service in the Armed Forces.

Officers are counseled also, with an emphasis on how to detect the signs and symptoms of drug abuse in personnel under their command.

Rehabilitation. Once a drug user is identified, he is offered a chance at counseling and rehabilitation. Therapists are available to help him identify his problem and find solutions. Some abusers are given a combination of counseling and out-patient treatment, while others are hospitalized, generally for six to eight weeks followed by a lengthy period of supervised care.

"One of the important goals of the program," says Algner, "is a restoration of productivity. The Army will try hard to retain the services of people who can make useful contributions."

If, after counseling and rehabilitation treatment, a soldier once again is proved to be a drug user, the penalty is swift and harsh. Users, and of course dealers, are booted out a lot more often than most people imagine. For example, in one recent three-year period, 51,000 people were separated from the services through courts-martial, administrative actions or nonjudicial punishments.

Random Drug Testing. The centerpiece of the effort in all the services is mandatory, random urinalysis, which has now been refined to the point where it can detect the presence of opiates such as morphine, amphetamines and PCP, as well as cocaine, marijuana and hashish. This screening is crucial, says Algner. "Without it, the program has no teeth."

Random Drug Testing

Testing for drugs began in the early 1970s when the DoD found evidence of abuse among military personnel in Southeast Asia, but it wasn't until 1982 that widespread screening got started. Now the services operate laboratories worldwide.

Military personnel never know when they will be required to submit to urinalysis. For example, at the submarine base in Bangor, Wash., a sign instructing all personnel whose Social Security numbers end in "8" to report for testing immediately, appeared one morning. In Cheyenne, Wyo., cars are randomly stopped at Warren AFB and passengers are required to undergo testing. Top brass, even the commanding general, are not exempt.

Experiences with the Military

We first learned about the effectiveness of workplace drug testing from our experience in the military. We learned that when you develop a procedure to detect the drug user and hold drug users accountable for their actions, changes occur. In fact, in the military, as I mentioned earlier, we saw drug use drop from 27 percent to under 5 percent, primarily as a result of implementing comprehensive random drug testing with treatment offered to those who wanted help and discharge for those who refused help.

Carlton E. Turner, speech delivered at The Heritage Foundation, March 20, 1990.

Since June 1988, all recruits in all services must test negative for drugs before they can be sworn in. The requirement was enacted by Congress and signed by President Ronald Reagan on Dec. 4, 1987. According to Sen. Ernest F. Hollings of South Carolina, sponsor of the amendment to a military authorization bill, "The time to start catching the users is before they join the Armed Forces."

The services perform 3 million drug tests annually at a cost of $15 each. The urine is delivered under the direct observation of someone unrelated to the individual being tested and clearly marked with an identifying number. The samples are placed in locked containers until delivered to a lab. If they show positive on ultra-sophisticated equipment, the samples are tested once again in a different lab at the same site to make certain no error was made. The military takes action only after a second test confirms the initial results.

A good deal of controversy has swirled around the scientific validity of the testing procedures. Opponents of drug tests have argued that errors can be made and that testing frequently is unable to identify specific drugs or how much of the substance has been used.

More Accurate Results

Now, however, drug testing produces extremely accurate results that, according to Navy Capt. Michael L. Pratt, "are rarely successfully contested in the courts." Pratt is Commanding Officer of a screening lab in Jacksonville, Fla.

Why has testing worked so well? Pratt's succinct answer: "It's very effective in scaring the hell out of these guys."

The military has indeed alarmed its personnel and in the process dramatically reduced the extent of drug abuse. The goal is to reduce the once-rampant scourge to a flat zero, and the Pentagon believes it can come very close.

The program costs about $175 million a year and requires several thousand man-hours of effort.

Could the military program be applied with the same degree of success to the civilian population? Because the services are closed organizations which must be run in an authoritarian way, experts say it may not be easy to put the same stringent policies into effect in society. Still, while the tough specifics probably cannot be taken over lock, stock and penalties, the Pentagon says the general principles can be adopted to curb civilian drug abuse.

Teaching Drug Hazards

• Education, the first prong in the military program, must blanket all segments of society.

A beginning has been made. The advertising industry, through the Partnership for a Drug Free America, has donated almost $800 million worth of media time and space from 1989 to 1991. $1 million is being spent every day on anti-drug commercials such as the fried-egg-and-brain campaign on television.

Across the nation, growing numbers of schools and colleges offer courses on drug abuse hazards, inviting prominent athletes and other respected adults to talk to students and form parent groups to battle abuse. Education departments should make these courses mandatory and, as in the military, continue them through a youngster's school years. . . .

Another idea schools could borrow from the Army: To combat drug abuse among children of soldiers, youth groups have been started to fight the menace through peer pressure and, in addition, youth task forces have been created to ferret out abusers and try to discourage them. "Peer pressure spreads drug use," President Bush says. "Peer pressure can help stop it."

• Treatment and rehabilitation, the second prong, must be sharply increased. "It's time we expand our treatment centers," President Bush said, "and do a better job of providing services to those who need them." Right now, there are about 2 million drug users in the country who may be able to kick their habit with proper treatment. But only 400,000 are receiving any help at all. . . .

A Legitimate Role

• Finally, the core of the military program—testing and harsh consequences for persons proved without any doubt to be abusers—should be adopted by businesses, professional organizations and all other areas of our society.

Controversy is still swirling around testing in the civilian world and court challenges are being filed but, according to the Society for the Advancement of Education, "drug testing is here to stay." L. Camille Herbert, law professor at Ohio State University, says the country's courts and legislatures have given employers wide latitude in testing their workers, adding: "I don't think an employee can expect not to be tested at all."

The U. S. Chamber of Commerce reports that testing is now "very extensive and increasing all the time in the nation's work places." More than half of America's major corporations and a large number of smaller ones already have made testing compulsory for all employees and the numbers are increasing monthly. The reason, the chamber says, is that there is no question that it works. Initial tests are now 92 percent to 98 percent accurate and the second confirmation process that all samples must go through is "virtually without any margin of error."

Mark A. de Bernardo, executive director of the Institute for a Drug-Free Workplace, says "Employers have a legitimate role in the war on drugs because drug abuse affects their bottom line." How severely? An estimated $100 billion a year is lost by the business community each year because of absenteeism, health-care costs and high accident rates because of drugs.

About 50 percent of Fortune 500 corporations have testing programs. They include IBM, Kodak, DuPont, Capital Cities/ABC and all defense contractors. In Baltimore, the Johns Hopkins Medical Institution has begun a random testing of all its new staff doctors.

Maricopa County in Arizona cracked down on users, with the anti-drug campaign slogan "Do Drugs, Do Time." To avoid felony charges, people who are nabbed must agree to attend weekly counseling sessions and undergo regular urinalysis. If they flunk the testing, they are prosecuted and go to jail, if convicted. A day or two in the pokey with hard-core criminals usually does the trick for "nice" people who do drugs casually. Heavy users generally welcome being caught. A chemist, who earns $50,000 a year and spent $150,000 a year on his habit, confesses, "I'm glad they got me. I was going to kill myself."

Airplane pilots as well as other transportation workers must submit to random tests for illegal drugs, according to new rules imposed by the Federal Aviation Administration and other U.S. transportation agencies. This testing is in addition to mandatory testing following any accident.

What's the bottom line? We are having limited success so far in controlling the supply of drugs flowing into the United States but the military has shown that a good job can be done on the demand side. The civilian population should listen, learn and act, quickly and decisively, or the social devastation will worsen. Sure, it will be a long, uphill fight, but the stakes are high.

It wouldn't be the first time the military has shown the way to win a war.

Periodical Bibliography

The following articles have been selected to supplement the diverse views presented in this chapter.

Judi Bailey	"Yes to Keeping Your Kids Drug Free," *The Family*, January 1993. Available from 50 St. Paul's Ave., Boston, MA 02130.
Alex G. Brumbaugh	"Acupuncture: New Perspectives in Chemical Dependency Treatment," *Journal of Substance Abuse Treatment*, February 1993. Available from Pergamon Press, 660 White Plains Rd., Tarrytown, NY 10591-5153.
Joseph A. Califano Jr.	"Overview: Drug Policy for the 1990s," *Yale Law & Policy Review*, vol. 8, no. 1, 1990. Available from 127 Wall St., New Haven, CT 06520.
John J. DiIulio Jr.	"A Limited War on Crime That We Can Win," *The Brookings Review*, Fall 1992.
Marc Galanter	"The End of Addiction," *Psychology Today*, November/December 1992.
Paul S. Jellinek and Ruby P. Hearn	"Fighting Drug Abuse at the Local Level," *Issues in Science and Technology*, Summer 1991.
Gerald W. Lynch and Roberta Blotner	"Legalizing Drugs Is Not the Solution," *America*, February 13, 1993.
Michael Massing	"Can We Cope with Drugs?" *Dissent*, Spring 1991.
Dee Dee Risher	"The Thirteenth Step," *The Other Side*, January/February 1993. Available from 300 W. Apsley St., Philadelphia, PA 19144.
Joanne Scognamiglio	"How to Help Addicts Kick Their Habits," *USA Today*, July 1990.
Stephen R. Shalom	"Drug Policy and Programs," *Z Papers*, vol. 1, no. 1, 1992.
Eric E. Sterling	"What Should We Do About Drugs?" *Vital Speeches of the Day*, August 1, 1991.
Genie Stoker	"To Stay Free of Drugs," *Christian Social Action*, December 1992. Available from 100 Maryland Ave. NE, Washington, DC 20002.
Thomas Szasz	"The Myth of Treatment," *The Drug Policy Letter*, Fall 1991. Available from 4801 Massachusetts Ave. NW, Suite 400, Washington, DC 20016-2087.
Reed Tuckson	"Doing Drugs to Numb the Pain," *Christian Social Action*, June 1990.

For Further Discussion

Chapter 1

1. In the first viewpoint, Mathea Falco uses the prevalence of drugs and of social problems related to drug abuse, such as crime and poverty, as evidence to support her contention that drug abuse is a serious problem. Does her evidence support her contention? Why or why not? What evidence might Sam Staley present to argue that it does not?

2. In his viewpoint, Mark Miller uses personal accounts of heroin abusers to support his main idea. Authors Mark A.R. Kleiman and Jonathan P. Caulkins use statistics as their evidence. Which type of evidence do you find more compelling? Why?

Chapter 2

1. Why does author Joseph D. Douglass Jr. contend that the war on drugs is a failure? What does he compare it to? Is his comparison valid? Why or why not? What solutions does Douglass suggest to counter the lack of will to win the war on drugs?

2. Authors Daniel K. Benjamin and Roger Leroy Miller believe the war on drugs is a failure. Compare their reasons for declaring the drug war a failure with Joseph D. Douglass Jr.'s. How do the two viewpoints differ? What do Benjamin and Miller propose and why?

3. Military involvement in the drug war has long been controversial. Advocates like Dale E. Brown argue that the military is far better equipped for the surveillance and intelligence aspects of the drug war than are civilian agencies. Brown is deputy chief of operations for Joint Task Force Six, the military's drug enforcement programs along the Southwest border of the United States. How might his position influence his viewpoint? Do you agree with his assertions? Why or why not?

4. The pair of viewpoints, one by Melvyn Levitsky and one by Eva Bertram and Peter Andreas, debate the validity of U.S. involvement in other countries' drug policies. Which viewpoint do you find more compelling? Do you believe future administrations should continue to be involved or do you think the policy should be altered? Give your reasons.

Chapter 3

1. Find examples of the following kinds of arguments in the chapter's viewpoints: bandwagon ("everybody knows or does this"); scare tactics ("something terrible will happen if you don't do as I suggest"); categorical statements ("this is obviously true"). How do these propaganda techniques affect the authors' arguments? Now that you have become aware of these techniques, do you think the arguments are weaker? Why or why not?

2. Eric Neisser and Robert L. DuPont both address the possibility of using coordination tests in place of drug testing. Compare their arguments. Which is more compelling? Why?

3. Glenn Berrien agrees with G. John Tysse and Garen E. Dodge that drug-using employees can cost an employer money. While Tysse and Dodge believe these costs are a burden to employers, Berrien thinks the money is well spent. Compare the financial and the human costs of following the advice in these two viewpoints.

Chapter 4

1. Authors Pete Stark and James R. Cooper discuss the Multiple Copy Prescription Program in their viewpoints. What is it? Why does Stark support such a measure? Why does Cooper consider it unnecessary? Which viewpoint do you consider more persuasive? Why?

2. After reading Eric P. Cohen's viewpoint, do you agree that prescription drug advertising is harmful? Or, after reading Paul H. Rubin's, do you believe these advertisements can benefit patients? Explain your answer. What effect do you think advertising prescription drugs has on health care?

Chapter 5

1. Mitchell S. Rosenthal vehemently opposes legalizing drugs as a solution to America's drug problem. Rosenthal is president of the Phoenix House Foundation, one of the nation's largest and most successful private drug treatment organizations. How might his background affect his view of drug legalization?

2. Compare Mitchell S. Rosenthal's view of legalizing drugs with author Ethan A. Nadelmann's. How do they differ in their assessment of the effects of legalization on the drug

problem? Are there any points on which they agree? If yes, what are they?

3. How might author Lester David's prescription for reducing drug abuse address Joseph D. Douglass Jr.'s criticism of the problem? How would Mathea Falco's community involvement solution respond to Douglass's viewpoint? Give reasons for your answers.

Organizations to Contact

The editors have compiled the following list of organizations that are concerned with the issues debated in this book. All have publications or information available for interested readers. For best results, allow as much time as possible for the organizations to respond. The descriptions below are derived from materials provided by the organizations. This list was compiled upon the date of publication. Names, addresses, and phone numbers of organizations are subject to change.

American Civil Liberties Union (ACLU)
132 W. 43rd St.
New York, NY 10036
(212) 944-9800

The ACLU, one of the oldest civil liberties organizations in the United States, favors decriminalization of drugs. It opposes indiscriminate drug testing as a violation of the right to privacy. The ACLU publishes information packets on drug legalization and decriminalization.

Cato Institute
1000 Massachusetts Ave. NW
Washington, DC 20001
(202) 546-0200

The institute is a public policy research foundation dedicated to limiting the control of government and to protecting individual liberty. It studies the drug problem and strongly favors drug legalization. It publishes the *Cato Journal* three times a year and the *Cato Policy Report* bimonthly.

Center for Substance Abuse Research (CESAR)
4321 Hartwick Rd., Suite 501
College Park, MD 20740
(800) 842-3828

CESAR maintains a library on substance abuse and provides information on substance abuse trends in Washington, D.C., and Maryland. The organization conducts research and provides training and assistance for local agencies and communities. CESAR operates an electronic bulletin board and publishes a weekly newsletter reporting the results of its research.

Committees of Correspondence
57 Conant St., Room 113
Danvers, MA 01923
(508) 774-2641

The committees, a national coalition of community groups, fights drug abuse among youth by publishing data about drugs and drug abuse. The coalition opposes drug legalization and advocates treatment for drug abusers. Publications include the quarterly *Drug Abuse Newsletter*; the periodic *Drug Prevention Resource Manual*; and related pamphlets, brochures, and article reprints.

Do It Now Foundation
6423 S. Ash Ave.
Tempe, AZ 85283
(602) 257-0797

The foundation fights drug abuse by providing students and adults with facts on legal and illegal drugs and drug abuse. Founded in 1968, Do It Now offered one of the first drug-abuse hotline services in the country. The foundation publishes books, posters, taped public-service announcements on drug abuse, and the pamphlets *Guide for Young People*, *Total Recovery*, and *Everyday Detox: A Guide to Living Without Chemicals*.

Drug Enforcement Administration (DEA)
1405 I St. NW
Washington, DC 20537
(202) 633-1000

The DEA is the federal agency charged with enforcing the nation's drug laws. The agency concentrates on stopping narcotics smuggling and distribution organizations in the United States and abroad. It publishes *Drug Enforcement Magazine* three times a year.

Drug Policy Foundation
4801 Massachusetts Ave. NW, #400
Washington, DC 20016
(202) 895-1634

The foundation supports legalizing many drugs and increasing the number of treatment programs for addicts. It distributes material on legislation regarding drug legalization. The foundation's publications include the bimonthly *Drug Policy Letter* and the books *The Great Drug War* and *1989-1990, A Reformer's Catalogue*. It also distributes *Press Clips*, an annual compilation of newspaper articles on drug legalization issues.

Drugs and Crime Data Center and Clearinghouse
1600 Research Blvd.
Rockville, MD 20850
(800) 666-3332

The clearinghouse, an office of the U.S. Justice Department, compiles and distributes information on drug-related crime for use by policymakers and other researchers. Its publications include *Federal Drug Data for National Policy* and *State Drug Resources: A National Directory*.

Drugs Anonymous
PO Box 772
Bronx, NY 10451
(212) 874-0700

Drugs Anonymous is a twelve-step self-help and support group based on the principles of Alcoholics Anonymous. Since 1975, the organization has helped those suffering addiction to prescription drugs.

The Heritage Foundation
214 Massachusetts Ave. NE
Washington, DC 20002
(202) 546-4400

The Heritage Foundation is a conservative public policy research institute that opposes the legalization of drugs and advocates strengthening law enforcement to stop drug abuse. It publishes position papers on a broad range of topics, including drug issues. Its regularly publications include the monthly *Policy Review*, the *Backgrounder* series of occasional papers, and the *Heritage Lectures* series.

International Narcotics Enforcement Officers Association (INEOA)
112 State St., Suite 1200
Albany, NY 12207
(518) 463-6232

INEOA examines national and international narcotics laws and seeks ways to improve those laws and prevent drug abuse. It also studies law enforcement methods to find the most effective ways to reduce illegal drug use. The association publishes *International Drug Report* and *Narc Officer*, both monthly journals, and a newsletter devoted to drug control issues.

Libertarian Party
1528 Pennsylvania Ave. SE
Washington, DC 20003
(202) 543-1988

The Libertarian party is a political party whose goal is to ensure respect for individual rights. It advocates the repeal of all laws prohibiting the production, sale, possession, or use of drugs. The party believes law enforcement should focus on preventing violent crimes against persons and property rather than on prosecuting people who use drugs. It publishes the bimonthly *Libertarian Party News* and periodic *Issue Papers* and distributes a compilation of articles supporting drug legalization.

Narcotic Educational Foundation of America (NEFA)
5055 Sunset Blvd.
Los Angeles, CA 90027
(213) 663-5171

NEFA provides educational materials on the dangers of drug use and abuse. It maintains a library on drug abuse topics and a reading room. Its publications include *Get the Answers—An Open Letter to Youth* and *Some Things You Should Know About Prescription Drugs*.

Narcotics Anonymous (NA)
PO Box 9999
Van Nuys, CA 91409
(818) 780-3951

NA, comprising more than eighteen thousand groups worldwide, is an organization of recovering drug addicts who meet regularly to help each other abstain from all drugs. It publishes *NA Way Magazine* and *Newsline* monthly.

National Acupuncture Detoxification Association (NADA)
PO Box 1927
Vancouver, WA 98668-1927
(206) 254-0186

NADA promotes acupuncture as a treatment for drug abuse. It favors government-funded drug treatment and opposes drug legalization. NADA publishes the *NADA Newsletter* annually.

National Clearinghouse for Alcohol and Drug Information (NCADI)
11426 Rockville Pike
Rockville, MD 20852
(800) 729-6686

NCADI is an information service of the Office for Substance Abuse Prevention of the U.S. Department of Health and Human Services. The clearinghouse provides alcohol and drug prevention and educational materials free, including technical reports, pamphlets, and posters. It publishes a bimonthly newsletter, *Prevention Pipeline: An Alcohol and Drug Awareness Service*, containing the latest available research, resources, and activities in the prevention field.

National Council on Patient Information and Education
666 11th St. NW, Suite 810
Washington, DC 20001
(202) 347-6711

The council consists of pharmaceutical manufacturers, health care professional organizations, and consumer groups. It provides information on the issue of prescription drugs and calls for increased discussion between doctors and patients regarding prescribed drugs. It publishes the *Directory of Prescription Drug Information and Education Programs and Resources.*

National Institute of Justice (NIJ)
PO Box 6000
Rockville, MD 20852
(800) 851-4320

The institute serves as a clearinghouse for information on the causes, prevention, and control of crime. Among the publications available are

Probing the Links Between Drugs and Crime and pamphlets on drug-free work environments, drug legalization, and information on specific drugs.

National Organization for the Reform of Marijuana Laws (NORML)
2001 S St. NW, Suite 640
Washington, DC 20009
(202) 483-5500

NORML fights to legalize marijuana and to help those who have been convicted and sentenced for possessing or selling marijuana. It publishes a newsletter, *Marijuana Highpoints*, on the progress of all legislation concerning the legalization of marijuana throughout the country.

Office of National Drug Control Policy
Executive Office of the President
Washington, DC 20500
(202) 467-9800

The Office of National Drug Control Policy, established by the National Narcotics Leadership Act of 1988, is responsible for the government's national drug strategy. It formulates the government's policy on illegal drug trafficking and coordinates the federal agencies responsible for stopping drug trafficking. Drug policy studies are available upon request.

Pharmaceutical Manufacturers Association (PMA)
1100 15th St. NW
Washington, DC 20005
(202) 835-3400

PMA is a nonprofit trade association of more than one hundred research-based pharmaceutical companies. It encourages high quality control standards for its member companies and for the research and development of new products. It opposes federally imposed price restrictions. PMA maintains an extensive book and periodical library and publishes a wide variety of material, including the report *Good Medicine: A Report on the Status of Pharmaceutical Research*, the weekly *Newsletter*, and the biweekly *State Capitol Reports*.

Phoenix House Foundation
164 W. 74th St.
New York, NY 10023
(212) 595-5810

Phoenix House, begun in 1967, is the largest private substance abuse treatment agency in the United States. It operates many outpatient and residential treatment programs across the country. It is opposed to legalization of drugs and believes that federal drug policy should focus more on stopping hard-core drug abuse. A variety of articles by and about Phoenix House is available upon request.

The RAND Corporation
Distribution Services
1700 Main St.
Santa Monica, CA 90406-2138
(310) 393-0411, ext. 6686

The RAND Corporation is a nonprofit research institution that seeks to improve public policy through research and analysis. RAND's Drug Policy Research Center (DPRC) publishes material on the costs, prevention, and treatment of alcohol and drug abuse as well as on trends in drug-law enforcement. Its extensive list of publications includes the book *Sealing the Borders* by Peter Reuter.

Bibliography of Books

Howard Abadinsky · *Drug Abuse: An Introduction*. Chicago: Nelson-Hall, 1989.

Daniel K. Benjamin and Roger Leroy Miller · *Undoing Drugs: Beyond Legalization*. New York: Basic Books, 1991.

David Boaz · *The Crisis in Drug Prohibition*. Washington, DC: Cato Institute, 1990.

Tony Bouza · *A Carpet of Blue*. St. Paul, MN: Deaconess Press, 1992.

Robert H. Coombs and Louis Jolyon West · *Drug Testing: Issues and Options*. New York: Oxford University Press, 1991.

Michael A. Corey · *Kicking the Drug Habit*. Springfield, IL: Charles C. Thomas, 1989.

Elliott Currie · *Dope and Trouble: Portraits of Delinquent Youth*. New York: Pantheon Books, 1991.

Elliott Currie · *Reckoning: Drugs, the Cities, and the American Future*. New York: Hill & Wang, 1993.

Robert DeCresce et al. · *Drug Testing in the Workplace*. Washington, DC: Bureau of National Affairs, 1989.

Jeffrey A. Eisenach · *Winning the Drug War: New Challenges for the 1990s*. Washington, DC: Heritage Foundation, 1991.

Mathea Falco · *The Making of a Drug-Free America*. New York: Random House, 1992.

Bryan S. Finkle, Robert V. Blanke, and J. Michael Walsh, eds. · *Technical, Scientific, and Procedural Issues of Employee Drug Testing: Consensus Report*. Washington, DC: U.S. Department of Health and Human Services, 1990.

Samuel R. Friedman · *Cocaine, AIDS, and Intravenous Drug Use*. Binghamton, NY: Haworth Press, 1991.

Dean R. Gerstein and Lawrence W. Green, eds. · *Preventing Drug Abuse*. Washington, DC: National Academy Press, 1993.

Ronald Hamowy, ed. · *Dealing with Drugs: Consequences of Government Control*. Lexington, MA: Lexington Books, 1987.

Abbie Hoffman with Jonathan Silvers · *Steal This Urine Test: Fighting Drug Hysteria in America*. New York: Penguin, 1987.

Robert L. Hubbard and Mary Ellen Marsden · *Drug Abuse Treatment: A National Study of Effectiveness*. Chapel Hill: University of North Carolina Press, 1989.

James A. Inciardi	*The War on Drugs II: The Continuing Epic of Heroin, Cocaine, Crack, Crime, AIDS, and Public Policy*. Mountain View, CA: Mayfield Publishing Co., 1992.
James A. Inciardi, Ruth Horowitz, and Anne E. Potteiger	*Street Kids, Street Drugs, Street Crime: An Examination of Drug Use and Serious Delinquency in Miami*. Belmont, CA: Wadsworth Publishing Co., 1993.
James A. Inciardi, ed.	*The Drug Legalization Debate*. Newbury Park, CA: Sage Publications, 1990.
Christina Jacqueline Johns	*Power, Ideology, and the War on Drugs: Nothing Succeeds Like Failure*. New York: Praeger, 1992.
Mark A.R. Kleiman	*Against Excess: Drug Policy for Results*. New York: Basic Books, 1992.
Melvyn B. Krauss and Edward P. Lazear	*Searching for Alternatives: Drug-Control Policy in the United States*. Stanford, CA: Hoover Institution Press, 1991.
Joyce H. Lowinson et al.	*Substance Abuse: A Comprehensive Textbook*. Baltimore: Williams and Wilkins, 1992.
Clarence Lusane	*Pipe Dream Blues*. Boston: South End Press, 1992.
Angela Browne Miller	*Working Dazed: Why Drugs Pervade the Workplace and What Can Be Done About It*. New York: Plenum Press, 1991.
Richard Lawrence Miller	*The Case for Legalizing Drugs*. New York: Praeger, 1991.
Chester Nelson Mitchell	*The Drug Solution*. Ottawa, Canada: Carleton University Press, 1990.
David F. Musto	*The American Disease: Origins of Narcotics Control*. Oxford: Oxford University Press, 1988.
Joseph Nowinski	*Substance Abuse in Adolescents and Young Adults*. New York: W.W. Norton, 1990.
Cardwell C. Nuckols	*Cocaine: From Dependency to Recovery*. 2d ed. Blue Ridge Summit, PA: Tab Books, 1989.
Office of National Drug Control Policy	*Building a Drug-Free Workforce*. Washington, DC: U.S. Government Printing Office, 1990.
James Ostrowski	*Thinking About Drug Legalization*. Washington, DC: Cato Institute, 1990.
Alfonso Paredes and David A. Gorelick	*Cocaine: Physiological and Physiopathological Effects*. Binghamton, NY: Haworth Press, 1993.
Stanton Peele and Archie Brodsky	*The Truth About Addiction and Recovery*. New York: Simon & Schuster, 1992.

Jennifer Rice-Licare and Katherine Delaney McLoughlin	*Cocaine Solutions*. Binghamton, NY: Haworth Press, 1990.
Bernard Segal, ed.	*Perspectives on Adolescent Drug Use*. Binghamton, NY: Haworth Press, 1989.
Peter H. Smith, ed.	*Drug Policy in the Americas*. Boulder: Westview Press, 1992.
Sam Staley	*Drug Policy and the Decline of the American City*. New Brunswick, NJ: Transaction Books, 1992.
Barry Stimmel	*The Facts About Drug Use*. Binghamton, NY: Haworth Press, 1992.
Thomas Szasz	*Our Right to Drugs: The Case For a Free Market*. New York: Praeger, 1992.
Harold H. Traver and Mark S. Gaylord, eds.	*Drugs, Law, and the State*. New Brunswick, NJ: Transaction Books, 1993.
Arnold S. Trebach and Kevin B. Zeese	*Drug Prohibition and the Conscience of Nations*. Washington, DC: Drug Policy Foundation, 1990.
Arnold S. Trebach and Kevin B. Zeese	*Friedman and Szasz on Liberty and Drugs*. Washington DC: Drug Policy Foundation, 1992.
Lamond Tullis	*Handbook of Research on the Illicit Drug Trade*. Westport, CT: Westport Publishing Group, 1991.
Carol J. Verburg	*Substance Abuse in America*. Washington, DC: National Academy Press, 1989.
J. Michael Walsh and Steven W. Gust, eds.	*Workplace Drug Abuse Policy: Considerations and Experience in the Business Community*. Washington, DC: National Institute on Drug Abuse, 1989.
Arnold Washton	*Cocaine Addiction*. New York: W.W. Norton, 1989.
Arnold Washton and Nannette Stone-Washton	*Step Zero*. San Francisco: Harper, 1991.
Terry Williams	*Crackhouse: Notes from the End of the Line*. Reading, MA: Addison-Wesley, 1992.
Steven Wisotsky	*Beyond the War on Drugs*. Washington, DC: Cato Institute, 1990.
Steven Wisotsky	*A Society of Suspects: The War on Drugs and Civil Liberties*. Washington, DC: Cato Institute, 1992.
Franklin E. Zimring and Gordon Hawkins	*The Search for Rational Drug Control*. New York: Cambridge University Press, 1992.

Index

255

257

258

259

Prohibition
  compared to drug laws, 193, 198
  compared to war on drugs, 67, 69
Pryor, David, 172-177
Public Citizen Health Research
  Group, 146, 160

Quayle, Dan, 179

Rangel, Charles B., 34, 48, 212
Reagan, Ronald
  drug testing and, 237
  war on drugs and, 59, 85, 102
Rehabilitation Act, 118-120
Reuter, Peter, 21, 88, 102, 203
Robert Wood Johnson Foundation,
  229
Rogers, Don, 21, 92
Rosenthal, Mitchell S., 200, 223
Rubin, Paul H., 159, 161

Sarokin, H. Lee, 133
Scalia, Antonin, 123
Schmoke, Kurt, 201
schools
  drug prevention programs in, 211,
    230-231, 232-233, 238-239
Select Committee on Narcotics Abuse
  and Control, 48
Shining Path insurgency, 88-89
Sid and Nancy, 33
South America
  efforts to win war on drugs, 75-82
  source of cocaine, 20, 78, 84
Spungen, Nancy, 33
Staley, Sam, 23
Stark, Pete, 142, 179
STAR prevention program, 227, 230,
  231
suicide
  drug abuse and, 152
Suriname
  cocaine industry in, 85
Synar, Mike, 177

television
  prescription drug ads on, 166, 167
  violates privacy, 133-134
Therapeutic Communities of
  America, 210
tobacco
  as addictive, 26-27, 41, 51, 196, 197
  deaths from, 27, 28
  education programs and, 198
  restrictions against should be
    tightened, 203
  use in America, 24-27, 194
  use is declining, 29

tranquilizers
  abuse of, 146-147, 149
Treatment Outcome Prospective
  Study (TOPS), 219-220, 221
treatment programs
  adolescents and, 211
  are successful, 67-68, 206-207, 208,
    219-220
    con, 216-224
  availability of, 223, 224
  benefits of, 221-222
  costs of, 211, 217-219
  dropout rates, 221
  funding for, 210
    should be increased, 209-215
    con, 216-224
  government mandated, 120
  inaccessible to poor, 210-214
  length of, 211, 212
  methadone, 218, 219, 220, 223
  military methods, 236
  outpatient, 218, 219, 220
  patient profiles, 220
  prisoners and, 213-214
  problems with, 211-212, 217
  programs are being cut, 48-49
  programs are full, 192, 222-223
    con, 223
  relapse rates, 221
  residential, 218-219, 220
  statistics on, 210, 217-219, 223
  twelve-step are successful, 222
  types of, 211, 217-218
  women and, 212-213
Trebach, Arnold, 53
tuberculosis
  drug abuse and, 208
Turner, Carlton E., 237
twelve-step programs, 218, 222
Tysse, G. John, 111

United States
  Defense Intelligence Agency, 105
  Department of Defense
    study on drug abuse, 235
    war on drugs and, 84, 88
      is effective, 91-98
        con, 99-107
      types of, 93-98, 103
  Department of Health and Human
    Services (HHS)
    prescription drug fraud and, 146,
      148
  drug abuse threatens way of life in,
    18, 21, 27, 59-64, 92, 204
  Drug Enforcement Administration,
    145
  drugs smuggled into, 20, 95-96

260

international aid for war on drugs, 84, 86, 88

national drug intelligence center (NDIC), 63-64

Office of National Drug Control Policy (ONDCP)
  National Drug Control Strategy, 61, 63

people prize their freedom, 71-72

Postal Service
  study on drug abuse and the workplace, 112-114, 118-123

Venezuela
  cocaine industry in, 85
  war on drugs and, 79

Wachsman, Harvey F., 173

war on drugs, 32
  compared to Vietnam War, 59, 61-62
  costs of, 59, 84, 101, 103, 106
  damages America's security, 86, 88-90
  destabilizes Latin American countries, 88-90
  drug seizures and, 79
  foreign countries do not cooperate, 62
  international aid for, 84, 86, 88

international measures can help win, 74-82
  con, 83-90
  is ineffective, 47, 54, 58-65, 70-71
  is misdirected, 85, 86, 100-101, 107
  myths about, 80-82
  should be abandoned, 66-73
  con, 58-65
  South American cooperation in, 75-82
  undercover operations, 71-72
  U.S. military involvement in, 84, 88
  is effective, 91-98
  con, 99-107
  types of, 93-98, 103
  Washington, D.C., as test case, 70-71

Waxman, Henry, 167, 222, 223

Weinberger, Caspar, 100

Wetherington, Gerald, 232

White House Office of Drug Control Policy, 107

Willard, Richard, 128

Williams, J.D., 179

Wolfe, Sidney, 160

women
  addiction and, 18-19, 21, 204, 213, 217
  heroin use and, 33, 35, 37
  treatment programs and, 212-213, 223, 231